Multicultural Education for Learners With Special Needs in the Twenty-First Century

A volume in
Contemporary Perspectives in Special Education
Anthony F. Rotatori and Festus E. Obiakor, *Series Editors*

Multicultural Education for Learners With Special Needs in the Twenty-First Century

edited by

Festus E. Obiakor
Valdosta State University

Anthony F. Rotatori
Saint Xavier University

INFORMATION AGE PUBLISHING, INC.
Charlotte, NC • www.infoagepub.com

Library of Congress Cataloging-in-Publication Data

A CIP record for this book is available from the Library of Congress
http://www.loc.gov

ISBN: 978-1-62396-580-8 (Paperback)
       978-1-62396-581-5 (Hardcover)
       978-1-62396-582-2 (ebook)

Printed in the United States of America

CONTENTS

LIST OF CONTRIBUTORS

Abdullah Khoifh Alodail	Ohio University Athens, Ohio
Jeffrey P. Bakken	Bradley University Peoria, Illinois
Tachelle Banks	Cleveland State University Cleveland, Ohio
Floyd D. Beachum	Lehigh University Bethlehem, Pennsylvania
Barbara J. Dray	University of Colorado Denver, Colorado
Laurel M. Garrick Duhaney	University of New York at New Paltz New Paltz, New York
Satasha L. Green	Chicago State University Chicago, Illinois
Ying Hui-Michael	Rhode Island College Providence, Rhode Island
Carlos R. McCray	Fordham University New York, New York
Tes Mehring	Emporia State University Emporia, Kansas
Festus E. Obiakor	Valdosta State University Valdosta, Georgia

Howard P. Parette Jr.   Illinois State University
                             Normal, Illinois

Anthony F. Rotatori   Saint Xavier University
                             Chicago, Illinois

Scott Sparks   Ohio University
                             Athens, Ohio

Cheryl A. Utley   Chicago State University
                             Chicago, Illinois

Peter Vigil   University of Colorado
                             Denver, Colorado

Sean Warner   Clark Atlanta University
                             Atlanta, Georgia

PREFACE

The United States has a very diverse population that continues to change. The changing demographics presents a challenge to educators in the 21st century as how to design effective educational practices that will accommodate diverse learners so that they reach their optimal potential. These practices are necessary not only in large metropolitan areas such as New York City, Chicago, and Los Angeles but small towns and villages where diverse families have transitioned as a way to enhance the quality of life for their children. While multicultural educational advances have occurred, there continue to be roadblocks that interfere with the implementation of effective practices such as misidentification, misassessment, miscategorization, misplacement, and misinstruction. *Multicultural Education for Learners With Special Needs in the Twenty-First Century* provides general and special educators innovative information that addresses the roadblocks to effective practice such that diverse learners will be appropriately: identified, assessed, categorized, placed, and instructed.

This volume provides general and special educators—who instruct diverse learners—comprehensive, creative, and best practice chapters by scholars in the area of multicultural education. Chapter 1 presents a system to reduce traditional education roadblocks that confront diverse learners called Culturally and Linguistically Responsive Teaching (CLRT). The CLRT system is designed to accomplish three objectives, namely, (a) to increase student achievement, (b) to help students develop skills to achieve economic sufficiency, and (c) allow students to acquire citizenship skills based on a realistic and thorough understanding of the political system. Chapter 2 discusses the pervasive problem of disproportionate

Multicultural Education for Learners with Special Needs in the Twenty-First Century, pages ix–x
Copyright © 2014 by Information Age Publishing
All rights of reproduction in any form reserved.

representation of students from diverse backgrounds in special education by examining what it is, who is impacted by it, why it is occurring, and how it can be addressed using promising strategies. Chapter 3 examines the use of authentic assessment to provide feedback for teachers and students, evaluate students' knowledge and understanding of key concepts and standards, and guide the instructional process by differentiating teaching to meet the educational needs of diverse learners. Chapters 4, 5, 6, and 7 address issues related to educating Latina/o Americans, African Americans, Asian Americans, and Native American in learners with special needs. Chapter 8 is a unique chapter that addresses the growing need to educate foreign-born immigrants who are now being referred to as "today's special learners in schools." This chapter delineates the use of the Comprehensive Support Model (CSM) to educate foreign-born learners who are identified by the authors as foreign-born English Language Learners (ELL). The CSM is recommended as a culturally sensitive intervention that integrates efforts of the self (i.e., learner), families, school, community, and government in responding to the needs of diverse learners. Chapter 9 provides a comprehensive discussion of how Culturally Relevant Leadership (CRL) can impact educational theory and practice. The authors delineate how CRL leads to reflective practices which position teachers and administrators to become leaders in school change that can increase student success for diverse learners. Chapter 10 provides illustrated content regarding the use of technology to educate multicultural learners with special needs. Chapter 11 delineates the culturally responsive infusion of effective behavior modification strategies that are designed to strengthen and facilitate positive behaviors for culturally and linguistically diverse learners with special needs.

—**Festus E. Obiakor**
Anthony F. Rotatori

CHAPTER 1

EDUCATING CULTURALLY AND LINGUISTICALLY DIVERSE LEARNERS WITH SPECIAL NEEDS

The Rationale

Festus E. Obiakor and Satasha L. Green

Educating culturally and linguistically diverse (CLD) learners with and without special needs appears to be in the dark and multicultural education is not getting the deserved attention in general and in special education. In many quarters, multicultural education has been cajoled and denigrated even though it is a progressive approach for transforming education that holistically critiques and addresses current shortcomings, failings, and discriminatory practices. It is a phenomenon grounded in the ideals of social justice, fairness, equity, and a dedication to facilitating educational experiences. Its emphasis is on students reaching their full potential as socially aware and active beings, locally, nationally, and globally. Multicultural education acknowledges that schools are essential to laying the foundation

Multicultural Education for Learners With Special Needs in the Twenty-First Century, pages 1–13
Copyright © 2014 by Information Age Publishing

1

for the transformation of society and the elimination of oppression and injustice (Gorski, 2000). It grew out of the civil rights movement of the 1960s (Banks, 2002; Banks & Banks, 1997; 2003) and has gone through many transformations both in theory and practice. As a field of study, it is as important as other theoretical frameworks such as humanistic education, behavioristic education, and cognitive education methodologies (Smith, Richards, MacGranley, & Obiakor, 2004). Researchers in the field have coined several definitions for the term multicultural education (Gollnick & Chinn, 2002, 2004; Gorski, 2000); and despite a multitude of differing conceptualizations, it is a movement that proposes to increase equity for victimized groups without limiting the opportunities of others (Banks, 2002; Banks & Banks, 1997; Diaz, 2001).

In the early nineties, multicultural education was aimed to create equal educational opportunities for students from CLD backgrounds (Banks & Banks, 1995; Obiakor, 2007; Smith et al., 2004). One of the major goals of multicultural education was to assist all students in acquiring the knowledge and skills needed to navigate effectively in a pluralistic society (Banks, 2002; Banks & Banks, 2001; Gorski, 2000). As an approach, it focused on reversing shortcomings, failures, and discriminatory practices in our educational system in several ways (Banks, 2002; Banks & Banks, 2003; Gorski & Covert, 2000) by (a) providing students with educational experiences based on an appreciation for variety, (b) focusing on socioeducational equity for CLD learners which has long been denied (Davidman & Davidman, 2001; Gorski & Covert, 2000), and (c) welcoming and viewing as assets students who come to school with different ethnic and racial identities (Banks, 2001, 2002; Gay, 2002; Rhee, 2002; Tantum, 1997).

An early view of multicultural education by Chisholm and Weztel (1997) stated that multicultural education is as essential to teaching as nurturing is to human development and its premise continues to hold true today. It has become increasingly clear that multicultural education utilizes a combination of concepts, paradigms, and theories from other fields of study such as ethnic and women studies, history, and social and behavioral sciences. It incorporates content from these fields and disciplines to pedagogy and curriculum development in educational settings (Banks, 2002; Banks & Banks, 2001). Additionally, its embodiments are in line with the intricacies of special education—it has now expanded in scope to the field of special education that is called *Multicultural Special Education* (Obiakor, 2007). As Obiakor (2007) printed out, multicultural special education encompasses educational programming that helps all learners who are at risk for misidentification, misassessment, miscategorization, misplacement, and misinstruction because of their racial, cultural, and linguistic differences. When teaching CLD learners with special needs, multicultural pedagogy is needed to build bridges between students' backgrounds and experiences and the teacher's frame of reference. Instruction must be responsive to students' learning styles and adapt and build on their existing skills. A multicultural approach accommodates students who are culturally or linguistically different through the use of teaching strategies that promote successful academic outcomes (Bennett, 2003; Gollnick & Chinn, 2004). Earlier, Irvine (2003) noted that one of the critical roles as a teacher is to incorporate daily experiences of students' prior knowledge within teaching new concepts. Teachers and service providers must connect students' personal cultural knowledge to learning objectives. By utilizing culturally familiar ways of instruction, educational professionals have the opportunity to encourage and include the cultural knowledge of their "special" learners in the curriculum (Irvine, 2003). However, the question remains, how can multicultural education be infused in the education of CLD learners with special needs? This chapter responds to this critical question.

TRADITIONAL PROBLEMS ASSOCIATED WITH DISPROPORTIONATE REPRESENTATION

In a 21st century classroom in the United States, the school population is increasingly diverse. Our public schools are attended by children from various racial, ethnic, and cultural groups and from various countries of the world. Therefore, special educators are working more and more in their classrooms with CLD students with a wide range of abilities (Erskine-Cullen & Sinclair, 1996; Piana, 2000). This in fact, raises the ante for how teachers are prepared to teach in 21st century schools. Clearly, new general and special education teachers must have the knowledge and skills to successfully work with CLD learners with special needs. CLD students come to school with home cultures and languages, ignoring these cultures and languages make it difficult for some educators to distinguish between cultural or linguistic differences and disabilities.

There are nearly 48.2 million students receiving a public school education in the United States (Lips, 2006). Disturbing numbers of CLD learners underachieve in these public schools (Garcia & Dominquez, 1997) and are placed into special education programs. These students are placed in special education at a much higher rate than their European American counterparts. The National Center for Culturally Responsive Educational Systems (NCCREST) (2006–2007) reported disproportionality by race for all disability categories within the United States. The highest disproportionality for African American students was in Utah, North Dakota, Oregon, and Wisconsin, while the lowest disproportionality for these students was in Arkansas, West Virginia, and Georgia (NCCREST). For Latino students, New York, Colorado, and Washington were the states with the highest disproportionality while the lowest disproportionality for these students was in Mississippi, West Virginia, and Missouri (NCCREST). The highest disproportionality for Asian/Pacific Islander students was in Wisconsin, Alaska, and Montana while the lowest disproportionality for these students was in New York, Louisiana, and Kentucky (NCCREST). American Indian/ Alaskan Native students had the highest disproportionality in Alaska, Nevada, and Minnesota while the lowest disproportionality was in South Carolina, Indiana, and Tennessee (NCCREST). White students had the highest chance of disproportionality in California, Georgia, and Nevada while the lowest disproportionality was in Montana, South Carolina, and Iowa (NC-CREST) (for a full representation of each state's disproportionality data readers can view the website: http://www.nccrest.org/).

African American and Latino American students make up a large percentage of CLD learners in U.S. public schools. While African Americans comprise 17% of all students in U.S. public schools, they account for: 31% of students identified as having cognitive/intellectual disabilities, 28% of students labeled as having emotional disturbance, and 21% of students with learning disabilities (National Association for the Education of African American Children with Learning Disabilities, 2012; Obiakor, 2007). Similarly, a large percentage of Latino American students are in special education programs' and they make up 14% of the special education population (Obiakor, 2007; United States Department of Education, 2001). The majority of Latino American students are referred for services related to speech, language, and/or reading-related learning disabilities. These linguistically different learners whose native language is not English are often misdiagnosed because they are perceived as having speech and language impairments. This occurs because speech language referral practices are primarily normed for students whose native language is English. This misdiagnosis occurs even with some CLD students whose native language is English and is socialized similarly to students from the dominant culture. Unfortunately, this misidentification results in overidentification and disproportionality of CLD learners in special education.

In an effort to compensate for misidentification and over-identification of CLD students, they are sometimes underidentified (Ovando & Collier, 1985) for special education services. Unfortunately, this is just as detrimental as being overidentified for special education services. Because of the heightened awareness of this underidentification phenomenon, there seems to be more sensitivity when assessing speech and language skills of linguistically diverse students. However, there still appears to be few trained, skilled, and certified special educators as well as speech and language pathologists who can effectively assess CLD learners. Consequently, monolingual special educators and speech and language pathologists are making decisions that may not be appropriate for CLD learners.

While the student population has become increasingly diverse, the vast majority of teachers continues to be monolingual, middle class, female, and do not live in communities in which they teach (Lovelace & Wheeler, 2006; Talbert-Johnson & Tillman, 1999; Weinstein, Tomlinson-Clarke, & Curran, 2004; Zeichner, 1992). To ensure that this population of students receives more appropriate placements, many school districts have added bilingual special education programs. Even with the addition of bilingual special education programs, it is imperative that special educators use multicultural education and culturally and linguistically appropriate and relevant methods to address diverse students' academic and emotional needs because of the mismatch between students and teachers' cultural linguistic backgrounds.

The needs of CLD students may vary from their peers because of differences in attitudes, values, beliefs, mores, and behaviors. These differences are further compounded when the student is CLD and exceptional because these differences can cause incongruities between the student's home and school cultures (Gay, 2000). To correct for these incongruities, culturally and linguistically appropriate and relevant methods need to be incorporated into the student's educational program. To be successful, these methods should focus on one's knowledge of and experiences with values, mores, beliefs, and traditions of cultures that are different from his/hers (Grant & Sleeter, 2006; Shujaa, 1995).

Special educators frequently benefit from knowing that when working with their CLD students, their students' cultures/ethnicities are also an important part of their identities and must be embraced and celebrated within the classroom. Additionally, these educators must hold realistic expectations for their students to learn and master the academic content of the curriculum (Connor & Craig, 2006; Obiakor, 1999; Ogbu, 2003; Sleeter & Grant, 1999). When this does not occur, the CLD learner's academic achievement can be negatively affected. This was reported by researchers (see Yero, 2002), who studied effective schools, and found that teachers' low and inappropriate expectations for CLD students negatively impacted their academic performance and perpetuated self-fulfilling prophecies. Unfortunately, the research literature reports that this situation is common for CLD learners. For example, the literature base has reported that CLD students are more likely to go to schools with poor teacher quality (Darling-Hammond, 1997, 2005; Haycock, Jerald, & Huang, 2001); and have more teachers with lower expectations (Connor & Craig, 2006; Obiakor, 1999; Ogbu, 2003; Stevenson, Chen, & Uttal, 1990).

While the above phenomenon is troublesome, it is exacerbated with students who have special needs because a disability further limits the expectation level from a teaching perspective and influences a teacher to focus on the negative behaviors of the students even though these same behaviors were observed in nonidentified students. This phenomenon is further complicated because the expectations for CLD students are not at equal levels with their counterparts who are European American mono-lingual English speaking peers. Also, there are negative expectation effects due to the CLD student being given a special education label which often has built in lowered expectation of school academic success. Lastly, these lower expectations and cultural deficit views transcend preservice and in-service preparations of teachers and service providers (Irvine, 2003).

CLD students have seldom been represented in instructional tools, such as textbooks and readers (Gay, 2002). Also, curricular materials and instruction utilized in today's schools do not accurately represent the student diversity within a classroom. This is particularly ironic for teaching in a 21st century classroom where students come from all over the world and many times their native language is other than English. Due to the above shortcomings, educators and service providers are often ill equipped to provide culturally and linguistically responsive curriculum and instruction for these students (Green, 2007). This causes educators to use traditional mono-cultural/mono-lingual approaches that propagate that there is only one way of knowing and only one way to assess, evaluate, teach, and instruct students in order for them to be academically successful. This can lead to disengagement between the student and teacher and can cause students to be perceived as not wanting to or caring about learning and their education. Unfortunately, this disengagement may lead to CLD students dropping out of school (Ledlow, 1992). To prevent this disengagement, educators and service providers need to be aware that multicultural education provides content that is culturally and linguistically responsive for all students (Green, 2007; Obiakor, 2008).

THE NEED FOR CULTURALLY
AND LINGUISTICALLY RESPONSIVE TEACHING

Schools are not culturally neutral terrains. However, the foundation and main functions of our education system have been shaped utilizing the dominant culture's values, ideals, and standards (Collins, 1979; Hurn, 1993). This creates a school system and educational process that may have negative effects on the academic achievement of CLD learners with special needs (Harrison, Newton, & Spickelmier, 1990; Trueba, Jacobs, & Kirton, 1990; Trueba, Rodriguez, Zou, & Cintrón, 1993). The intent of culturally and linguistically responsive teaching (CLRT) is to (a) increase student achievement, (b) help students develop skills to achieve economic self-sufficiency, and (c) develop citizenship skills based on a realistic and thorough understanding of the political system (see Shujaa, 1995). CLRT empowers students intellectually, socially, emotionally, and politically by using cultural referents to impart knowledge, skills, and attitudes (Ladson-Billings, 1992). In addition, it requires educators and service providers to recognize who they are racially, culturally, linguistically, and economically and how they view others who are racially, culturally, linguistically, and economically different from themselves (see Shujaa, 1995).

It is common knowledge that the student's culture and language may contribute to the development of a student's identity, self-worth, and academic achievement. As a result, educators of CLD learners with special needs must develop specific knowledge and skills to assist them in promoting respect for diversity in the classroom as well as addressing students' individual learning styles and needs. Cultural and linguistic differences include patterns of communication as well as behavior. Recognition that behavior is not interpreted homogeneously and that expectations are different across cultures may assist educators in adapting instructional strategies to embrace cultural and linguistic patterns of socialization. Schools typically practice traditional instruction, which is often characterized by tracking (Banks & Banks, 2001; Oakes & Wells, 1998). Academic tracking has appealed to those who support a narrow range of learning styles and curricula and it excludes the contributions of people of diverse cultures and languages (Banks & Banks, 2001; Gollnick & Chinn, 2002). According to Denbo (2002), the effectiveness of a school is influenced by a school's culture, which can be expressed through its policies, practices, and beliefs. School culture may affect the quality of social and emotional climates of the school, student achievement expectations, student and teacher relationships, and school and community associations.

In more ways than one, CLRT recognizes, accepts, and focuses on the strengths that CLD students with special needs bring into the classroom; therefore, classrooms should be consistently reflective of students' cultural and linguistic orientations (Gay, 2000). The use of cultural knowledge, prior experiences, frames of reference, and performance styles of CLD students make learning more relevant and effective (see Obiakor, 2008). CLRT expresses the fact that teacher's low expectations for students have negative effects on their academic performance (National Research Council, 2002). Teachers and related professionals who apply CLRT have more positive perceptions and expectations of underachieving CLD students than those who do not utilize CLRT. Educators and service providers who utilize CLRT, acknowledge the presence of cultural and linguistic diversity and find ways for students to connect with a variety of content materials (Montgomery, 2001); and these students are more motivated to learn and perform better academically (Gay, 2002; Green, 2007; McIntyre, 1996).

While educators and service providers benefit from the development of specific knowledge and skills that assist them in promoting respect for students' diversity in their classrooms, they also benefit from the use of CLRT. For example, CLRT's recognition, acceptance, and emphasis on CLD students' strengths displayed in the classroom are essential in the teaching and learning process. In other words, the recognition for racial, ethnic, and linguistic varieties through the use of CRLT strengthens the well-being of CLD students with special needs. As noted earlier, many teachers and service providers are unprepared or ill prepared for this. CLRT helps these professionals to deconstruct their own cultural, linguistic, and learning experiences from when they were in school as well as examine the cultural divide between being a teacher and the experiences of their K–12 students. Additionally, CLRT helps professionals to challenge themselves to examine their beliefs, attitudes, and instructional practices as well as to develop multicultural awareness and cultural competence (Green, 2007, 2009; Hitchcock, Prater, & Chang, 2009; Obiakor, 2008).

MULTICULTURAL EDUCATION: A LOOK AT THE FUTURE

When teaching CLD students with special needs, multicultural education is needed to build bridges between the students' home culture, language experiences, and the teacher's frame of reference not only about the student's culture and language but also about his/her disability. Instruction must be responsive to students' learning styles and adapted to build on their existing skills. A multicultural education approach accommodates students who are CLD with special needs through the use of teaching strategies that promote successful academic outcomes (Gollnick & Chinn, 2002; Obiakor, 2007). In addition, teachers and service providers must nurture students' cultural and language developments by validating and appreciating their cultures and native languages within the classroom.

It is imperative and futuristic that special educators and related professionals utilize multicultural education and culturally and linguistically responsive approaches to teach in our increasingly pluralistic classrooms. However, many teachers and service providers may not be prepared to deal with such a diverse student population and they may interpret cultural and language differences as deficits. Therefore, it is important for general education and special education teachers to have knowledge and skills to successfully work CLD students. These teachers must make a conscious effort to reflect on their practices by examining how they design, deliver, and implement curriculum and instruction. They must deconstruct the relevance of a mono-cultural/mono-lingual approach to teaching and construct a multicultural/multilingual approach that addresses a diverse K–12 student body. Practitioners and professionals at all service levels must weigh in on how their own success in school was achieved.

As a futuristic move, we must recognize that the educational system needs a structural change that not only values diversity but incorporates diverse ways of knowing. In order to successfully and effectively meet these changes that target the needs of CLD students with special needs, we must begin to align curriculum and instruction with culturally and linguistically responsive approaches (Ladson-Billings, 2001). To a large extent, the use of multicultural education and the study of CLRT must be situated in teacher preparation programs as the core concept or theory. Multicultural education and CLRT must be implemented as a continuous body of knowledge supplemented by collaborative field experiences with schools and school personnel working with CLD populations, families, and communities. Providing field-based experiences in urban school districts where there is a diverse student population, for example, will give opportunities for preservice as well as in-service teachers to learn about students' individual differences. By doing all of these, we might, in a realistic fashion, move towards more culturally and linguistically responsive practices in general and special education.

CONCLUSION

This chapter addresses issues related to the education of CLD learners with special needs. It also emphasizes the need for multicultural education as an equalizing element in reducing the traditional misidentification, misassessment, miscategorization, misplacement, and misinstruction that CLD learners have consistently endured. We believe CLRT is one way to reduce traditional education dilemma that confront CLD learners. Another way is to prepare teachers through preservice and in-service trainings to acknowledge, value, and infuse the voices of CLD populations in their programming and plans. We cannot afford to silence these voices because they are different, unique, nontraditional, and multicultural.

This chapter sets the stage for other chapters in this book. It recognizes that we can all make a difference, especially if and when we collaborate, consult, and cooperate with CLD students, families, school personnel, communities, and governmental agencies. We cannot continue to downplay the impact of partnerships as we redesign and institute new ideas, themes, constructs, models, and programs in special education. We must move outside the comfort zone of our sacred existence and we must revisit our concepts of "see no evil, hear no evil, and speak no evil" about the entrenched Eurocentric nature of our educational system. On the other hand, just being African American, Latina/Latino, or Asian American is not enough! We must go beyond our narrow scope and continue to support professionals who help CLD learners with and without special needs to maximize their fullest potential. Finally, we must challenge when necessary and build when necessary, especially if we are interested in developing the spirits of our own humanity.

REFERENCES

Banks, J. A. (2001). Multicultural education: Its effect on students' racial and gender role attitudes. In J. A. Banks & C.A.M. Banks (Eds.), *Handbook of research on multicultural education* (pp. 123–150). San Francisco: Jossey-Bass.

Banks, J. A. (2002). An introduction to multicultural education (3rd ed.). Boston: Allyn and Bacon.

Banks, J. A., & Banks, C. A. M. (Eds.). (1995). Handbook of research on multicultural education. New York: Macmillan.

Banks, J. A., & Banks, C. A. M. (Eds.). (1997). Multicultural education: Issues and perspectives (3rd ed.). Boston: Allyn and Bacon.

Banks, J. A., & Banks, C. A. M. (Eds.). (2001). Handbook of research on multicultural education. San Francisco: Jossey-Bass.

Banks, J. A., & Banks, C. A. M. (Eds.) (2003). Multicultural education: Issues and perspectives (4th ed.). New York: John Wiley and Sons.

Bennett, C. I. (2003). Comprehensive multicultural education: Theory and practice (5th ed.). Boston: Allyn and Bacon.

Chisholm, I. M., & Wetzel, K. (1997). Lessons learned from a technology integrated curriculum for multicultural classrooms. Journal of Technology and Teacher Education, 5(4), 293–317.

Collins, R. (1979). The credential society. New York: Academic Press.

Connor, C., & Craig, H. (2006). African American preschoolers' language, emergent literacy skills, and use of AAE: A complex relation. JSLHR, 49, 771–792.

Darling-Hammond, L. (1997). The right to learn: A blueprint for creating schools that work. San Francisco: Jossey-Bass.

Darling-Hammond, L. (2005). A good teacher in every classroom: Preparing the highly qualified teachers our children deserve. San Francisco: Jossey-Bass.

Davidman, L., & Davidman, P. T. (2001). Teaching with a multicultural perspective: A practical guide (3rd ed.). New York: Longman.

Denbo, S. J. (2002). Why can't we close the achievement gap? In S. J. Denbo & L. Moore Beaulieu (Eds.), Improving schools for African American students (pp. 13–18). Springfield, IL: Charles C. Thomas.

Diaz, C. F. (2001). Multicultural education in the 21st century. New York: Longman Library.

Erskine-Cullen, E., & Sinclair, A. M. (1996). Preparing teachers for urban schools: A view from the field. *Canadian Journal of Educational Administration and Policy, 6.* Retrieved from http://www.umanitoba.ca/publications/ cjeap/articles/cullensinc.html

Garcia, S., & Dominquez, L. (1997). Cultural contexts that influence learning and academic performance. *Child and Adolescent Psychiatric Clinics of North America, 6,* 621–655.

Gay, G. (2000). *Culturally responsive teaching: Theory, research and practice.* New York: Teachers College Press.

Gay, G. (2002). Culturally responsive teaching in special education for ethnically diverse students: Setting the stage. *Qualitative Studies in Education, 15*(6), 613–629.

Gollnick, D. M., & Chinn P. C. (2002). *Multicultural education in a pluralistic society.* Washington: Merrill-Prentice Hall.

Gollnick, D. M., & Chinn, P. C. (2004). *Multicultural education in a pluralistic society.* Upper Saddle River: Pearson Education.

Gorski, P. (2000). Narrative of whiteness and multicultural education. *Electronic Magazine of Multicultural Education* [online], *2* (1), 43.

Gorski, P., & Covert, B. (2000). *Multicultural pavilion: Defining multicultural education.* Retrieved from http://curry.edschool.virginia.edu/go/multicultural/initial.html.

Grant, C., & Sleeter, C. (2006). *Turning on learning: Five approaches to multicultural teaching plans for race, class, gender, and disability.* Upper Saddle River; NJ: Prentice-Hall.

Green, S. L. (2007). Preparing special educators to work with culturally and linguistically diverse students. *The Black History Bulletin, 70* (1), 12–19.

Green, S. L. (2009). *Motivating African learners in reading; Using culturally and linguistically responsive scientifically-based reading instruction.* Saarbrucken, DE: VDM Publishing House.

Harrison, D. S., Newton, A. R., Spickelmier, A. L., & Barnes, T. J. (1990). Electronic CAD frameworks. *Proceedings of the IEEE, 78*(2), 393–417.

Haycock, K., Jerald, C., & Huang, S. (2001). *Status and trends in the education of Blacks* (NCES, 2003-2034). Washington: Education Trust, Thinking K–16.

Hitchcock, C. H., Prater, M. A., & Chang, C. (2009). Developing multicultural proficiency: Effects of a multiple activity workshop in elementary school personnel in an Asian Pacific setting. *Multicultural Learning and Teaching, 4*(2), 1–24.

Hurn, C. J. (1993). *The limits and possibilities of schooling: An introduction to the sociology of education* (3rd ed.). Needham Heights, MA: Allyn and Bacon.

Irvine, J. J. (2003). *Educating teachers for diversity: Seeing with a cultural eye.* New York: Teachers College Press.

Ladson-Billings, G. (1992). Liberatory consequences of literacy: A case of culturally relevant instruction for African American students. *Journal of Negro Education, 61*(3), 378–391

Ladson-Billings, G. (2001). *Crossing over to Canaan.* San Francisco: Jossey-Bass.

Ledlow, S. (1992). Is cultural discontinuity an adequate explanation for dropping out? *Journal of American Indian Education, 31*(3), 21–36.

Lips, D. (2006). America's opportunity scholarships for kids: School choice for students in underperforming public schools. *Research Education,* Retrieved from http://new.heritage.org/Research/Education/bg1939.cfm

Lovelace, S., & Wheeler, T. R. (2006). Cultural discontinuity between home and school language socialization patterns: Implications for teachers. *ERIC, 127*(2), 303–309.

McIntyre, T. (1996). Guidelines for providing appropriate services to culturally diverse students with emotional and/or behavioral disorders. *Behavioral Disorders, 21*(2), 137–144.

Montgomery, W. (2001). Creating culturally responsive, inclusive classrooms. *Teaching Exceptional Children, 33*(4), 4–9.

National Association for the Education of African American Children with Learning Disabilities (2012). Retrieved from: http://www.aacld.org/

National Center for Culturally Responsive Education Systems (2006–2007). Data maps. Retrieved from: http://www.nccrest.eddata.net.

National Research Council (2002). *Minority students in special education and gifted education.* Washington: National Academy Press.

Oakes, J., & Wells, A. (1998). Detracking for high student achievement. *Educational Leadership,* 56, 38–41.

Obiakor, F. E. (1999). Teacher expectations of minority exceptional learners: Impact on "accuracy" of self-concepts. *Exceptional Children, 66,* 39–53.

Obiakor, F. E. (2007). *Multicultural special education: Culturally responsive teaching.* Upper Saddle River, NJ: Pearson Merrill/Prentice Hall.

Obiakor, F. E. (2008). *The eight-step approach to multicultural learning and teaching* (3rd ed.). Dubuque; IA: Kendall Hunt.

Ogbu, J.U. (2003). *Black American students in an affluent suburb: A study of academic disengagement.* Mahwah, NJ: Erlbaum.

Ovando, C. J., & Collier, V. (1985). *Bilingual and ESL classrooms: Teaching in multicultural contexts.* New York: McGraw Hill.

Piana, L. D. (2000). *Still separate. Still unequal: 46 years after Brown v. Board of Education* (Fact-sheet on Educational Inequality). Oakland, CA: Applied Research Center.

Rhee, E. (2002). *Professor researches the effects of racial identity on children.* Retrieved from http://www.udel.edu/PR/UDaily/01-02/rhee112202.html

Shujaa, M. (1995). Cultural self meets cultural other in the African American experience: Teachers' response to a curriculum content reform. *Theory Into Practice, 34*(5), 194–201.

Sleeter, E. S., & Grant C. A., (1999). *Making choices for multicultural education: Five approaches to race, class, and gender.* New York: John Wiley & Sons.

Smith, T. B., Richards, P. S., MacGranley, H., & Obiakor, F. E. (2004). Practicing multiculturalism: An introduction. In T. B. Smith (Ed.), *Practicing multiculturalism: Affirming diversity in counseling and psychology* (pp. 3–16). Boston: Pearson/Allyn & Bacon.

Stevenson, H. W., Chen, C., & Uttal, D. H. (1990). Beliefs and achievement: A study of Black, White, and Hispanic children. *Children Development, 61,* 508–523.

Talbert-Johnson, C., & Tillman, B. (1999). "Perspectives on color in teacher education programs: Prominent Issues." *Journal of Teacher Education, 50*(3), 200–208.

Tantum, B. D. (1997). *Why are all the black kids sitting together in the cafeteria? And other conversations about race.* New York: Basic Books.

Trueba, H. T., Jacobs, L., & Kirton, E. (1990). *Cultural conflict and adaptation: The case of Hmong children in American society.* New York: The Falmer Press.

Trueba, H. T., Rodriguez, C., Zou, Y., & Cintron, J. (1993). *Healing multicultural America: Mexican immigrants rise to power in rural California.* Washington, DC: The Falmer Press.

United States Department of Education (2001). *Twenty-sixth annual report to Congress on the implementation of individuals with disabilities act.* Washington, DC: U.S. Government Printing Office.

Weinstein C., Tomlinson-Clarke S., & Curran M. (2004). Toward a conception of culturally responsive classroom management. *Journal of Teacher Education, 55*(1), 25–38.

Yero, J. L. (2002). *Standards and expectations.* Retrieved from Teacher's Mind Resources: http://www.TeachersMind.com

Zeichner, K. (1992). Rethinking the practicum in the professional development school partnership. *Journal of Teacher Education, 43*, 296–307.

CHAPTER 2

DISPROPORTIONATE REPRESENTATION IN SPECIAL EDUCATION

A Persistent Stain on the Field

Laurel M. Garrick Duhaney

More than 40 years following Lloyd Dunn's (1968) classic article characterizing failures in special education, the educational literature continues to systematically document a persistent problem of disproportionate representation of students from culturally and linguistically diverse (CLD) backgrounds (i.e., students from racial, ethnic, linguistic, geographic, and economically disadvantaged minority groups) in special education (Artiles, Kozleski, Trent, Osher, & Ortiz, 2010; Harry & Klingner, 2006; McCall & Skrtic, 2009; Salend, Garrick Duhaney, & Montgomery, 2002; Samson & Lesaux, 2009; Skiba et al., 2008; Sullivan, 2011). In his seminal work, Dunn critiqued the racially biased, instructionally inferior, and psycho-socially damaging nature of segregated special education programs and suggested that the disproportionate representation of ethnically and linguistically diverse students in segregated special education classrooms should raise sig-

Multicultural Education for Learners with Special Needs in the Twenty-First Century, pages 15–40
Copyright © 2014 by Information Age Publishing

nificant educational concerns (Skiba et al., 2008). In addition to being the focus of much attention in the academic literature, nationally, the problem of disproportionality also has garnered much attention, having been studied twice by the National Research Council (NRC, 1982; 2002).

Although the literature abounds with evidence of ongoing efforts to improve policy, practices, and services to students with disabilities and their families (see Artiles et al., 2010; Schiller, O'Reilly, & Fiore, 2006; Sullivan & Kozleski, 2008), disproportionate representation remains a "wicked problem" (McCall & Skrtic, 2009, p. 4). This problem has not been obliterated despite litigation and legislation designed to advance equity in schools (e.g., *Brown v. Board of Education,* 1954; the Education for All Handicapped Children Act of 1975 since reauthorized and currently renamed the Individuals With Disabilities Education Improvement Act (IDEIA); *Mills v. Board of Education,* 1972; *Pennsylvania Association for Retarded Children (PARC) v. the Commonwealth of Pennsylvania,* 1972; and *Plyler v. Doe,* 1982). In addition, even though several initiatives have been implemented in response to educational outcomes data indicating that CLD students are achieving below their potential and at a level incommensurate with their White peers, advocacy groups have found sufficient cause to raise concern about the disproportionate representation of students from CLD backgrounds in special education (Salend & Garrick Duhaney, 2011; Smith, Gallagher, Owen, & Skrtic, 2009; Books, 2007). In light of the foregoing, this chapter revisits (see Salend & Garrick Duhaney, 2005) the issue of the disproportionate representation of students from CLD backgrounds by examining how it is defined, how it is measured, why it is a problem, who is impacted by it, why it is occurring, how it can be curtailed, and how to evaluate efforts to minimize it.

HOW IS DISPROPORTIONATE REPRESENTATION DEFINED?

Disproportionate representation—also referred to as disproportionality—means that there are more or fewer students with particular characteristics in certain educational settings than one would envision given their representation in the general school population (Salend & Garrick Duhaney, 2005; Skiba et al., 2008). It relates to the pervasiveness of inequities in accessibility to learning opportunities, resources, and educational capital (Brayboy, Castagno, & Maughan, 2007). Disproportionate representation includes *underrepresentation* and *overrepresentation* of students with respect to such variables as educational classification, placement, and treatment (Salend & Garrick Duhaney, 2005). *Overrepresentation* is evident in schools where certain groups of students are in special education at rates that are higher than their prevalence in the general population of students (Salend,

2011). Such is the case for English language learners (ELLs) who are over-represented in special education in select school districts (Artiles et al., 2005; Sullivan, 2011; Velenzuela, Copeland, Qi, & Park, 2006) and in special education generally (Samson & Lesaux, 2009). In contrast, underrepresentation is manifested when particular groups participate in educational programming at rates that are lower than their prevalence in the general student population (Salend, 2011). Thus, we find that African American, Latino/a, and American Indian/Alaska Native students are underrepresented in gifted education by more than 40 percent (Ford, Grantham, & Whiting, 2008) and also in advanced placement classes (The College Board, 2002).

HOW IS DISPROPORTIONATE
REPRESENTATION MEASURED?

An approach that has been used to measure disproportionate representation is the application of formulas; namely, the composition index, the risk ratio, and the risk index. The composition index represents the percentage of a given disability or placement category that is represented by a specific group (i.e., Total number of students in a disability or placement category ÷ Number of students from a particular racial/ethnic category in that disability or placement category) (National Research Council, 2002; Skiba et al., 2008). Although the composition index is regarded as an uncomplicated measure by some, there are problems with its use, including the absence of a criterion for determining significance and homogeneity within ethnic groups (Chinn & Hughes, 1987; Coutinho & Oswald, 2004; Skiba et al., 2008).

An epidemiological statistic referred to as the risk ratio "is commonly used in analysis of binary outcomes, and is a measure of effect size commonly employed in medical research" (Sullivan, 2011, p. 323). Within the disproportionality literature, the risk ratio has been used to determine the extent to which a group is considered eligible for service at a rate differing from that of other groups (Skiba et al., 2008). Stated differently, the risk ratio has been used to estimate the risk for specific outcomes for a particular group based on the proportion of the group that is served in a given category. Within the literature, a risk ratio of 1.0 represents exact proportionality, while ratios below and above indicate under- and overrepresentation. Consistent with these cutoffs, here is an illustration of how the risk ratio is computed. In early 2000, 2.64% of African Americans in the nation's public schools were identified as having mental retardation (MR) (Donovan & Cross, 2002). The use of this percentage (2.64%) to compute African American students' risk for MR with a risk index of 1.21 for White students for the MR category results in a risk ratio of 2.18 (i.e., $2.64/1.21 = 2.18$), implying that African Americans are over two times as likely as White students to be served in the MR category. Like the composition index which some regard as problematic, concern also has been raised about the risk ratio, which is viewed as not particularly meaningful with small samples (see Hosp & Reschly, 2004; Skiba et al., 2008). The risk index is defined as the percentage of a given population in a given category (Skiba et al., 2006). It is calculated as: Number of Racial/Ethnic (e.g., African American students) category in a given disability or placement category ÷ Total enrollment of Racial/Ethnic category (e.g., African American students) in the state. The risk index for a particular CLD group is interpreted by comparing it to the risk index for another group or to the risk index for all other students combined, producing a relative risk ratio (Skiba et al., 2006).

There remains significant variability in quantifying disproportionate representation despite some progress in standardizing its measurement. This is due, in part, to an absence of agreement regarding the referent group against which to contrast a target group's risk index and the lack of definitive criteria in determining disproportionality (Skiba et al., 2008). This variance in measuring disproportionate representation undoubtedly contributes to the fluctuations in rates of overrepresentation at the national, state, and district levels, where we find, for example, some states showing no disproportionate placement rates and districts within those states showing high disproportionality patterns (Waitoller, Artiles, & Cheney, 2010). Cutoffs for determining disproportionality have included 2.0 (Parrish, 2002) and 1.0 to over 4.0 in some states (Sullivan, Kozleski, & Smith, 2008).

WHY IS DISPROPORTIONATE REPRESENTATION A PROBLEM?

Disproportionate representation of CLD students in special education is problematic for a variety of reasons. First, as a field, special education is founded on the principle of fairness and established in the civil rights movement. However, the overplacement of CLD students in special education is inequitable and biased, and results in special education labeling and placement, stereotyping, lowered expectations, inferior instruction, substandard curriculum, segregated classrooms, and poor educational opportunities for these students. Other consequences of disproportionate representation include inferior graduation and employment rates, lack of readiness for postsecondary studies, and higher arrest rates compared to disabled White and nondisabled peers (Affleck, Edgar, Levine, & Kortering, 1990; Blanchett, 2006; Losen & Wellner, 2001; Sullivan et al., 2009). Although disproportionality is a complex problem, requiring multidimensional resolutions, teachers have the power to create inclusive classrooms and opportunities for students to succeed (Sullivan et al., 2009).

WHO IS IMPACTED
BY DISPROPORTIONATE REPRESENTATION?

Disproportionate representation is discussed primarily as a problem of racial and ethnic inequality in special education referral, identification, placement, disciplinary consequences, academic performance, and graduation from special education (Artiles et al., 2005; Blanchett, 2006; Cartledge, Singh, & Gibson, 2008; Ford et al., 2008; Harry & Klingner, 2006; Skiba et al., 2006; Skiba, Michael, Nardo, & Peterson, 2002). However, a number of researchers also see it as a problem that intersects with socioeconomic status, class, gender, age, language, geography, and inequality (Artiles et al., 2005; Harry & Klingner, 2006; Sullivan, 2011). Moreover, poor, working class, and linguistically diverse students also are disproportionately represented in special education programs (Artiles et al., 2005; Connor & Ferri, 2007; Harry & Klingner, 2006; Skiba et al., 2008). While there is a wide range of opinions regarding the problem of disproportionality and its impacts, there is general consensus that African Americans, Latinos/as, and Native Americans are most significantly impacted by it (Losen & Orfield, 2002). These students are overrepresented in the high-incidence disability categories of emotional and behavioral disorders (EBD), learning disabilities (LD), mild mental retardation (MMR), and speech/language impairments (SLI) (U.S. Department of Education, 2006). Nationally, African American students are overrepresented in the categories of mental retardation (MR) and EBD, in more restrictive than less restrictive educational settings (Cartledge, Singh, & Gibson, 2008; Skiba et al., 2008), have a higher rate of office referrals and out-of-school suspensions and expulsions, and are punished more harshly than their peers (Children's Defense Fund, 1975; Gregory, 1997; Shaw & Braden, 1990). African American students also have a greater failure rate on state and national standards in basic subjects such as mathematics and language arts than their white peers (National Research Council [NCR], 2002). American Indian/Alaska Native students are disproportionately enrolled in the LD and EBD categories at the national and statewide levels (Artiles et al., 2010; Artiles, Rueda, Salazar, & Higareda, 2002; Chinn & Hughes, 1987; Donovan & Cross, 2002; National Center on Culturally Responsive Educational Systems, NCCRESt, 2006; U.S. Department of Education, 2006).

Disproportionality is evident in the number of males that are served in special education. Males outnumber girls 2 to 1 among those receiving special education services (Wehmeyer & Schwartz, 2001). Furthermore, the

1992 report to Congress on the implementation of IDEA found that 68.5% of secondary age students served in special education were males. Males were disproportionately represented in the learning and emotional disabilities categories, with males comprising 73.4% and 76.4% of each, respectively. The report also stated that males were overrepresented in every disability category except for deaf-blindness. Regarding evidence of disproportionality in programs for the gifted and talented, there is limited research on gifted students who are culturally and linguistically diverse. Nevertheless, the research that is available shows that African American, Latino/a, and American Indian students are underrepresented in gifted education by greater than 40% in all instances, especially males, and there has been an increase in underrepresentation for African American students each year (Ford et al., 2008). Conversely, Asian American students are amply represented in gifted education programs (Ford et al., 2008).

Although disproportionality has persisted for decades, there is limited research investigating whether ELLs are under or overrepresented in special education. Studies that have been done reveal patterns of overrepresented in the high-incidence categories of LD, MMR, and SLI categories at rates more than twice that of their White peers. The studies also reveal that ELLs are in more restrictive placements, are underrepresented in kindergarten through second grade, and that older ELLs are overrepresented in special education (Samson & Lesaux, 2009; Skiba et al., 2008; Sullivan, 2011; Valenzuela, Copeland, Qi, & Park, 2006). Although there is considerable consistency in the research investigating African American disproportionality, the research exploring Latino/a disproportionality is inconsistent (Skiba et al., 2008). National studies trend toward underrepresentation of Latinos/as in overall special education services and in a majority of disability categories (Chinn & Hughes, 1987; NCCRESt, 2006). State- and district-level studies show Latino/a overrepresentation in special education (Artiles, Rueda, Salazar, & Higareda, 2002), particularly in the LD category and somewhat so in the hearing impaired category (Sullivan, 2011).

The preponderance of research on disproportionate representation reveals some general characteristics. African Americans are as a group more often investigated than Latinos, ELLs, Native Americans, and Asians, and are the most overrepresented in special education programs in almost every state (Donavan & Cross, 2002; Parrish 2002). On the national level, African American and Native American students are most affected by disproportionate representation and Latinos are disproportionately represented in certain regions and states (Artiles, Sullivan, Waitoller, & Neal, 2010). Although kindergarten and first grade ELLs are underrepresented in special education, special education identification of ELLs has been found to increase beginning in fifth grade and becomes increasingly pronounced in secondary school (Samson & Lesaux, 2009). The high-incidence categories of MMR and EBD regularly show overrepresentation of African American students while Native American students frequently are overrepresented in the LD category. Students with high-incidence disabilities comprise between 90%–95% of the students with disabilities. Thus, disproportionate representation is greater in socially-constructed disability categories that require the use of judgment than in the biologically-based disability categories (e.g., hearing impairment, speech/language impairment, orthopedic impairment, visual impairment) (Donovan & Cross, 2002; Salend, 2011). Students from CLD backgrounds are overrepresented in more restrictive special education settings and underrepresented in less restrictive educational settings such as gifted education and advanced placement classes (Ford et al., 2008).

WHY IS DISPROPORTIONATE REPRESENTATION OCCURRING?

The factors contributing to disproportionate representation are multidimensional. They include schooling and societal factors, issues of gender and age, sociogeographic, and socioeconomic variables. For example, the correlation between poverty and subaverage performance in school has been examined as a factor in the overrepresentation of CLD students in special education (see for example, Skiba et al., 2008). Although the majority of poor children are White, a greater proportion of students from CLD backgrounds (a) grow up in persistent poverty, (b) are more likely than their White peers to experience failure in school, (c) have delayed language development and limited English proficiency, and (d) experience social and emotional skill deficits. However, these issues alone do not explain the significant and ongoing disparity in the placement rates of CLD students into special education classrooms (Donovan & Cross, 2002; Losen & Orfield, 2002; Oakes & Lipton, 2007; Salend, 2011). It appears as though students' race, ethnicity, and gender appear to be important factors that result in large numbers of students being referred to and placed in special education (e.g., Coutinho, Oswald, & Best, 2002; Knotek 2003). The inappropriate placement of students from CLD backgrounds in special education also may be attributed to issues discussed in the following sections.

Limited Use of Culturally Relevant Assessments

The assessments used in placing students in special education should be examined to determine not only their impact on the disproportionate representation of CLD students in these educational settings, but also to ascertain whether they are culturally based. For example, there has been extensive research on the impact of psychometric testing—that is, testing that is concerned with the educational and psychological measurement of such things as abilities, knowledge, interests, personality traits, and attitudes—and its correlation to disproportionate representation of students from CLD backgrounds in special education. Findings from this research have tended to exclude test bias as a factor in the placement of CLD students in special education setting (Brown, Reynolds, & Whitaker, 1999; Jensen, 1980; Reynolds, 2000; Shepard, 1987). However, test bias cannot be conclusively ruled out as a cause of disproportionality (Abedi, 2004; Skiba et al., 2008; Fuchs & Fuchs, 1986). Furthermore, even if some researchers maintain that standardized tests are unbiased, uncritical interpretations of the results of such tests that fail to account for differential access to educational resources on students from CLD backgrounds poses significant problems.

Culturally competent assessments examine many factors including the cultural competence of the examiner and assessment strategies. Because disproportionality is most evident in the categories where there is heavy reliance on professional judgment (i.e., in such categories as MR, EBD, and LD), those who determine students' eligibility for special education placement should have in-depth understanding of CLD students and of the assessments that are most appropriate for use with these students. Such assessments strategies include direct assessment approaches (e.g., curriculum-based measurement and functional assessments) that are useful in planning and evaluating remediation without the need to classify or place students within special education (Skiba, Knesting, & Bush, 2002).

Subjectivity in Special Education Referral, Decision Making, and Placement

Teacher bias in teacher referral, decision making, and placement has been attributed to the overrepresentation of students from CLD backgrounds in special and education (Ford et al., 2008; Harry & Klingner, 2006) and also to their underrepresentation in gifted education (Donovan & Cross, 2002; Elhoweris, Mutua, Negmeldin, & Holloway, 2005; Ford et al., 2008; Garrick Duhaney, 1998). For example, research suggests that the overrepresentation of males in special education is influenced by gender bias on the referral, classification, and placement processes, and that teacher bias stems from gender-stereotyped societal norms and expectations for girls and boys, with respect to such variables as behavior and achievement (Kratovil & Bailey, 1986; Wehmeyer & Schwartz, 2001).

Inadequate Preparation of Teachers to Work With a Diverse Student Population

Teachers' readiness to teach CLD students has been called into question (Blanchett, 2006). Consequently, this issue has to garner greater attention in attempts to resolve disproportionate representation. Improvement in teachers' proficiency to work with CLD students is likely to enrich students' learning (Darling-Hammond, 2004), preclude their placement in special education (Harry & Klingner, 2006), and improve their in-school and out-of-school outcomes. In training preservice teachers, teacher preparation programs (TEPs) should help teacher candidates to deconstruct issues of class, power, and privilege and to reflect on how these could negatively affect their decisions regarding placement of CLD students in special education (Blanchett, 2006; Sleeter, 1993). These programs can utilize a variety of pedagogical approaches (e.g., case studies, videos, hyperlink materials, reflective activities, and autobiographical sketches) to develop and broaden teacher candidates' knowledge and awareness of multicultural issues. They also can provide teacher candidates' clinical experiences in high-needs school districts with students from CLD backgrounds so they can learn about these students, and to help them make connections between theory and practice.

Misinterpretation or Pathologization of Culturally Different Behaviors

The disproportionately high placement of CLD students in special education classrooms has been associated with the misinterpretation of their behaviors as indicators of the presence of a disorder or disability (Donovan & Cross, 2002; Salend, 2011; Skiba et al., 2008). Given that behaviorally-based special education referrals are prevalent, there is a need for teachers to examine cultural factors that underline CLD students' behaviors (Hershfeldt et al., 2009). Here is one example that provides a rationale for doing so. Some cultures allow unstructured collegial interaction among classmates during class time while western cultures such as the United States do not encourage it. Teachers lacking training and sensitivity to this kind of cultural behavioral norm may view the students' interactional behavior as problematic (Hershfeldt et al., 2009) and refer them to special education. Once in special education, students may face disproportionate disciplinary actions from teachers who are more likely to resort to office referrals, suspensions, expulsions, or place these students in more restrictive classroom settings (Krezmien, Leon, & Achilles, 2006; Lo & Cartledge, 2007). With a majority of teachers being White and with more and more students being from CLD backgrounds, there is an urgent need to prepare teachers to use culturally appropriate behavioral interventions (Hershfeldt et al., 2009).

Differential Appropriation of Educational Funding and Resources

Differential access to educational resources and the gross inequity in school funding results in students in wealthier, mostly White school districts getting much more school resources than students in poorer, high-minority school districts (e.g., uncertified and inadequately prepared teachers, state-of-the art equipment and up-to-date materials and resources, modern buildings) (Books, 2007; Kozol, 2005). With high-poverty schools typically enrolling students from CLD backgrounds, many of these students have limited access to educational resources, high-quality prereferral, Response-to-Intervention (RTI), ancillary services, and licensed professionals, which hinders their educational advancement and postschool outcomes (Salend, 2011).

Lack of Home-School Collaboration

Although a central principle of the Individuals With Disabilities Education Improvement Act of 2004 is family participation, there have been obstacles to the participation of parents and families of students from CLD backgrounds (Harry, 2008). Barriers to parental participation include teachers' misperceptions of parental roles in the placement process; historical legacy of prejudice, exclusion, and marginalization of CLD groups; and differential definition of disability across cultures that often results in miscommunication between service providers and families (Harry, 2008; Kalyanpur & Harry, 1999; Lo, 2005). Schools can foster home–school communication by providing ESL and literacy training to parents and families who speak languages other than English and by learning about the families' belief systems, child rearing practices, developmental expectations, and perceptions about disability (Salend, 2011).

HOW CAN WE CURTAIL DISPROPORTIONATE REPRESENTATION?

Because the factors that contribute to the problem of disproportionality are multifaceted, a comprehensive and multifaceted intervention approach needs to be implemented to address it. Delivering a wide variety of evidence-based, culturally sensitive educational services and practices within the general education classroom that supports student learning and family involvement can help curtail the problem of disproportionate representation. Such services and practices should address students' unique needs, strengths, opportunities, experiences, sociocultural, and linguistic needs as well as home–school collaborations (Salend & Garrick Duhaney, 2005; Salend, 2011). Effective practices that can minimize the likelihood of disproportionality follow.

Providing Certified, Academically Competent, and Caring Teachers

Good teaching is the single greatest predictor in promoting or deterring student achievement (National Commission on Teaching and America's Future, 1996; Nieto, 2006). Because students' success in the classroom is directly correlated to their opportunity to learn, it is not difficult to predict that those with limited educational opportunities and unskilled teachers are more likely to be referred for special education services (Salend, 2011). Certified teachers who are highly trained and educated, are ready to embrace the challenges and opportunities of teaching in multicultural school settings, are education advocates for students and their families, and are reflective about their own teaching practice and how they can minimize the problem of disproportionality and improve student achievement (Oakes & Lipton, 2007; Salend, Whittaker, Garrick Duhaney, & Smith, 2003).

Qualified teachers are effective and competent in content areas, and are conversant with philosophical underpinnings, rationales, and beliefs that support instructional decisions and actions. Consequently, school districts should ensure that all students have access to qualified teachers as failure to do so results in minimal impact of school reforms on student achievement (Darling-Hammond & Falk, 1997; Gay, 1997). Competent teachers are aware of the impact of sociological factors (e.g., their attitudes and interpersonal skills about different groups) on learning. Thus, they create democratic classroom environments where students experience a sense of belonging. Such teachers bring out the very best in each of their students; are uncompromising, yet caring; demanding, yet encouraging; and warm, yet reserved. They connect with their students and have invaluable insights into their backgrounds, challenges, and problems. They maintain proactive contact with their students, both in and outside of the classroom. Students know these teachers care about their academic progress because they demonstrate it day-after-day by holding them to high academic standards and expectations, and by pushing them to do their best. Such teachers respect and trust their students, provide them with emotional support (e.g., when they are emotionally upset due to the loss of a friendship, family member, or pet), and celebrate their accomplishments and special milestones (e.g., academic and athletic accomplishments, birthdays).

Likewise, competent teachers are often those who care enough to accept teaching positions in urban school districts. These are the teachers who know each student by name and are able to establish relationships with students who feel disconnected from academics and its related outcomes. They are adept at enabling students to make meaning of who they are, to believe in themselves, to set challenging and meaningful goals, and to work toward attaining those goals. They observe how students relate to each other and purposely implement classroom activities that enable their students to develop social and cross-cultural relationships. Such teachers understand that the disparities in the academic achievement between White and CLD students can be mitigated when teachers demonstrate care, respect, and trust in the classroom, when students are motivated, challenged, and engaged in their schoolwork, and when students have good relationships with their teachers and peers (Noddings, 1992; Wentzel, 1997).

Fostering Culturally Sensitive Instructional Classroom Environments

Qualified and caring teachers are aware of the rich and ever-increasing cultural and linguistic diversity of our schools, and of the imperative to use culturally sensitive instructional strategies that are differentiated. They are teachers who acknowledge students' experiential, cultural, and linguistic backgrounds; learning styles; and developmental ages (Banks, 2009; Cartledge & Kourea, 2008; Garrick Duhaney & Whittington-Couse, 1998; Garrick Duhaney, 2005; Gay, 2000; Gollnick & Chinn, 2009; Obiakor, 2007; Taylor & Whittaker, 2009). Culturally sensitive teachers use teaching strategies that promote equity in educational outcomes, are aware of their students' cultural values and of the importance that parents and families place on academic success, homework, school discipline, and teacher authority, and of the need to establish alliances with students and families from CLD backgrounds (Diaz-Rico & Weed, 2010; Gay, 2000; Gollnick & Chinn, 2009; Ladson-Billings, 1994, 1999; Taylor & Whittaker, 2009). Such teachers are introspective, constantly review the literature, and try out various teaching strategies in the interest of improving their students' learning (Ladson-Billings, 1994).

Effective culturally responsive classroom instructional strategies have been highlighted in the educational literature (Banks et al., 2005; Boykin, Tyler, & Miller, 2005; Friend & Bursuck, 2009; Klingner & Soltero-González, 2009), and include relating instruction to what is familiar and meaningful to students (e.g., many African American, Latino/a, and Asian American students are responsive to cooperative rather than competitive teaching and learning environments). Culturally responsive instructional strategies promote the linking of instruction to goals that are especially relevant to students, curriculum content modification, and the use of verbal response options (e.g., chorus responding in large-group situations or one-on-one with the teacher, dub or rap poetry, storytelling, group recitations and discussions, and role playing), and the use of physical stimulation and high-energy, high-action, purposeful movement in the classroom. Classroom arrangements that affirm the family and community orientations that are common to CLD groups, that promote divergent thinking (e.g., brainstorming, debates, and group discussions), and frequent assessment of students' progress also are effective classroom instructional approaches.

Employing Culturally Responsive Evidence-Based Behavioral Practices

As previously discussed, there is disproportionality in disciplinary actions—both in quantity and severity—for students from CLD backgrounds with disabilities. This substantiates the need for principals and their teachers to employ culturally responsive behavior management practices that are informed by policies, guidelines, and ongoing professional development, as well as research activities that foster introspection on cultural underpinnings of behavior (Cartledge & Kourea, 2008; Garrick Duhaney, 2000; Gay, 2000; Hershfeldt et al., 2009; Ladson-Billings, 1999; Salend & Garrick Duhaney, 2005). Teachers who adhere to the principles and practices of culturally responsive pedagogy use various *primary* level school wide and class wide behavior management strategies to create disciplined environments rather than punitive ones. For example, they adapt the classroom design, including the placement of the teacher's desk, use active supervision and student engagement, multiple procedures to respond to inappropriate student behavior, clear and effective communication, more positive than negative student–teacher interactions, orchestrate smooth transitions and continuous momentum throughout the school day, carry out routine classroom tasks promptly and efficiently, and develop authentic relationships with their students (Hershfeldt et al., 2009; Salend, 2011).

When students are unresponsive to primary level behavior interventions and need *secondary* or more direct interventions, teachers can use social skills instruction. Social skills instruction includes telling the student what the desired behavior is, showing the student how to perform the behavior, giving the student sufficient opportunity to practice the behavior with corrective and reinforcing feedback, and allowing opportunities for maintenance and transfer of the behavior (Cartledge & Kourea, 2008; Cartledge & Milburn, 1996). Students with and at risk for behavior disorders may benefit from *tertiary* interventions. Such interventions might include the use of culturally sensitive functional behavior assessments (FBAs) and behavior intervention plans (BIPs) to ascertain the importance of a behavior and teaching a student how to replace a disruptive behavior with an appropriate one (Cartledge & Kourea, 2008; Salend, 2011). Parents and families can partner with teachers in teaching their children/students how to behave in socially appropriate ways.

Employing Evidence-Based Prereferral Strategies

The provision of evidence-based prereferral systems and services can reduce the referrals of students from CLD backgrounds to special education (Gravois & Rosenfield, 2006; Knotek, 2003). Prereferral services include identification of students' educational performance, their medical history, and their cultural backgrounds and experiences (Salend, 2011). Teachers who employ prereferral interventions should assess them and use the data gathered to determine the success or failure of the interventions (Salend & Garrick Duhaney, 2005). Consonant with this approach, assessment results for an instructional consultant model showed reduction in the number of special education referral and identification, and in the racial and ethnic discrepancies in rates of referral and identification for special education (Gravois & Rosenfield, 2006).

When students fail to progress in the general education classroom their teachers should determine whether more individualized and specialized educational services are needed. A prereferral intervention team (also referred to as a multidisciplinary planning team, child study team, or general education assistance team) comprising a diverse group of competent and culturally sensitive professionals, the student (when appropriate), and the student's parents can help teachers determine whether students need more intensive educational services, and also can help to combat bias in the prereferral process (Salend, 2011; Salend & Garrick Duhaney, 2005). Although not mandated, the multidisciplinary planning team may be expanded to include professionals and community members who (a) understand the student's native language and culture, (b) can identify the difference between a linguistic or cultural difference and a learning difficulty, (c) have knowledge of classroom based assessment alternatives, and (d) can translate assessment data in culturally appropriate ways to enhance the team's ability to make more appropriate educational decisions to address students' learning challenges and opportunities (Fielder et al., 2008; García & Ortiz, 2006; Garrick Duhaney, 2005; Salend, 2011).

Implementing Culturally Responsive Response-to-Intervention Models

Response to Intervention (RTI)—a multi-tiered, research-validated, comprehensive instructional model—is an alternative to an IQ-achievement discrepancy formula that the Individuals with Disabilities Education Improvement Act of 2004 allows schools to use for special education eligibility decisions (Brown & Doolittle, 2008; Fuchs & Fuchs, 2007; Klingner & Edwards, 2006). Based on the concept of treatment validity, RTI attempts to minimize inappropriate referrals to special education through early screening; consideration of factors that contribute to a student's academic failures (e.g., inadequate, inconsistent, or improperly delivered classroom instruction); brief assessments of a student's performance on target skills (e.g., oral reading fluency); and the provision of systematic, research-based instruction and appropriate interventions that are correlated to students' needs. RTI typically has three levels of intervention. The first level, which comprises early assessment, identification, and implementation of instructional support, is referred to as Tier 1. In Tier II more intensive instructional and behavioral supports as well as progress monitoring are provided to the student in the general education classroom. In Tier III, the last tier in some models, the student who does not respond to the targeted intervention or who does not make sufficient progress in Tier II receives individualized, intensive, supplementary interventions targeted to the skill deficits. For models with only three tiers, the student would be receiving this intensive, supplemental instruction in the general education classroom while he or she is simultaneously being tested for special education supports and services. For models with a fourth tier, this is the stage where testing for determining eligibility for special education would be conducted (Brown & Doolittle, 2008; Fuchs & Fuchs, 2007; Salend, 2011; Stecker, 2007; Vanderheyden, 2011).

When using RTI with CLD students, educators should ensure that it is compatible with their prior experiences. The interventions and assessments used should be culturally responsive and should address student, classroom, and home–community factors. The interventions and assessments also should be compatible with research-based practices for working with CLD students. Additionally, the instructional methods used should be validated for use with CLD students, adhere to bias-reducing practices and strategies, and be evaluated relative to the cultural context within which they are used (e.g., acculturation levels, prior experiences, cultural values) (Klingner & Edwards, 2006; Salend, 2011).

Incorporating the Principles of Universal Design for Learning

Universal design for learning (UDL) provides a framework to help all students to access the general education curriculum through differentiated curriculum and instruction and to be successful (Dukes & Lamar-Dukes, 2009; Salend, 2011). In UDL teachers present information and materials in many formats (e.g., demonstration, lectures, simulations, visual, auditory, and digital); provide students with a number of ways to demonstrate their learning (e.g., orally, written, technologically, graphically, tests, group projects); use various means to engage, challenge, and motivate students to learn; and assess whether students' are meeting educational goals. Examples of assessment approaches that educators can use include report cards; standardized tests; informal assessments such as teacher-made tests; rating scales that address such things as attitude, behavior, and interests; classroom work samples such as projects and assignments; and classroom observation. Thus, UDL supports the development of adjustable materials, a variety of instructional methods, and practical assessment approaches (Kurtts, Matthews, & Smallwood, 2009; Salend, 2011; Sopko, 2008).

Using Authentic Assessments

In the past decade or so, there has been a rise in large-scale educational assessment to hold schools accountable for students' learning. However, for students with significant disabilities who cannot be included in state and district educational assessment, IDEA 1997 allows schools to develop and use alternative assessments (Towles-Reeves, Kleinert, & Muhomba, 2009). Consequently, teachers have the autonomy to use authentic or classroom-based assessments in addition to prereferral intervention strategies, RTI, and UDL in their efforts to prevent a referral to determine eligibility for special education. These assessment alternatives should be linked to a student's individualized education program (IEP), and would have the advantage of including parents and families in the selection and use of these strategies, thereby providing a more comprehensive picture of the student's educational strengths and challenges (Salend & Garrick Duhaney, 2005).

Salend (2011), Reese and Levy (2009), and Roeber (2002) outlined authentic assessment approaches that teachers may employ in their classrooms, and a few of these are presented here:

- *E-Portfolios* can provide conclusive evidence of learning over time. They can be used to assess a body of evidence or continuous collection of student work over time that is assessed against predetermined scoring criteria (e.g., rubric). Teachers using e-portfolios for assessment should ensure that students know the purposes for which the e-portfolio is being created (e.g., to document achievement for grading purposes, to document progress towards attainment of standards, or to place students appropriately), the processes to follow in developing their e-portfolios, and how they should select their work for inclusion in the e-portfolios. They also should create opportunities for their students to reflect on their work products, and they should establish how and when the e-portfolio will be evaluated.
- *Curriculum-based measurement* (CBM) can be used to enhance student achievement. It permits the teacher to conduct continuous and repeated measurements of students' progress and of their teaching effectiveness. Advantages of CBM include sensitivity to changes in students' progress over short durations of time, ease of administration, and cost-effectiveness.
- *Checklists* can help teachers to identify whether students are able to perform a specific educational task or activity, or how well they know a particular subject. Teachers who use checklists for assessment should clarify their intended purpose and establish well-defined criteria for performance.
- *Learning journals or logs* can be used to assess students' learning progress. For example, after teaching a lesson, a teacher can ask students to write in their journal on what they have learned and what they do not understand.
- *Rubrics* describe criteria associated with different levels of proficiency for evaluating students' performance. They are useful in communicating the teacher's expectations and allow for objective and consistent feedback to students.

Using Practical and Well-Established Strategies to Set the Stage for Academic Success

Students from CLD backgrounds who have or at-risk for disabilities have the greatest need for practical, evidence-based teaching strategies that have the greatest potential to improve students' academic success. Numerous such strategies from the academic literature include efficiency in preparing for teaching, getting students settled and ready for instruction, taking attendance, distributing materials, transitioning from one subject or activity or setting to another, managing classroom behavior, presenting interactive instruction, and monitoring seatwork. Other strategies include posting daily schedules in areas that are highly visible to students, arranging the classroom space for easy flow, and using only a few positively stated classroom rules. Teacher efficiency in these strategies results in higher student on-task behavior and higher achievement in students from CLD backgrounds, non-English-speaking students, and students from low socioeconomic backgrounds (Evertson & Emmer, 1980; Good & Grouws, 1979; Stallings, Cory, Fairweather, & Needels, 1978).

Working With Families

School partnership and collaboration with parents and families from CLD backgrounds is not only important for students' educational success but can help to reduce disproportionality. Recognizing the importance of parental participation in schools, the IDEA requires that schools make every effort to involve parents and families in their children's education (Harry, 2008; Yssel et al., 2007). Teachers can involve parents and families in schools by including them in curriculum planning; individualized education program (IEP) development; school events; and by soliciting information from them about child rearing practices and their children's interests, strengths, challenges, and opportunities; and by offering them educational programs (Salend, 2011). School–parent–family partnerships will have the greatest opportunity for success if educators are collaborative, respectful, trustworthy, and understand the cultural values of the family (Salend & Garrick Duhaney, 2005).

Teachers should pay careful attention to how and what tools they use in communicating with parents and families. Several strategies to consider include using open ended questions, careful and empathetic listening, and good communication strategies that reflects a knowledge of the parents' language and culture and uses clear and courteous language. Educators also can use technology-based communication such emails, multilingual hotlines, automated notification systems, and interactive videoconferencing if they know that parents and families prefer these modes of communication (Salend, 2011).

HOW CAN EFFORTS TO MINIMIZE DISPROPORTIONATE REPRESENTATION BE EVALUATED?

Educators should evaluate their efforts to eliminate disproportionate representation. Among the strategies that they can employ to accomplish this objective is to comply with federal policies and guidelines. For example, the IDEIA requires school districts and state education agencies to establish databases to ensure that students from CLD backgrounds are not over identified as being eligible for special education services. The databases should be examined for inconsistencies in the prereferral, RTI, referral, identification, and placement processes and should be disaggregated by race, gender, and income status. If disproportionate representation exists, school districts are required to take steps to address it. The IDEIA also requires school districts to measure the academic progress of students who have disabilities, either by including them in standardized assessments other students take or, for students with significant intellectual disabilities, by using an alternate assessments (requirements are clarified in the No Child Left Behind Act [NCLB], 2002). These student learning outcomes assessment data should be analyzed to determine whether students are inappropriately placed in special education. Examples of questions that can guide the review of the data are: What percentage of students from CLD backgrounds versus White students exit special education? Are students being challenged by the curriculum?

Finally, educators can collaborate with others to design assessments to determine the effectiveness of the strategies and programs they implement to reduce disproportionate representation. For example, they can bring in a university-based consulting team to work with them in developing tools and strategies to evaluate how well the anticipated outcomes and impacts of the strategies they implemented have been achieved. Similarly, questionnaire and interview data on the perceptions of parents and families regarding strategies and policies can be collected and examined. Not to be overlooked, educators also should evaluate their own perceptions, beliefs, and practices about diversity. They can do so by asking themselves a series of questions (e.g., What are my perceptions about students from CLD backgrounds? What are my thoughts about disproportionate representation? What steps have I taken to safeguard against contributing to this problem?). The answers to these and other questions could be recorded in a journal and examined with a view toward taking corrective action when necessary.

CONCLUSION

This chapter has discussed the pervasive problem of disproportionate representation of students from CLD backgrounds in special education. Disproportionate representation is a complex problem and a combination of factors contributes to it. Predictors vary by cultural and linguistic group and the disability studied. Because the promise of ending educational inequalities and the poor school outcomes for students from CLD back-grounds rests, in part, in bringing an end to the persistent stain of dispro-portionate representation, this chapter has examined what it is, who is im-pacted by it, why it is occurring, and how it can be addressed by discussing several strategies that hold promise for reducing this problem. Finally, this chapter presented strategies for evaluating the success of efforts to mini-mize disproportionate representation.

REFERENCES

Abedi, J. (2004). The No Child Left Behind Act and English language learners: As-sessment and accountability issues. *Educational Researcher, 33*(1), 4–14.

Affleck, J. Q., Edgar, E., Levine, P., & Kortering, L. (1990). Post-school status of students classified as mildly mentally retarded, learning disabled or non-handicapped: Does it get better with time? *Education and Training in Mental Retardation, 25*(4), 315–324.

Artiles, A. J., Kozleski, E. B., Trent, S. C., Osher, D., & Ortiz, A. (2010). Justifying and explaining disproportionality, 1968–2008: A critique of underlying views of culture. *Exceptional Children, 76*(3), 279–299.

Artiles, A. J., Rueda, R., Salazar, J. J., & Higareda, I. (2002). English language learner representation in special education in California urban school districts. In D. J. Losen & G. Orfield (Eds.), *Racial inequality in special education* (pp. 117–135). Cambridge, MA: Harvard Education Publishing Group.

Artiles, A. J., Rueda, R., Salazar, J. J., & Higareda, I. (2005). Within-group diversity in minority disproportionate representation: English language learners in ur-ban school districts. *Exceptional Children, 71*, 283–300.

Artiles, A. J., Sullivan, A., Waitoller, F., & Neil, R. (2010). Latinos in special educa-tion: Equity issues at the intersection of language, culture, and ability differ-ences. In E. Murillo (Ed.), *Handbook of Latinos in education* (pp. 361–381). Mahwah, NJ: Erlbaum.

Banks, J., Cochran-Smith, M., Moll, L., Richert, A., Zeichner, K., LePage, P., et al. (2005). Teaching diverse learners. In L. Darling-Hammond & J. Bransford (Eds.), *Preparing teachers for a changing world: What teachers should learn and be able to do* (pp. 232–274). San Francisco: Jossey-Bass.

Banks, J. A. (2009). *Teaching strategies for ethnic studies* (8th ed.). Boston: Allyn & Bacon.

Blanchett, W. (2006). Disproportionate representation of African American stu-dents in special education: Acknowledging the role of White privilege and racism. *Educational Researcher, 35*, 24–28.

Books, S. (Ed.). (2007). *Invisible children in the society and its schools* (3rd ed.). Mah-wah, NJ: Lawrence Erlbaum.

Boykin, A. W., Tyler, K. M., & Miller, O. (2005). In search of cultural themes and their expressions in the dynamics of classroom life. *Urban Education, 40*, 521–549.

Brayboy, B. M. J., Castagno, A. E., & Maughan, E. (2007). Equality and justice for all? Examining race in education scholarship. *Review of Research in Education, 31,* 159–194. *Brown v. Board of Education,* 347 U.S. 483 (1954).

Brown, J. E., & Doolittle, J. (2008). A cultural, linguistic, and ecological framework for response to intervention with English language learners. *Teaching Exceptional Children, 40*(5), 66–72.

Brown, R. T., Reynolds, C. R., & Whitaker, J. S. (1999). Bias in mental testing since *Bias in Mental Testing. School Psychology Quarterly, 14,* 208–238.

Cartledge, G., & Kourea, L. (2008). Culturally responsive classrooms for culturally diverse students with and at risk for disabilities. *Exceptional Children, 74*(3), 351–371.

Cartledge, G., & Milburn, J. F. (1996). *Cultural diversity and social skill instruction: Understanding ethnic and gender differences.* Champaign, IL: Research press.

Cartledge, G., Singh, A., & Gibson, L. (2008). Practical behavior-management techniques to close the accessibility gap for students who are culturally and linguistically diverse. *Preventing School Failure, 52,* 29–38.

Children's Defense Fund. (1975). *School suspensions: Are they helping children?* Cambridge, MA: Washington Research Project.

Chinn, P. C., & Hughes, S. (1987). Representation of minority students in special education classes. *Remedial and Special Education, 8,* 41–46.

Connor, D. J., & Ferri, B. A. (2007). The conflict within: Resistance to inclusion and other paradoxes in special education. *Disability and Society, 22*(1), 63–77.

Coutinho, M. J., & Oswald, D. P. (2004). *Disproportionate representation of culturally and linguistically diverse students in special education: Measuring the problem.* Tempe, Arizona: National Center for Culturally Responsive Educational Systems.

Coutinho, M. J., Oswald, D. P., & Best. A. M. (2002). The influence of sociodemographics on the disproportionate identification of minority students as having learning disabilities. *Remedial and Special Education, 23,* 49–59.

Darling-Hammond, L. (2004). Inequality and the right to learn: Access to qualified teachers in California's public schools. *Teachers College Record, 106,* 1936–1966.

Darling-Hammond, L., & Falk, B. (1997). Using standards and assessments to support student learning. *Phi Delta Kappan, 79*(3), 190–199.

Diaz-Rico, L. T., & Weed, K. Z. (2010). *Crosscultural, language, and academic development handbook: The complete K–12 reference guide* (4th ed.). Boston: Allyn & Bacon.

Donovan, M. S., & Cross, C. T. (Eds.). (2002). *Minority students in special and gifted education.* Washington, DC: National Academy Press.

Dukes, C., & Lamar-Dukes, P. (2009). Inclusion by design: Engineering inclusive practices in secondary schools. *Teaching Exceptional Children, 41*(3), 16–23.

Dunn, L. M. (1968). Special education for the mildly retarded: Is much of it justifiable? *Exceptional Children, 35,* 5–22.

Elhoweris, H., Mutua, K., Negmeldin, A., & Holloway, P. (2005). The effects of the child's ethnicity on teachers' referral and recommendation decisions in gifted and talented programs. *Remedial and Special Education, 26,* 25–31.

Evertson, C., & Emmer, E. (1980). *Effective management at the beginning of the school year in junior high classes.* Austin, TX: University of Texas, Research and Development Center for Teacher Education.

Fielder, C. R., Chiang, B., Van Haren, B., Jorgensen, J., Halberg, S., & Boreson, L. (2008). Culturally responsive practices in schools: A checklist to address disproportionality in special education. *Teaching Exceptional Children, 40*(5), 52–59.

Ford, D. Y., Grantham, T.C., & Whiting, G.W. (2008). Culturally and linguistically diverse students in gifted education: Recruitment and retention issues. *Exceptional Children, 74,* 289–306.

Friend, M., & Bursuck, W. D. (2009). *Including students with special needs: A practical guide for classroom teachers* (5th ed.). Upper Saddle River, NJ: Pearson Education.

Fuchs, D., & Fuchs, L. S. (1986). Test procedure bias: A meta-analysis of examiner familiarity effects. *Review of Educational Research, 56,* 243–262.

Fuchs, L. S., & Fuchs, D. (2007). A model for implementing responsiveness to intervention. *Teaching Exceptional Children, 39*(5), 14–23.

Garcia, S. B., & Ortiz, A. A. (2006). Preventing disproportionate representation: Culturally and linguistically responsive prereferral interventions. *Teaching Exceptional Children, 38*(4), 64–67.

Garrick Duhaney, L. M. (1998). A multicultural teaching model for the 21st century. *Gems of AGATE, 22*(1), 26–27.

Garrick Duhaney, L. M. (2000). Culturally sensitive strategies for violence prevention. *Multicultural Education, 7*(4), 10–17.

Garrick Duhaney, L. M. (2005). Fostering equity curriculum and pedagogy: Educating students with dialectical variations. In R. Hoosain & F. Salili (Eds.), *Language in multicultural education* (pp. 95–114). Greenwich, CT: Information Age.

Garrick Duhaney, L. M., & Whittington-Couse, M. (1998, April). *Using learning styles and strategies to enhance academic learning for linguistically and culturally diverse students.* Paper presented at the Conference on Providing Appropriate Instruction and Services to Culturally and Linguistically Diverse Learners, Fishkill, NY.

Gay, G. (1997). Multicultural infusion in teacher education: Foundations and applications. *Peabody Journal of Education, 22*(1), 150–177.

Gay, G. (2000). *Culturally responsive teaching: Theory, research, and practice.* New York: Teachers College Press.

Gollnick, D. M., & Chinn, P. C. (2009). *Multicultural education in a pluralistic society* (8th ed.). Upper Saddle River, NJ: Merrill/Pearson Education.

Good, T. L., & Grouws, D. A. (1979). The Missouri mathematics effectiveness project. *Journal of Educational Psychology, 71,* 355–362.

Gravois, T. A., & Rosenfield, S. A. (2006). Impact of instructional consultation teams on the disproportionate referral and placement of minority students in special education. *Remedial and Special Education, 27*(1), 42–52.

Gregory, J. E. (1997). Three strikes and they're out: African American boys and American schools' responses to misbehavior. *International Journal of Adolescence and Youth, 7*(1), 25–34.

Harry, B. (2008). Collaboration with culturally and linguistically diverse families: Ideal versus reality. *Council for Exceptional Children, 74*(3), 372–388.

Harry, B., & Klingner, J. (2006). *Why are so many minority students in special education? Understanding race and disability in schools.* New York: Teachers College Press.

Hershfeldt, P. A., Sechrest, R., Pell, K. L., Rosenberg, M. S., Bradshaw, C. P., & Leaf, P. L. (2009). Double-check: A framework of cultural responsiveness applied to classroom behavior. *Teaching Exceptional Children Plus, 6*(2) Article 5. Retrieved September 15, 2012, from http://escholarship.bc.edu/education/tecplus/vol6/iss2/art5.

Hosp, J. L. & Reschly, D. J. (2004). Disproportionate representation of minority students in special education: Academic, demographic, and economic predictors. *Exceptional Children, 70,* 185–199.

Individuals With Disabilities Education Act Regulations, 34 C.F.R. 300.1 et seq.

Individuals With Disabilities Education Act Amendments of 1997 (IDEA), Pub. L. No. 105–17, 20 U.S.C. §§1400 et seq.

Jensen, A. R. (1980). *Bias in mental testing.* New York: Free Press.

Kalyanpur, M., & Harry, B. (1999). *Culture in special education: Building reciprocal family-professional relationships.* Baltimore: Paul H. Brookes.

Klingner, J. K., & Edwards, P. A. (2006). Cultural considerations with response to intervention models. *Reading Research Quarterly, 41*(1), 108–115.

Klingner, J., & Soltero-González, L. (2009). Culturally and linguistically responsive literacy instruction for English language learners with learning disabilities. *Multiple Voices, 12*(1), 4–20.

Knotek, S. (2003). Bias in problem-solving and the social process of student study teams: A qualitative investigation. *The Journal of Special Education, 37*(1), 2–14.

Kozol, J. (2005). *The shame of the nation: The restoration of apartheid schooling in America.* New York: Crown.

Kratovil, J., & Bailey, S.M. (1986). Sex equity and disabled students. *Theory Into Practice, 25,* 250–256.

Krezmien, M. P., Leone, P. E., & Achilles, G. M. (2006). Suspension, race, and disability: Analysis of statewide practices and reporting. *Journal of Emotional and Behavioral Disorders, 14,* 217–226.

Kurtts, S. A., Matthews, C. E., & Smallwood, T. (2009). (Dis)solving the differences: A physical science lesson using universal design. *Intervention in School and Clinic, 44*(3), 151–159.

Ladson-Billings, G. (1994). Who will teach our children: Preparing teachers to successfully teach African American students. In E. R. Hollins, J. E. King, & W. C. Hayman (Eds.), *Teaching diverse populations: Formulating a knowledge base* (pp. 129–142). Albany, NY: State University of New York Press.

Ladson-Billings, G. (1999). Preparing teachers for diverse student populations: A critical race theory perspective. In A. Iran-Nejad & D. Pearson (Eds.), *Review of research in education, Vol. 24* (pp. 211–248). Washington, DC: American Educational Research Association.

Lo, Y. (2005). Barriers to successful partnerships with Chinese-speaking parents of children with disabilities in urban schools. *Multiple Voices, 8*(1), 84–95.

Lo, Y., & Cartledge, G. (2007). Office disciplinary referrals in an urban elementary school. *Multicultural Learning and Teaching, 2*(1), 20–38.

Losen, D., & Orfield, G. (Eds.). (2002). *Racial inequality in special education.* Cambridge, MA: Harvard Educational Press.

Losen, D., & Wellner, K. (2001). Disabling discrimination in our public schools: Comprehensive legal challenges to inappropriate and inadequate special education services for minority students. *Civil Liberties Law Review, 36*(2), 407–260.

McCall, Z., & Skrtic, T. (2009). Intersectional needs politics: A policy frame for the wicked problem of disproportionality. *Multiple Voices, 11*(2), 3–23.

Mills v. Board of Education of the District of Columbia, 348 F. Supp. 866 (d.D.C., 1972).

National Center on Culturally Responsive Educational Systems. (2006). Disproportionality by race and disability 2003-2004 [Data file]. Retrieved June 29, 2010, from http://nccrest.eddata.net/data/index.php?id=476fI=2003-2004&f2=Hispanic.

National Commission on Teaching and America's Future. (1996). *What matters most: Teaching for America's future.* New York: National Commission on Teaching and America's Future.

National Research Council. (1982). *Placing children in special education: A strategy of equity.* Washington, DC: National Academy Press.

National Research Council. (2002). *Minority students in special and gifted education.* Washington, DC: National Academy Press.

Nieto, S. (2006). Solidarity, courage and heart: What teacher educators can learn from a new generation of teachers. *Intercultural Education, 17*(5), 457–473.

No Child Left Behind (NCLB) Act of 2001, Pub. L. No. 107-110, § 115, Stat. 1425 (2002).

Noddings, N. (1992). *The challenge to care in schools: An alternative approach to education.* New York: Teachers College Press.

Oakes, J., & Lipton, M. (2007). *Teaching to change the world* (6th ed.). New York: McGraw Hill.

Obiakor, F. E. (2007). *Multicultural special education: Culturally responsive teaching.* Upper Saddle River, NJ: Merrill/Pearson Education.

Parrish, T. (2002). Racial disparities in the identification, funding, and provision of special education. In D. J. Losen & G. Orfield (Eds.), *Racial inequity in special education* (pp. 15–37). Cambridge, MA: Harvard Education Press.

Pennsylvania Association for Retarded Children v. Commonwealth of Pennsylvania, 343 F. Supp. 279 (E.D. Pa., 1972).

Plyler v. Doe, 457 U.S. 202 (1982).

Reese, M., & Levy, R. (2009, February). Assessing the future: E-Portfolio trends, uses, and options in higher education. (Research Bulletin, Issue 4). Boulder, CO: EDUCAUSE Center for Applied Research. Available from http://www.educause.edu/ecar.

Reynolds, C. R. (2000). Why is psychometric research on bias in mental testing so often ignored? *Psychology, Public Policy, and Law, 6,* 144–150.

Roeber, E. D. ((2002, November). *Appropriate inclusion of students in state accountability systems.* Retrieved August 3, 2004, from Education Commission of the States website, www.ecs.org/clearinghouse/40/11/4011.htm.

Salend, S. J. (2011). *Creating inclusive classrooms: Effective and reflective practices* (7th ed.). Upper Saddle River, NJ: Pearson Education.

Salend, S. J., & Garrick Duhaney, L. M. (2005). Understanding and addressing the disproportionate representation of students of color in special education. *Intervention in School and Clinic, 40*(4), 213–221.

Salend, S. J., & Garrick Duhaney, L. M. (2011). Historical and philosophical changes in the education of students with exceptionalities. In A. F. Rotatori, F. E. Obiakor, & J. P. Bakken (Eds.), *Advances in special education* (pp. 1-20), Bingley, Great Britain: Emerald Group.

Salend, S. J., Garrick Duhaney, L. M., & Montgomery, W. (2002). A comprehensive approach to identifying and addressing issues of disproportionate representation. *Remedial and Special Education, 23*(5), 289–299.

Salend, S. J., Whittaker, C. R., Garrick Duhaney, L. M., & Smith, R. M. (2003). Diversifying teacher education programs to recruit and graduate culturally and linguistically diverse teachers. *Teacher Education and Special Education, 26*(4), 315–327.

Samson, J. F., & Lesaux, N. K. (2009). Language-minority learners in special education: Rates and predictors of identification for services. *Journal of Learning Disabilities, 42*(2), 148–162.

Schiller, E., O'Reilly, F., & Fiore, T. (2006). *Marking the progress of IDEA Implementation: The study of state and local implementation and impact of IDEA.* Bethesda, MD: Abt Associates.

Shaw, S. R., & Braden, J. P. (1990). Race and gender bias in the administration of corporal punishment. *School Psychology Review, 19*, 378–383.

Shepard, L. A. (1987). The case for bias in tests of achievement and scholastic aptitude. In S. Modgil & C. Modgil (Eds.), *Arthur Jensen: Consensus and controversy* (pp. 177–190). New York: Falmer Press.

Skiba, R. J., Knesting, K., & Bush, L. D. (2002). Culturally competent assessment: More than nonbiased tests. *Journal of Child and Family Studies, 11, 61–78*

Skiba, R. J., Michael, R. S., Nardo, A. C., & Peterson, R. L. (2002). The color of discipline: Sources of racial and gender disproportionality in school punishment. *Urban Review, 34*, 317–342.

Skiba, R. J., Poloni-Staudinger-Poloni, L., Gallini, S., Simmons, A. B., & Feffins-Azziz, R. (2006). Disparate access: The disproportionality of African American students with disabilities across educational environments. *Exceptional Children, 72*(4), 411–424.

Skiba, R. J., Simmons, A. B., Ritter, S., Gibb, A. C., Rausch, M. K., Caudrado, J., & Chung, C. G. (2008). Achieving equity in special education: History, status, and current challenges. *Exceptional Children, 74*(3), 264–288.

Sleeter, C. E. (1993). How White teachers construct race. In C. McCarthy & W. Crichlow (Eds.), *Race identity and representation in education* (pp. 157–171). New York: Routledge.

Smith, R. M., Gallagher, D., Owen, V., & Skrtic, T. M. (2009). Disability studies in education: Guidelines and ethical practice for educators. In J. Andrzejewski, M. P. Baltodano, & L. Symcox (Eds.), *Social justice, peace, and environmental education* (pp. 235–251) New York: Routledge.

Sopko, K. M. (2008). *Universal design for learning: Implementation in six local education agencies.* Alexandria, VA: National Association of State Directors of Special Education.

Stallings, J., Cory, R., Fairweather, J., & Needels, M. (1978). *A study of basic reading skills taught in secondary schools.* Menlo Park: CA: SRI International.

Stecker, P. M. (2007). Tertiary intervention: Using progressive monitoring with intensive services. *Teaching Exceptional Children, 39*(5), 50–57.

Sullivan, A. L. (2011). Disproportionality in special education identification and placement of English Language Learners. *Exceptional Children, 77*(3), 317–334.

Sullivan, A. L., & Kozleski, E. B. (2008). *Part B Annual Performance Report Analysis: Indicator 5, LRE.* Tempe: AZ: National Institute for urban School Improvement.

Sullivan, A. L., Kozleski, E. B., & Smith, A. (2008, March). *Understanding the current context of minority disproportionality in special education: Federal response, state activities, and implications for technical assistance.* Paper presented at the American Educational Research Association Annual Meeting. New York, NY.

Sullivan, A. L., A'Vant, E., Baker, J., Chandler, D., Graves, S., McKinney, E., & Sayles, T. (2009). Confronting inequity in special education, part I: Understanding the problem of disproportionality. NASP *Communiqué, 38*(1), Available at http://www.nasponline.org/publications/cq/mocq381disproportionality.aspx.

Taylor, L. S., & Whittaker, C. R. (2009). *Bridging multiple worlds: Case studies of diverse educational communities* (2nd ed.). Boston: Allyn & Bacon.

The College Board. (2002). *Opening classroom doors: Strategies for expanding access to AP: AP teacher survey results.* Washington, DC: Author.

Towles-Reeves, E., Kleinert, H., & Muhomba, M. (2009). Alternate assessment: Have we learned anything new? *Exceptional Children, 75*(2), 233–252.

U.S. Department of Education. (2006). *26th annual report to Congress on the implementation of the Individuals with Disabilities Education Act, 2004.* Jessup, MD: Ed Pubs. (ERIC Document Reproduction Service No. ED494709).

Valenzuela, J. S., Copeland, S. R., Qi, C. H., & Park, M. (2006). Examining educational equity: Revisiting the disproportionate representation of minority students in special education. *Exceptional Children, 72*, 425–441.

Vanderheyden, A. M. (2011). Technical adequacy of response to intervention decisions. *Exceptional Children, 77*(3), 335–350.

Waitoller, F. R., Artiles, A. J., & Cheney, D. A. (2010). The miner's canary: A review of overrepresentation research and explanations. *The Journal of Special Education, 44*(1), 29–49.

Wehmeyer, M. L., & Schwartz, M. (2001). Disproportionate representation of males in special education services: Biology, behavior, or bias? *Education and Treatment of Children, 24*(1), 28–45

Wentzel, K. (1997). Student motivation in middle school: The role of perceived pedagogical caring. *Journal of Educational Psychology, 89*(3), 411–419.

Yssel, N., Engelbrecht, P., Oswald, M. M., Eloff, I., & Swart, E. (2007). Views of inclusion: A comparative study parents' perceptions in South Africa and United States. *Remedial and Special Education, 28*(6), 356–365.

CHAPTER 3

MAKING ASSESSMENT AUTHENTIC FOR MULTICULTURAL LEARNERS WITH SPECIAL NEEDS

Tes Mehring

America's classrooms are becoming increasingly diverse. We are becoming the most ethnically, culturally, and linguistically diverse society that has ever existed. Consider the following statistics:

- Today, approximately 40 percent of students enrolled in public schools in the United States are minority students (Gargiulo, 2009).
- Twenty percent of students live in poverty (Gargiulo, 2009).
- Approximately 13 percent of the 48 million students in U.S. schools have special needs that interfere with their ability to learn (O'Donnell, Reeves, & Smith, 2009).
- By the year 2020, multicultural households will account for more than 40 percent of the U.S. population and that percentage will likely grow to 50 percent by 2050 (Gargiulo, 2009).

Multicultural Education for Learners with Special Needs in the Twenty-First Century, pages 41–48
Copyright © 2014 by Information Age Publishing
All rights of reproduction in any form reserved.

- By 2020, students of color are projected to make up almost one half of all school-age youth (Gollnick & Chinn, 2009).
- By the year 2050, the U.S. population is projected to be 53 percent Anglo, 24 percent Latino, 13 percent black, 9 percent Asian, and 1 percent Native American (Chinn, 2002).
- About one in five individuals (approximately 19 percent of the U.S. population over the age of 5 speaks a language other than English at home (U.S. Census Bureau, 2007).
- The number of students who are culturally and linguistically diverse and disabled is estimated at approximately 530,000 (Baca, Baca, & Valenzuela, 2004).

The appropriate assessment of all students has been a longstanding concern among special educators for more than three decades. Appropriate assessment is an especially critical issue for children from minority populations. According to Gargiulo (2009), assessment is the "primary vehicle through which access to services is determined and progress is evaluated, using a variety of formal and informal means. Assessment should be a dynamic, multifaceted, multipurpose decision-making process whose primary goal is to evaluate the academic and behavioral progress of a student" (p. 101). The growing number of culturally and linguistically diverse (CLD) students in the nation's classrooms and the tightening of school, district, and state accountability expectations are resulting in a reexamination of the assessment measures we use to refer, diagnose the need for special education services, and document student progress in learning goals. Assessment and instructional practices in American schools were neither created nor designed to be responsive to the range of diversity represented in today's school population. There are several roadblocks to the goal of achieving meaningful and valid assessments of students who are culturally and linguistically diverse. Standardized testing has frequently been criticized for its failure to consider the cultural and experiential background of culturally and linguistically diverse students. Most standardized academic achievement tests require students to have specific culturally-based information in order to perform well on the test (Grassi & Barker, 2010). Many tests are culturally biased toward the mainstream—White, English only, middle to upper class students (Baca et al., 2004).

Many factors must be considered in achieving inclusive and equitable assessment for diverse students. These include the "prior knowledge and language skills that assessment tasks require; whether test content, procedures, or scoring criteria are biased; whether tests are valid for the population being assessed; and whether all students have had the opportunity to learn the material assessed" (Lachat, 2004, p. 67). Assessment must be inclusive, fair, relevant, comprehensive, valid, and yield meaningful information

(Gottlieb, 2006). Educators must understand the power of assessment data in helping to provide the evidence that our students are learning and making progress. Ultimately, it is our responsibility to create a bridge, through sound assessment, to ensure the academic success of our students, especially those who come from diverse backgrounds. To large measure, concern about test bias has resulted in efforts to reduce bias through focusing on the test instruments themselves. Many tests were revised in an effort to reduce the number of culturally specific test items (content bias) and the reliance on culturally specific language. Tests were also renormed, or restandardized to reflect the growing diversity of children in schools (Gargiulo, 2009). Even the testing environment and the race of the examiner and his or her interactions with the student have been analyzed. Many school districts, searching for better ways of assessing diverse students are moving more and more toward more authentic, performance-based assessment strategies (Friend & Bursuck, 2006).

CHARACTERISTICS OF AUTHENTIC ASSESSMENTS

Authentic assessment is widely viewed as offering a means to measure student progress on learning standards and as being more responsive to diversity than traditional assessments. When standards are linked to authentic assessment, students must demonstrate their skills and abilities through a range of "performances," and emphasis is placed on student work that involves higher-order thinking and complex problem solving. Students are asked to apply the skills and competence they have learned to "authentic" tasks that represent practical or "real-life" contexts. According to Lachat (2004), authentic assessments have the key features listed below. These assessments

- measure student achievement against a continuum of agreed-upon standards of proficiency;
- emphasize the importance of context through real-life tasks that are "authentic" to the learner;
- focus on higher-order thinking processes and how students integrate information and skills in performing tasks;
- require students to display what they know and are able to do by solving problems (performance tasks) of varying complexity, some of which involve multiple steps, several types of performance, and significant student time; and
- often involve group as well as individual performance on a task.

Ronis (2007) noted that an assessment is considered to be authentic "when it involves students in tasks that are worthwhile, significant, and meaningful; occurs over time (not just one day); is open-ended; and allows for students to demonstrate competence in a variety of ways" (p. 2). Such assessments involve higher-order thinking skills along with the use of a broad range of knowledge. Authentic assessments are brain compatible. They emphasize learning and thinking, especially higher order skills involved in problem solving. Authentic assessments use meaningful tasks that reflect real-life, interdisciplinary challenges. They present students with complex, ambiguous, open-ended problems and tasks that integrate their knowledge and skills. Such assessments usually culminate in student products or performances that recognize and value each student's multiple abilities, varied learning styles, and individual background.

Authentic assessments are more student oriented than traditional assessments and less concerned with the formal characteristics of assessment formats. They also tend to relate more closely both to instruction and to real-life applications of the knowledge and skills involved. Examples of authentic assessments might include the following:

- *Observation* of student behavior in a natural setting (e.g., playground, bus, classroom, cafeteria, etc.) using rating scales, observational recording systems, anecdotal records, or audio recordings
- *Demonstrations/Presentations* that provide opportunities for students to show their learning in oral and media performances or exhibitions
- *Interviews* obtained orally or in writing from significant individuals in a student's life (e.g., parents, teachers, siblings, peers, or the pupil him or herself)
- *Projects and Demonstrations* that provide opportunities for students to show their learning in oral and media performances or exhibitions (e.g., poster, oral or written report, production, skit, speech, Web page, etc.)
- *Work Samples/Permanent Products* that provide evidence of a pupil's classroom performance, typically focused on particular skills (e.g., quizzes, tests, homework, assignments, etc.)
- *Simulations* that provide role-playing tasks that allow students to demonstrate connections among concepts and ability to apply learning in contexts that replicate real-life problem solving
- *Learning Logs/Reflective Journals* in which students reflect on what they have learned and/or their own performance using written or audio recordings
- Portfolios that document a wide range of examples of a student's emerging growth, abilities, and accomplishments over time (e.g., a unit of study, semester, academic year, or multiple years of school-

ing) through a collection of student work that might include any of the types of authentic assessments presented above. Bohlin, Durwin, and Reese-Weber (2009) indicated that a portfolio is "a systematic collection of students; work that demonstrates accomplishments, growth, and reflection on their learning" (p. 470).

Clearly, one aspect most authentic assessments have in common is that they usually result in a student product or performance. This type of assessment has become increasingly popular because it relates more closely to activities one actually does in life (O'Donnell, Reeve, & Smith, 2009).

ADVANTAGES OF AUTHENTIC ASSESSMENT

O'Donnell, Reeve, and Smith (2009) cited several advantages supporting the use of authentic assessments. These assessments are directly related to the skill being assessed. For example, the best way to determine whether students can write legibly using cursive or manuscript is to collect a permanent product that provides samples of student handwriting. Authentic assessments cause students to prepare for the assessment in ways that are conducive to learning. Authentic assessments also tend to be more engaging for students than standardized assessments. Lachat (2004) cites several additional advantages for authentic assessments with diverse learners. These assessments promote active student learning and support instruction. They assist teachers to make instructional decisions by actively involving both students and teachers in the learning process. Authentic assessments minimize the likelihood of drawing conclusions from limited performance opportunities. They offer children from different backgrounds varied ways to display their knowledge and abilities. These assessments provide information that can be used to form a profile of a student's individual strengths and weaknesses. Authentic assessments allow teachers to document the broad-based process of learning, follow children's development, and create differentiated profiles of student's accomplishments. Teachers and students often collaborate in the learning process. These assessments allow students to display proficiencies in a wide variety of ways, allow more dynamic approaches to assessing student learning, and allow developmental learning to be profiled over time. Meisels, Dorfman, and Steele (1995) suggest that authentic assessments provide teachers with evidence to monitor student progress over time and to adjust instruction appropriately. Farr and Trumbull (1997) stated the following advantages:

> Because authentic assessments involve multiple ways of demonstrating proficiency, they invite students to draw on multiple intelligences and to display

varied cognitive and communicative styles. As a result, these assessments provide a wider range of opportunities for students to show what they know and can do. Because they make greater cognitive demands on students than traditional standardized tests, authentic tasks invite a fuller range of responses, provide a richer picture of what students have learned, and allow for the ongoing assessment of their higher-order thinking skills. (p. 89)

Lachat (2004) indicated that the flexibility of authentic assessments allows teachers to vary the methods used to diagnose the learning of students whose cognitive and cultural styles may cause them to perform poorly on standardized tests. "By offering a range of contexts—including opportunities to work alone, in pairs, or in groups—teachers can vary assessment settings to reflect cultural preferences and also to evaluate the impact of these contexts on particular students' progress. By examining how students solve tasks, teachers can better differentiate between learning problems caused by poverty or language competence, and those caused by limited content knowledge" (p. 89). As it appears, authentic assessments are brain compatible. Ronis (2007) stated that

When correctly designed, they emphasize learning and thinking, especially those higher-order thinking skills involved in problem solving. Authentic assessments comprise meaningful tasks that reflect real-life, interdisciplinary challenges; they present students with complex, ambiguous, open-ended problems and tasks that integrate their knowledge and skills. Such assessments usually culminate in student products that integrate their knowledge and skills. Such assessments usually culminate in student products or performances that recognize and value each students' multiple abilities, varied learning styles, and individual background. (p. 13)

DISADVANTAGES TO AUTHENTIC ASSESSMENTS

There can also be disadvantages to authentic assessments. These tools can be difficult to objectively score. Bias can also enter into scoring of these assessments even if criteria are explicit. For example, a general classroom teacher who is frequently challenged by disruptive behavior from an African American student with behavior disorder, may inadvertently or overtly score his orally presented speech about early settlers in Alaska lower than peers who tend to be compliant and engaged in class sessions even though a scoring rubric is very explicit. Performance anxiety might also be a problem in authentic assessment because some students are very reluctant to engage in any kind of performance in front of their peers. If authentic assessments involve work conducted outside the classroom, it can be difficult to know if the student completed the assessment activity independently, or if they had assistance from family members or even friends. Finally, authentic assessment can be very time consuming.

CONCLUSION

Despite criticisms that standardized tests do not always assess what students are learning, and that their emphasis is on mostly factual knowledge rather than higher-order thinking and application, Burke (2009) indicated that they are still the "yardstick that the public and policymakers use to measure educational progress. Standardized tests are viewed by many people as being valid and reliable and, for the most part, the most effective method to compare students, schools, districts, states, and countries" (p. 1). Hargreaves and Shirley (2008) indicated that the data on these existing assessment foci and the economic need for increased innovation and creativity has necessitated a shift in education reform. Although research-based instructional strategies and classroom management strategies are critical components of teaching, the research on authentic assessment indicates that it is one of the major factors that improve student achievement. As Marzano (2006) pointed out, "To the surprise of some educators, major reviews of the research on the effects of classroom assessment indicate that it might be one of the most powerful weapons in a teacher's arsenal" (p. 2).

Authentic assessments provide feedback for teachers and students, evaluate students' knowledge and understanding of key concepts and standards, and guide the instructional process by differentiating teaching to meet the diverse needs of all learners. Authentic assessments that are frequent and integrated seamlessly with instruction provide a continuous feedback loop that informs instruction. Stiggins (2004) concluded that the educational system will continue to use both standardized tests and authentic assessments and both will continue to provide valuable information for important decision making. Clearly, authentic assessments are valuable teaching tools that should be used to promote meaningful learning for all students. Most advocates of authentic assessment do not want to totally eliminate traditional tests. What they seek is a good mix of assessment practices. As educators, we are constantly challenged to make informed decisions about our students. We plan, gather, and analyze information from multiple sources over time so that the results are meaningful to teaching and learning. If reliable, valid, and fair for our students, assessment can be the bridge to educational equity. Using multiple assessment measures in multiple contexts to obtain a more accurate assessment of student's proficiency levels provides a more accurate interpretation of functioning. Authentic assessments provide an option for assisting educators to accomplish this goal.

REFERENCES

Baca, L., Baca, E., & Valenzuela, J. (2004). Background and rationale for bilingual special education. In L. Baca & H. T. Cervantes (Eds.), *The bilingual special education interface* (4th ed., pp. 1–23)). Upper Saddle River, NJ: Pearson Education.

Bohlin, L., Durwin, C. C., & Reese-Weber, M. (2009). *EdPsych modules*. Boston: McGraw Hill Higher Education.

Burke, K. (2009). *How to assess authentic learning* (5th ed.). Thousand Oaks, CA: Corwin Press.

Chinn, P. (2002). *Changing demographics in America*. Nashville, TN: Alliance Project, Vanderbilt University.

Farr, B. P., & Trumbull, E. (1997). *Alternate assessments for diverse classrooms*. Norwood, MA: Christopher-Gordon.

Friend, M., & Bursuck, W. (2006). *Including students with special needs* (4th ed.). Boston: Allyn and Bacon.

Gargiulo, R. M. (2009) *Special education in contemporary society* (5th ed.). Los Angeles, CA: SAGE.

Gollnick, D., & Chinn, P. (2009). *Multicultural education in a pluralistic society* (8th ed.). Upper Saddle River, NJ: Pearson Education.

Gottlieb, M. (2006). *Assessing English language learners: Bridges from language proficiency to academic achievement*. Thousand Oaks, CA: Corwin Press.

Grassi, E. A., & Barker, H. B. (2010). Culturally and linguistically diverse exceptional students: Strategies for teaching and assessment. Thousand Oaks, CA: Sage.

Hargreaves, A., & Shirley, D. (2008). Beyond standardization: Powerful principles for improvement. *Phi Delta Kappan, 90*(2), 135–143.

Lachat, M. A. (2004). *Standards-based instruction and assessment for English language learners*. Thousand Oaks, CA: Corwin Press.

Marzano, R. J. (2006). *What works in schools: Translating research into action*. Alexandria, VA: Association for Supervision and Curriculum Development.

Meisels, S. J., Dorfman, A., & Steele, D. (1995). Equity and excellence in group-administered and performance-based assessments. In M. Nettles & A. Nettles (Eds.), *Equity and excellence in educational testing and assessment*. Boston: Kluwer Academic.

O'Donnell, A. M., Reeve, J., & Smith, J. K. (2009). *Educational psychology: Reflection for action*. Danvers, MA: John Wiley & Sons, Inc.

Ronis, D. (2007). *Brain-compatible assessments* (2nd ed.). Thousand Oaks, CA: Corwin Press.

Stiggins, R. J. (2004). *Student-involved assessment for learning*. Upper Saddle River, NJ: Merrill/Prentice Hall.

U.S. Census Bureau. (2007). Statistical abstract of the United States: 2008 (127th ed.). Washington, DC: Author.

CHAPTER 4

EDUCATING LATINA/O STUDENTS WITH SPECIAL NEEDS

Barbara J. Dray and Peter Vigil

Hispanic and Latino are terms used to denote individuals from Mexican, Central/South American and Caribbean Islands where Spanish is the primary language. Chicano, a term popularized in the 1960's, was originally designated for Mexican Americans primarily from economically oppressed urban environments as an empowering sociopolitical term, which is still used today by some from the Mexican American community. Similarly *Diasporican* is a term used to describe the sociopolitical realities of Puerto Ricans who have settled across various regions of the United States thus being influenced not only by Puerto Rican identity but the situated realities of the region settled in the United States (Valldejuli & Flores, 2000).

While Hispanic and Latino are the most common terms used today, the preference is to use specific terms of origin such as Puerto Rican, Mexican, Peruvian, Bolivian, etc. The reason is that the more specific term of origin more accurately reflects the sociopolitical and cultural experiences of the individual. For example, students from Dominican background are more likely to have African American heritage, whereas, a student from a

Multicultural Education for Learners with Special Needs in the Twenty-First Century, pages 49–65
Copyright © 2014 by Information Age Publishing

Mexican background may have indigenous heritage while a Hispanic student from New Mexico may be of Spaniard descent. Therefore the sociopolitical realities are embedded within the terms used by a subset of the Latino population to reflect their lived experiences and cultural identities.

The ethnic and national identity of an individual can tell a different story and account for the diaspora of what it means to be Hispanic or Latino. Diaspora refers to the phenomenon of how groups have been scattered or dispersed (like seeds of wildflowers) in their settlement away from the homeland and yet recreate certain aspects through social formation, culture, and identity that is uniquely linked to their homeland, in essence being bicultural or multicultural with strong ties to their homeland (Kavazanjian, n.d.). Such factors as where a person settles, occupation, access to others from a similar background, and language dominance all feed into one's identity. Additionally, in some communities it is common to make frequent trips or send money back to the home country thus becoming a *transnational citizen*, which denotes a fluid movement across the border between the home country and United States (Nieto & Bode, 2012). For example, in the Puerto Rican community, which is a commonwealth of the United States, it is common for families to have a more fluid relationship with the United States and Puerto Rico spending periods of time in both. This phenomenon of going back and forth from home country to the United Sates and back again is called *circular migration* (most common among Mexican and Puerto Rican communities due to proximity and relationship with the United States).

Throughout this chapter, we explore the topic of educating *Latina/o* students in special education by tending to critical features of linguistic and cultural identity. We begin by examining the Latino landscape in the United States through demographic growth, immigration patterns, and language dominance. Next, we reveal the impact on K–12 education and unintended consequences in special education in particular. The second half of the chapter is focused on recommendations for educating bilingual Latino students in special education to ensure appropriate referral, program placement and planning, as well as ongoing professional development of educational staff.

THE LATINO LANDSCAPE IN THE UNITED STATES

During the first decade of the new millennium, there has continued to be a dramatic increase in the numbers of both native born and immigrant Latinos living in the United States. The 2010 U.S. census counted 50.5 million *Hispanics* in the United States, making up 16.3% of the total population, with the *Hispanic* population accounting for most of the nation's growth

(56%) from 2000 to 2010 (United States Census, 2010). It's important to note that the definition of Hispanic or Latino origin used in the 2010 census refers to a person of Cuban, Mexican, Puerto Rican, South or Central American, or Spanish (language) culture or origin regardless of race. The census report notes that "the terms Hispanic or Latino are used interchangeably in this report" (Humes, Jones, & Ramirez, 2011, p. 2). Another subset of the population, undocumented Latino immigrants, represents a sizeable population that remains unaccounted for with formal measures such as the United States Census. The Pew Research Center notes however that as of March 2010 there were 11.2 million unauthorized immigrants living in the United States with Latino immigrants comprising 81% or 9.1 million of the total (as cited in Fry & Lopez, 2012). Collectively that puts the total number of Latinos living in the United States at nearly 60 million.

This sustained growth of native and foreign-born Hispanics nationwide has resulted in a broader distribution of Latinos into areas of the United States that have traditionally had very few if any Latinos. The term *New Latino Diaspora* has been used to describe the social phenomenon of Latinos settling both temporarily and permanently in the small towns, rural areas, and more isolated communities of the regions of the Northeast, the Southeast, the Midwest and the mountain west because in addition to their country of origin, their experiences are so varied given where they settle (Murillo & Villenas, 1997). As evidenced in the 2010 United States Census, the *New Latino Diaspora* can be seen in states with the largest percent growth that more than doubled in their Latino population to include nine states —seven in the Southeast: Alabama, Arkansas, Kentucky, Mississippi, North Carolina, Tennessee, and South Carolina; one in the Mideast: Maryland; and another in the Midwest: South Dakota (United States Census Bureau, 2011).

Unfortunately, the term *Latino* has too frequently been viewed from the monolithic perspective that there is some sort of universal characteristic, language presumably, that defines the United States *Latino* population. However other characteristics such as immigration status (e.g., first, second or third generation), acculturation level (e.g., the extent to which the family identifies with their ethnic heritage and United States culture), region of settlement in the United States (e.g., Northeast, Southeast, Midwest, West Coast, etc.), reason for immigrating, family ties in the United States or home country, etc. are equally important to consider. That being said, language is an important variable when considering the educational implications of the *New Latino Diaspora* as described here. A statistical portrait of Latinos living in the United States in 2009 provides intriguing data that helps to highlight the variance and diversity among Latinos. According to a 2009 Pew Center Report, nearly 7 million *Hispanics* age 5–17 years speak a language other than English at home with that number swelling to over

24 million for *Hispanics* over the age of 18 years. The numbers are further
disaggregated into categories of "English spoken very well" and "English
spoken less than very well" (as cited in Fry & Lopez, 2012). The critical
point here is that rather than some mythical commonality shared among
all Latinos living in the United States, first and/or second language proficiency represent important distinctions because it cannot be assumed that
all Latinos are learning English as a second language, in fact many are native English speakers.

Immigration experience and country of origin are two additional characteristics that help illustrate the diversity among Latinos in the United States.
The immigrant populations, who largely comprise the *New Latino Diaspora*,
not only come from different countries of origin than their counterparts
of 10 years ago, but also have very different immigration experiences when
compared to Latino immigrants who arrived to the United States prior to
the year 2000. Latino immigration patterns prior to the turn of the century
revealed the bulk of newcomers arriving from Mexico and the Caribbean islands of Cuba, Dominican Republic, and Puerto Rico. Mexican immigrants
mainly settled in the Southwestern United States, and Latinos from the Caribbean mainly settled in Florida and New York, respectively. While destina-
tions such as California and Arizona located in the Southwest were by no
means safe havens for Latino immigrants of Mexican descent, there were
family or community members already there to ease and assist with the acculturation process. By contrast, today's fastest growing number of Latinos
by country of origin come from Guatemala, El Salvador, and Colombia, and
as mentioned before, they are settling in portions of the United States with
very little history or precedent for accommodating immigrant populations.

It is difficult to say how community members from different areas of the
United States will react when confronted with the changes that are inherent to this New Latino Diaspora. Will the traditional community members
treat the newcomers *con respeto* (Valdes, 1996) or see their culture and language as a problem (Ruiz, 1984)? Will community members who view the
newcomers as problems respond with punitive and subtractive schooling
that serves to assimilate and subtract their home culture identity in favor of
United States dominant mainstream culture (Valenzuela, 2010)?

What is known is the fact that the public schools will play a part in this
unfolding dynamic. For example, Levinson (2002) points out how new
social relations and cultural identities have emerged in these regions of
the New Latino Diaspora and describes how public schools become fundamental sites of socialization and cultural transmission. In addition, public
schools are frequently the places where values and assumptions about cultural differences get played out in various policies and practices (Levinson,
2002). Although newcomer Latino immigrant families bring well-defined
beliefs about schooling and family values to their new communities, they

are often confronted with educational systems that under value their *funds of knowledge* and stress assimilation (Moll, Amanti, Neff, & Gonzalez, 1992). Regrettably, the response in certain communities affected by the new Latino Diaspora has been educational practices that at the very least constrain the academic achievement of the newcomer students. We have recently witnessed how fears and assumptions about immigrants can be played out in the worst way with policies such as those recently passed in Arizona and Alabama. Both states have passed far-reaching immigration bills, which cover all aspects of immigrants' lives including employment, housing, and schooling. Both SN 1070 in Arizona and HB56 in Alabama allow police to question anyone suspected of being an illegal alien, with the Alabama bill going as far as to require public schools to check the status of all immigrant students. What remains to be seen are the educational decisions and practices that will develop as substantial portions of the Southeastern and Midwestern United States face fundamental shifts in their school age population.

THE DEMOGRAPHIC IMPERATIVE OF LATINA/O IN K–12 EDUCATION

The continuing trend in the overall population of Latinos in the United States is reflected in a 39% increase in the number of Latino school age children over the last decade (Fry & Lopez, 2012). The consistent rate of Latino immigrants over a longer period has resulted in a rise in the number of children ages 5–17 years who spoke a language other than English at home from 4.7 to 11.2 million between 1980 and 2009, or from 10 to 21 percent of the population in this age range (Snyder & Dillow, 2012).

The last report of the Office of Civil Rights (2006) projected that roughly 20% of the school age population is Hispanic (non-White). Nearly 13% of the overall school age population is classified as having a disability either under the Individuals with Disabilities Education Act (IDEA) or Part 504. Of those classified with a disability and who are Hispanic, 15% are classified with Intellectual Disabilities (IT), 11% classified with Emotional Disturbance (ED), and 21% classified with a Specific Learning Disability (SLD) (Office of Civil Rights [OCR], 2006). The United States Department of Education (USDOE), Office of Special Education and Rehabilitative Services, Office of Special Education Programs (2009) reported that 16% of students receiving special education services ages 6–12 years were Hispanic, roughly 974,638 students. This is a 2% increase since the OCR report in 2006 and points to the potential for continued growth. According to the Working Group on ELL Policy (2010), "U.S. schools now serve more than 5 million ELLs, who thus comprise over 10 percent of the national public

school enrollment" (p. 1). Of those identified as English language learners (ELLs), Spanish remains the predominant language spoken with nearly
80% of ELLs identifies Spanish as the primary language other than English
and in some districts or schools this number can far exceed 80% (OELA,
2008). Since 1994, 12 states have experienced as much as a 200% growth
rate in the ELL population (e.g., Nevada, Arkansas, Georgia, and Puerto
Rico) and some states have experienced as much as 300% increase in ELL
population (e.g., Alabama, Indiana, Kentucky, Nebraska, North Carolina,
South Carolina, and Tennessee) (USDOE, 2009). What is most notable is
that contrary to popular belief most English language learners are Ameri-
can-born citizens with only 24% of ELLs being foreign born of the elementary school population and only 44% of ELLs being foreign born of the
secondary school population (Loeffler, 2007).

Historically, ELLs have been inappropriately referred for special education and in particular experienced overidentification under the categories
of speech language impaired and learning disability (Artiles & Ortiz, 2002;
Cummins, 1984; Hamayan, Marler, Sanchez-Lopez, & Damico, 2007). However, this is not a consistent pattern across the board as some districts have
experienced an under-referral of ELLs particularly in programs that provide more time for ELLs to transition and learn English (Artiles & Ortiz,
2002). Also, research conducted in California after the implementation of
proposition 227 (English only mandate) demonstrated that ELLs of Hispanic descent (Spanish-speaking) who have limited language supports tend
to be over-represented in the categories of IT and SLD (Artiles, Rueda,
Salazar, & Higareda, 2005).

UNINTENDED CONSEQUENCES IN SPECIAL EDUCATION

Given the high numbers of Latino students represented within the ELL
population, it is important to consider the trajectories and experiences of
this population in general to better understand how educators can best
meet the needs of such learners. For example, Artiles et al. (2005) found
that ELLs were more likely to be placed in special education in grades
6–12 and the percentage of ELLs increased as they progressed through
high school. As language supports were reduced, ELLs were more likely
to be placed in special education (Artiles et al., 2005) while ELLs in English Immersion (English only) programs were three times as likely to be
placed in special education as ELLs in Bilingual programs (Artiles et al.,
2005). ELLs who have limited proficiency in both their first language (L1)
and second language (L2) are the most vulnerable for special education
placement (Artiles et al.. 2005). Additional research on English learners in
special education suggests that ELLs, who are placed in special education,

are more likely to be placed in the most restrictive and segregated programs (de Valenzuela, Copeland, & Park, 2006). Once placed in special education, ELLs are less likely to receive language supports (e.g., native language instruction, English as a Second Language (ESL), or Sheltered Content Instruction) and were more likely to receive instruction in English only (Zehler, Fleischman, Hopstock, Pendzick, & Stephenson, 2003). Schools with the highest percentages of ELLs are more likely to place these students with novice teachers or teachers without bilingual education or ESL certification (Kushner, 2008; Tyler, Yzquierdo, Lopez-Reyna, & Saunders Flippin, 2004).

Given the realities of educational and sociopolitical experiences of the Latino Diaspora in the United States and the resulting educational implications introduced here, the essential questions remain: How do we accurately and efficiently identify the academic strengths and needs of *Latino* students at risk for or identified with special needs? And; how do we prepare educators to build on the strengths and meet the special needs of the highly diverse so-called *Latino* students in K–12 classrooms?

EDUCATING LATINO/A STUDENTS WITH SPECIAL NEEDS

Figueroa (2005) noted the nuanced concerns for the *Latino*/a diaspora in the United States who are at risk for being labeled with a disability instead of a difference. He stated that:

> Among the many factors associated with Latino students' educational outcomes, two stand out: culture and bilingualism. The first manifests itself in multiple national origins, traditions, and histories. These interact with American culture, producing unique sociocultural and socioeconomic outcomes. More than anything, however, what impacts Latino populations in the United States is the failure of the American educational system to meet the needs of students who manage two language systems." (p. 163)

As such the focus of this section of the chapter is on Latino students who are negotiating in two languages—Spanish and English.

All too often when teachers see a student struggling, they assume that there must be something inherently wrong with the child versus examining the environment and teaching contexts that might be triggering or inadequately addressing the learning needs of the student (Hamayan, Marler, Sanchez-Lopez, & Damico, 2007). For instance, is the student struggling because the language of instruction is too high or not well matched to be comprehensible for the student's English proficiency? Or could it be that the teaching techniques are not a good match for the cultural learning style of the student? Maybe the student is from a migrant family and has frequently moved around thus having interrupted educational experiences?

Teachers cannot answer the above questions unless they take the time to gather and analyze data to describe the student and the context? It is critical that teachers spend time observing and gathering data about the student in multiple contexts (i.e., academic, social) and across settings (i.e., type of instruction, content area, etc.) to better understand the students' behavior, as well as describe what is happening during times of need or when the student is doing well. It's important to understand why a student is responding in a certain way given the circumstances and/or unique characteristics of the student. In other words, teachers first need to describe a student's behavior before diagnosing a student with a disability and take the time to really understand multiple parameters that may be interacting that present as an academic challenge (Hamayan et. al, 2007; García & Ortiz, 2008; Ortiz & Garcia, 1988). With this process in mind, Table 4.1 lists factors that should be considered and addressed to ensure appropriate programming and placement of Latino students who are negotiating in two languages.

Providing Access to Optimal Language Supports

Research (Oller & Eilers, 2002; Ramirez, Yuen, Ramey, & Pasta, 1991; Thomas & Collier, 2002) suggests that it is optimal to provide instruction for bilingual Latino students with minimal English proficiency in the native language of the student with high quality English as a Second Language supports. As students acquire proficiency both socially and academically in both languages across the domains of listening, speaking, reading, and writing—transition to English dominant instruction can occur. However, the benefits of bilingualism and maintaining the native language while acquiring English are most optimal and typically yield the highest academic results in English. Countless studies have found that developmental or

TABLE 4.1 Recommendations for Educating Latino Students in Special Education

1. Provide *optimal language supports.*
2. Use *culturally and linguistically responsive curriculum and instruction.*
3. Routinely collect data systematically to *monitor student's progress* in both the native language and English.
4. Convene a multi-disciplinary *academic support team.*
5. Administer *culturally and linguistically responsive assessments.*
6. Implement a *schoolwide problem-solving process.*
7. Attend *professional development* workshops/trainings regularly.

additive bilingual programs yield the highest results of English acquisition and academic achievement in English (Oller & Eilers, 2002; Ramírez et al., 1991; Thomas & Collier, 2002). When certified Spanish proficient personnel are not available, students MUST have access to English as a Second Language (ESL) and Sheltered English instruction in the content areas to promote optimal language growth (Echevarria & Graves, 2010). It's important to keep in mind that language and cognition are intricately linked, so if a student does not have full access to language or interrupted language acquisition this will impact their ability to learn at higher levels. Thus, the goal of education should not only be focused on content and skills but also increasing language repertoire so students can fully process information and interact with (express) the new content and skills. That said, listening and speaking tend to develop at faster rates than reading and writing—so it is important to use listening and speaking as pathways for higher level thinking and in the development of reading and writing. Even as the beginning stages of language learning, students can be exposed to higher level content knowledge with scaffolded supports.

Using Culturally and Linguistically Responsive Instruction /Curriculum

To ensure that the environment builds on the experiences of the students and views cultural and linguistic differences as an asset within the larger context of society, teachers need to: create positive learning environments by believing that all children can learn, take responsibility to meet the individual needs of all learners, and use instructional practices known to be effective for Latino students and students learning English as a second language. Some examples of the above include:

- Respect and affirm students' cultural and linguistic diversity keeping in mind that each Latino student has their own unique identity and experiences (Nieto & Bode, 2012).
- Develop meaningful relationships with students by providing a caring, supportive environment that engages students personally as well as academically (Antrop-Gonzalez & DeJesus, 2006; Valenzuela, 2010).
- Seek to gain a deeper understanding and knowledge of students' families so that you are aware of the individual experiences and culture that shapes who the student is as an individual and learner (Jimenez & Rose, 2010; Kalyanpur & Harry, 1999; Moll & Gonzalez, 1997).
- Connect instruction and curriculum to students' cultural and linguistic background and community (i.e., life experiences) (Antrop-Gonzalez & DeJesus, 2006; Jimenez & Rose, 2010).

- Make instruction comprehensible, meaningful, and intellectually challenging. Move beyond meaningless disconnected content that requires students to respond in a rote manner. Provide opportunities for students to write bilingually. Incorporate Spanish as a gateway to understanding concepts in English while building on the skills students bring to support their growth academically (Luke, Woods, Dooley 2010; Valenzuela, 2010).
- Continuously reflect mindfully on your own biases and assumptions about interactions in the classroom and learn more about the cultural preferences of the individual student to help you develop culturally responsive practices (Dray & Wisneski, 2011).

Research (Irizarry, 2007) has shown that culturally connected teachers understand the hybridity of identity and realize that students have membership in more than one community that is socioculturally situated. Teachers need not be from the same cultural or linguistic background to successfully implement culturally (and linguistically) responsive practices, but they must have the sensibility of being culturally connected (i.e., understanding that culture is not monolithic and that culture is dynamic, fluid and contextually or socioculturally situated) (Irizarry, 2007). What is most critical is that teachers develop authentic relationships with students in a manner that not only validates and respects their students hybrid identities but also embeds such information or experiences during instructional activities (e.g., connecting to students cultural or national heritage as well as age, region, gender specific referents) (Jimenez & Rose, 2010). Additionally, teachers who are not proficient in Spanish can be effective when instructing bilingual Latino students with and without disabilities when they understand the process of first and second language acquisition, institute ESL and/or sheltered instruction, and incorporate ways for students to interact with content in the Spanish/English (García & Dray, 2006).

KEY POINTS ABOUT THE FUTURE

It is important to routinely collect data systematically to monitor student's progress across content and skills in both Spanish and English. For bilingual Latino students, it is critical to gather data in both languages across the four domains (e.g., listening, speaking, reading, and writing) as bilingual students in the process of learning English as a second language tend to display sporadic skills in each language (Gottlieb, 2006). Composite skills in both languages reveal a more accurate picture of the student's abilities. Progress monitoring data should be used to measure student's skills, content knowledge, and response to a variety of instructional practices, so that decisions can be made on how to continue to support optimal language development as well as academic growth. Progress monitoring tools should be relevant and authentic (not arbitrary or convenient) to the content knowledge and skills being taught so that data may be used to inform instruction and continue to support students' growth. Teachers are often provided with district-mandated assessments, however, one needs to ask if they are relevant and authentic to the language of instruction, content, and skills being taught and consider ways that this information will support instructional development to support student's academic and linguistic growth. In addition to district-mandated assessments, teachers should incorporate other forms of data such as portfolios, teacher made tests, checklists, student self assessment, etc. to ensure that instruction is being informed by data so that students can continue to make gains both academically and linguistically (Gottlieb, 2006; Hamayan, et. al., 2007).

Education of ELLs can be enhanced by teachers convening a multi-disciplinary *academic support team* (sometimes referred to as teacher assistance team, child study team, or RtI support team). Typically, the academic support group consists of individuals who represent a variety of expertise such as general education, bilingual and/or ESL, special education, community members or parents as well as ancillary service providers such as school psychology, speech language, social worker, etc. Using such expertise results in a better understanding of how a student's culture and language impacts on: their learning, the interface between bilingualism and special education, and instructional methods. Ideally, teachers meet regularly (monthly) to review instructional data on students' who are struggling or are at risk for a disability. During this process, it is important that teachers gather a variety of data (e.g., achievement test scores, language proficiency levels, interviews, observations, work samples, etc.) across various settings (e.g., social as well as academic) and content areas that includes a variety of perspectives (e.g., teachers, family members, peers, etc.) (García & Ortiz, 2008). Teams should be prepared to make recommendations that teachers can implement and continue data collection to inform instruction. Once a variety of techniques have been implemented and data has been collected and analyzed over a period of time (typically 6–8 weeks), the educational team may determine appropriateness of a referral to special education (Vaughn & Fuchs, 2003). Table 4.2 outlines questions to consider when bilingual Latino students are struggling academically to tease out linguistic and cultural factors to be addressed. This is important because there is a delicate balance of not referring too early before implementing more individualized and appropriate instruction to meet the needs of a learner and too late when students continue to fail and fall further behind.

To a large measure, teachers must administer *culturally and linguistically responsive assessments*. For bilingual Latino youth, be sure to assess the child in their native language as well as English as appropriate. Teachers need to assess the child's native language proficiency and English language in the four domains of listening, speaking, reading, and writing as well as acculturation level. Tables 4.3 and 4.4 can assist teaches in this endeavor. Table 4.3 provides a list of common characteristics shared by English learners

TABLE 4.2 Questions to Consider When Bilingual Latino Students Struggle

- Are the interventions normed for Latino students?
- Are optimal language supports being provided?
- Does the teacher understand the child's culture or cultural norms?
- To what extent is the child in the process of acquiring language?
- How is acculturation playing a role?
- To what extent has the student had access to optimal language supports?
- Have multiple research-based interventions been tried?
- Are interventions culturally and linguistically responsive?
- Is there documented evidence of the disability in both languages?
- Are teachers with special education and linguistically diverse knowledge on the instructional team or have they been consulted?

TABLE 4.3 Common Characteristics of Students Who are Learning English as a Second Language and/or Have a Disability

- Extended periods of silence
- Confusion with locus of control
- Indifference to time
- Shy, social withdrawal
- Acting out/aggressive behavior
- Short attention span
- Frequently off-task
- Forgets easily
- Difficulty with independent work
- Limited task completion behaviors
- Increased Anxiety
- Perceived lack of significance of school achievement
- Poor motivation
- Distractible
- Low self-esteem

TABLE 4.4 How Do We Know When a Bilingual Latino Has a Disability?

- Language or learning delays present in both languages.
- Significantly interferes with one's learning, often regardless of instructional method used.
- Multiple instructional approaches implemented, yet limited response.

and students with disabilities and Table 4.4 provides the key characteristics for knowing when a disability exists. It's important to gain a deep understanding of the extent to which second language, second culture learning is impacting the student's behaviors in the classroom because some of these characteristics can appear to be a disability when in fact they are part of the natural progression of acculturation and bilingual development. Additionally, even when a bilingual Latino student has a disability, language and culture are still impacting the student's identity as a learner so it is important to continue to provide services and instruction to address these needs.

Teachers need to keep in mind that not all Latino students speak Spanish, as many are monolingual native English speaking. Because of this, it is essential for teachers to check whether assessments have been normed for the population, which they are testing. Furthermore, teachers need to consider cultural and linguistic differences that may impact the validity of the scores. It is a best assessment practice to involve native or proficient speakers of Spanish who are certified in education, culturally connected, and/ or work with the specific Latino community to appropriately administer and interpret results. Lastly, teachers must be cognizant that not all Latino students have the same experiences or cultural values, factors such as country of origin, dialect of Spanish, immigration status/citizenship, which may influence their understanding, performance and acclimation to school culture (Hollins, 1996; Rhodes, Ochoa, & Ortiz, 2005).

Another imperative point is the need to implement a *schoolwide problem-solving process* to discuss issues and practices that may be contributing to academic supports or failure (e.g., disproportionate representation) and identify areas of growth for your school (Fiedler et al., 2008). Also, teachers need to consider the extent to which culturally and linguistically responsive practices are being implemented for Latino students within policies, practices, and beliefs across the continuum of services provided at your school (e.g., general education classroom, early intervening services, prereferral, referral, and specialized services—Title I, special education, bilingual, ESL, etc). A tool that can assist teachers in this process is the *Culturally Responsive Practices in Schools: The Checklist to address Disproportionality* developed by the Madison Metropolitan School District, the University of Wisconsin-Madison, and the Wisconsin Department of Public Instruction, which can be found at http://www.dpi.wi.gov/sped/spp-disp.html.

This above process can also be used to generate specific professional development topics and goals. To keep current, teachers must attend *professional development* workshops/in-service trainings on the instruction of Latina/o students with special needs, regularly, since research on the New Latino Diaspora as well as language development for bilingual learners is so dynamic and continues to grow. It is critical for teachers who primarily work with bilingual Latino youth to have professional development in the following: first and second language acquisition, effective strategies and techniques for developing native language and English as a second language, cultural influences on children's socialization at school as well as the teaching and learning process, progress monitoring approaches for bilingual Latino students, and approaches for working with Latino families (targeted for the specific ethnic community served in your program) (Kushner, 2008; Nieto & Bode, 2012). Lastly, teachers may want to invite community leaders and family members to their class to talk about their experiences which can lead to a better understand of the aspirations, issues, and needs of the Latino community.

CONCLUSION

In today's world where the Latino population continues to increase in diversity, it is important to continue to be open to learning about the identities and unique characteristics of our Latino students while also recognizing that identity is fluid and dynamic with multiple variables impacting upon them as individuals and learners especially in a context where cultures are in contact and influence each other. In this chapter, we explored the topic of educating Latino students in special education with a particular focus on linguistic and cultural factors that impact learning. As Latino populations continue to shift and move throughout the United States, it will be increasingly important to learn of each populations' unique and shared characteristics and experiences. Not only should we uphold high expectations for academic achievement and linguistic development of our Latina/o students, but we should do so in a context that recognizes the role of race, culture, language, ability and other sociocultural identities that influence their experience while affirming and building on their varied identities. Being Latino is much more than having Spanish speaking heritage and in some cases this cannot be assumed. Rather, being Latino needs to be unpacked within the unique sociocultural context of the individual's experiences.

REFERENCES

Antrop-González, R., & De Jesús, A. (2006). Toward a theory of *critical care* in urban small school reform: Examining structures and pedagogies of caring in two Latino community-based schools. *International Journal of Qualitative Studies in Education, 19*(4), 409–433.

Artiles, A., & Ortiz, A. (2002). *English language learners with special education needs: Identification, assessment, and instruction.* Washington, D.C.: Center for Applied Linguistics.

Artiles, A. J., Rueda, R. Salazar, J. J., & Higareda, I. (2005). With-in group diversity in minority disproportionate representation: English language learners in urban school districts. *Exceptional Children, 71*(3), 283–300.

Cummins, J. (1984). *Bilingualism and special education: Issues in assessment and pedagogy.* Clevedon, UK: Multilingual Matters.

de Valenzuela, J. S., Copeland, S. R., Qi, C. H., & Park, M. (2006). Examining educational equity: Revisiting the disproportionate representation of minority students in special education. *Exceptional Children, 72*(4), 425–441.

Dray, B. J., & Wisneski, D. B. (2011). Mindful reflection as a process for developing culturally responsive practices. *TEACHING Exceptional Children, 44*(1), 28–36.

Echevarria, J., & Graves, A. (2010). *Sheltered content instruction: Teaching ELLs with diverse abilities* (4th ed). Boston, MA: Allyn & Bacon.

Fiedler, C. R., Chiang, B., Van Haren, B., Jorgensen, J., Halberg, S., & Boreson, L. (2008). Culturally responsive practices in schools: A checklist to address disproportionality in special education. *TEACHING Exceptional Children, 40*(5), 52–59.

Figueroa, R. (2005). Dificultades O desabilidades de aprendizaje? *Learning Disability Quarterly, 28*(2), 163–168.

Fry, R., & Lopez, M. (2012). Hispanic student enrollments reach new highs in 2011. *Pew Hispanic Center.* Retrieved from http://www.pewhispanic.org/files/2012/08/Hispanic-Student-Enrollments-Reach-New-Highs-in-2011_FINAL.pdf

Garcia, S. B., & Dray, B. J. (2006). Bilingualism and special education. In F. Obiakor (Ed.), *Multicultural special education: Culturally responsive teaching* (pp.18–33). Upper Saddle River, NJ: Prentice Hall.

García, S. B., & Ortiz, A. A. (2008). A framework for culturally and linguistically responsive design of Response-to-Intervention models. *Multiple Voices, 11*(1), 24–41.

Gottlieb, M. (2006). *Assessing English language learners: Bridges from language proficiency to achievement.* Thousand Oaks, CA: Corwin.

Hamayan, E., Marler, B., Sanchez-Lopez, C., & Damico, J. (2007). *Special education considerations for English language learners: Delivering a continuum of services.* Philadelphia, PA: Caslon.

Hollins, E. (1996). *Culture in school learning: Revealing the deep meaning.* New York: Routledge.

Humes, K. R., Jones, N. A., & Ramirez, R. R. (2011). Overview of Race and Hispanic Origin: 2010. *2010 Census Briefs.* Washington, DC: US Department of Commerce, Economics and Statistics Administration, US Census Bureau. Retrieved from www.census.gov/prod/cen2010/briefs/c2010br-02.pdf

Irizarry, J. (2007). Ethnic and urban intersections in the classroom: Latino students, hybrid identities, and culturally responsive pedagogy. *Multicultural Perspectives, 9*(3), 21–28.

Jimenez, R. T., & Rose, B. C. (2010). Knowing how to know: Building meaningful relationships through instruction that meets the needs of students learning English. *Journal of Teacher Education, 61*(5), 403–412.

Kalyanpur, M. & Harry, B. (1999). *Culture in Special Education.* Baltimore, MD: Paul H. Brookes.

Kavazanjian, C. (n.d.). *What is Diaspora? International Institute for Diaspora Studies.* Retrieved at http://www.diasporastudies.org/Whatis.html

Kushner, M. (2008). Preparing highly qualified teachers for English language learners with disabilities and at risk of disabilities. *Multiple Voices for Ethnically Diverse Exceptional Learners, 11*(1), 42–57.

Levinson, B. (2002). Forward. In S. Wortham, E. Murillo Jr. & E. Hamann (Eds.), *Education in the new Latino diaspora: Policy and the politics of identity (pp.45–68).* Westport, CT: Ablex Publishing.

Loeffer, M. (2007). *NCELA Fast FAQ 4: What languages do ELLs speak?* Washington, DC: National Clearing House for English-Language Acquisition and Language Instruction.

Luke, A., Woods, A., & Dooley, K. (2011). Comprehension as social and intellectual practice: Rebuilding curriculum in low socioeconomic and cultural minority schools. *Theory Into Practice, 50*(2), 157–164.

Moll, L., Amanti, C., Neff, D., & Gonzalez, N. (1992). Funds of knowledge for teaching: Using a qualitative approach to connect homes and classrooms. *Theory into Practice, 31*(1), 132–141.

Moll, L. C., & González, N. (1997). Teachers as social scientists: Learning about culture from household research. In P. M. Hall (Ed.), *Race, ethnicity, and multiculturalism* (pp. 89–114). New York: Garland.

Murillo Jr., E., & Villenas, S. (1997). *East of Atzlan: Typologies of resistance in North Carolina communities.* Paper presented at the Reclaiming Voices: Ethnographic Research in a Postmodernism Age, Los Angeles, CA.

Nieto, S., & Bode, P. (2012). *Affirming diversity: The sociopolitical context of multicultural education* (6th ed.). New York: Pearson.

Office of Civil Rights (2006). *Civil Rights Data Collection (CRDC) Projections and Documentation.* 2006 National Projections. Retrieved from http://ocrdata.ed.gov/Projections_2006.aspx.

Office of English Language Acquisition, Language Enhancement, and Academic Achievement for Limited English Proficient Students (2008). *Biennial Report to Congress on the Implementation of the Title III State Formula Grant Program, School Years 2004–06.* Washington, DC: Author.

Oller, K., & Eilers, R. (Eds.). (2002). *Language and literacy in bilingual children.* Clevedon, UK: Multilingual Matters.

Ortiz, A., & Garcia, S. (1988). *Preventing inappropriate referrals of language minority students to special education.* (Prepared for Office of Bilingual Education and Minority Language Affairs [OBEMLA], U.S. Department of Education). NCBE New Focus, 5. Silver Spring, MD: National Clearinghouse for Bilingual Education. No. 300-86-0069.

Ramírez J. S., Yuen, D., Ramey, S., & Pasta, D. (1991). Final report longitudinal study of structured English immersion strategy, early exit and late-exit bilingual education programs for language minority children (Vol. I). (Prepared for U.S. Department of Education). San Mateo, CA: Aguirre International. No. 300-87-0156.

Rhodes, R. L., Ochoa, S. H., & Ortiz, S. O. (2005) *Assessing culturally and linguistically diverse students: A practical guide.* New York: Guilford Press.

Ruiz, R. (1984). Orientations in language planning. *NABE Journal, 8*(2), 15–34.

Snyder, T. D., & Dillow, S. A. (2012). *Digest of Education Statistics, 2011.* Washington, D.C.: National Center for Education Statistics, Institute of Education Sciences, U.S. Department of Education. http://nces.ed.gov/pubsearch/pubsinfo.asp?pubid=2012001

Thomas, C. J., & Collier, V. P. (2002). *A national study of school effectiveness for language minority students' long-term academic achievement.* Center for Research on Education, Diversity, and Excellence. Available at www.usc.edu/dept/education/CMMR/CollierThomasExReport.pdf.

Tyler, N. C., Yzquierdo, Z., Lopez-Reyna, N., & Saunders Flippin, S. (2004). Cultural and linguistic diversity and the special education workforce: A critical overview. *Journal of Special Education, 38*(1), 22–38.

United States Census Bureau. (2011). *Overview of race and Hispanic origin: 2010.* Washington D.C. Retrieved from http://www.census.gov/prod/cen2010/briefs/c2010br-02.pdf

U.S. Department of Education, Office of Special Education and Rehabilitative Services, Office of Special Education Programs. (2009). *28th Annual Report to Congress on the Implementation of the Individuals with Disabilities Education Act, 2006,* (vol. 2). Washington, DC: Author.

Valdés, G. (1996). *Con respeto: Bridging the distances between culturally diverse families and schools: An ethnographic portrait.* New York: Teachers College Press.

Valenzuela, A. (2010). *Subtractive schooling: U.S.-Mexican youth and the politics of caring.* Albany, NY: SUNY Press.

Valldejuli, J. M., & Flores, J. (2000). New Rican voices: Un muestraria/o sampler at the millennium. *Journal of the Center for Puerto Rican Studies, 12*(1) 49–26.

Vaughn, S., & Fuchs L. (2003). Redefining learning disabilities as inadequate response to instruction: The promise and potential problems. *Learning Disabilities: Research & Practice, 18,* 137–146.

Working Group on ELL Policy (2010). Improving educational outcomes for English language learners: Recommendations for the reauthorization of the Elementary and Secondary Education Act (updated May 25, 2010). Author. Retrieved at: http://ellpolicy.org/wp-content/uploads/ESEAFinal.pdf

Zehler, A. M., Fleischman, H. L., Hopstock, P. J., Pendzick, M. L., & Stephenson, T. G. (2003). *Descriptive study of services to LEP students and LEP students with disabilities: Findings on special education LEP students* (Special Topic Report #4). Washington, DC: Office of English Language Acquisition, U.S. Department of Education (Contract No. ED–00–CO–0089).

CHAPTER 5

EDUCATING AFRICAN AMERICAN LEARNERS WITH SPECIAL NEEDS

Tachelle Banks

Culturally and linguistically diverse (CLD) children with disabilities all too often experience inadequate services, low-quality curriculum and instruction, and unnecessary isolation from their nondisabled peers. Moreover, inappropriate practices in both general and special education classrooms have resulted in overrepresentation, misclassification, and hardship for CLD students, particularly African American children. In 2009, the U.S. Department of Education (2010) estimates showed that about 5.8 million of the nation's schoolchildren, ages 6 to 21, were receiving special education services through the Individuals with Disabilities Education Act (IDEA). Approximately 61% of those students have specific learning disabilities or speech and language impairments. Only about 8% are diagnosed with significant cognitive disabilities, such as cognitive disability or traumatic brain injury.

Access to the general education curriculum is an important issue for all students with disabilities, especially for African American students. More than half of all students with disabilities spend at least 80% of their time in the regular classroom. The overrepresentation of African American

Multicultural Education for Learners with Special Needs in the Twenty-First Century, pages 67–83
Copyright © 2014 by Information Age Publishing
All rights of reproduction in any form reserved.

students typically occurs in the categories of disability that are the most subjective to identify (Donovan & Cross, 2002). Some scholars attribute this overrepresentation in special education to the use of identification tools, such as IQ tests, which they claim can be culturally biased (Losen & Orfield, 2002). This chapter reviews the historical precedent and current state of special education. In addition, it critically examines salient topics that impact the education of African American learners with special educational needs.

HISTORICAL PRECEDENT OF SPECIAL EDUCATION FOR AFRICAN AMERICAN STUDENTS

When identifying factors that define the state of special education in the nation's schools, attention should be paid to certain issues that can help to strengthen future efforts of both policymakers and educators. In the classic critique of the field, Dunn's (1968) article introduced the educational community to the disproportionate representation of CLD students. Prior to the critique, in the case *Hobson v. Hansen* (1967), Judge Wright found that denying children from low socioeconomic status backgrounds the same opportunity afforded to affluent children was a violation of the Due Process Clause of the Fifth Amendment. Underwood and Mead (1995) asserted that "not only are plaintiffs and their class denied the publicly supported education to which they are entitled, many are suspended or expelled from regular schooling or specialized instruction or reassigned without any prior hearing and are given no periodic review thereafter. Due process of law requires a hearing prior to exclusion, termination of classification into a special program" (p. 61). Dunn's critique built upon prior legislation and a history of structural inequalities that have helped to underscore overrepresentation concerns.

In the early years of special education, children that were from CLD backgrounds were excluded from school (Dunn, 1968; Hollingworth, 1923). As Dunn (1968) pointed out, the advent of compulsory attendance laws "resulted in the establishment of self-contained special schools and classes as a method of transferring these 'misfits' out of regular grades" (p. 5). Not surprisingly, approximately 60% to 80% of the students being serviced were from CLD backgrounds. Moreover, "this extensive proliferation of self-contained special schools and classes raises serious educational and civil rights issues which must be squarely faced" (Dunn, 1968, p. 6).

Since the call for an investigation was made by Dunn in 1968, continued challenges were brought to court for litigation in order to provide equal access in education. In *Larry P. v. Riles* (1979), an initial complaint was filed by six African American school children from the San Francisco Unified School District. The complaint was that IQ tests used by the school system to place children into special education for the educable cognitive disability violated the Equal Protection Clause of the United States and federal statutes. Underwood and Mead (1995) confirmed that "the court enjoined the use of nonvalidated intelligence tests and ordered the reevaluation of all African American children whose placements were based on the use of invalid IQ tests" (p. 88).

SPECIAL EDUCATION TODAY

The nation's public school systems collectively educate more than 6 million students with disabilities, about 9% of the school-age population. Nearly one-third of those students with disabilities are of traditional high school age. More than at any other time in the history of American education, youth with disabilities receive instruction in school settings similar to those serving the general student population, continuing the trend of mainstreaming. This movement toward greater educational inclusion has resulted from decades of litigation, federal law, and policymaking. The total number of students in special education programs is also on the rise, a development fueled in large part by the rapid growth in two particular disability categories—Other Health Impairments (which includes attention deficit hyperactivity disorder or ADHD) and Specific Learning Disabilities (which encompasses a wide variety of diagnoses that do not fit under other existing classifications).

The choice of method for diagnosing disabilities remains a contentious issue. A new approach (i.e., Response-to-Intervention [RTI]) to identifying learning disabilities recognized by the 2004 reauthorization of the federal IDEA has emerged as an alternative to traditional discrepancy-based models. The severity of disabilities generally falls along a wide continuum. As a result, it can prove difficult to accurately identify certain conditions or to distinguish between a student who exhibits low achievement due to a disability and one whose low performance is attributable to other factors. The sensitivity and accuracy of procedures for diagnosing disabilities are, therefore, critical factors in the provision of special education services.

In terms of school experiences and outcomes, students with special education needs are generally more likely to become involved in major disciplinary incidents (i.e., suspensions and expulsions) than are their peers in general education programs. Likewise, students with disabilities attain significantly lower levels of academic performance than the average student. In both cases, however, we observe a great deal of variation within the special education population, with certain disability classifications much more likely to be associated with negative educational outcomes. Such achievement gaps have gained new salience given the rise of performance-based school accountability and the increasing inclusion of students with disabilities in both federal and state testing and accountability systems.

ACHIEVEMENT OF AFRICAN AMERICAN STUDENTS

The term "achievement gap" is often defined as the differences between the test scores of CLD and/or low-income students and the test scores of their White and Asian peers. But, achievement gaps in test scores affect many different groups. Some groups may trail at particular points, for example, boys in the early years and girls in high school math and science. Differences between the scores of students from different backgrounds (i.e., ethnic, racial, gender, disability, and income) are evident on large-scale standardized tests. Test score gaps often lead to longer-term gaps, including high school and college completion and the kinds of jobs students secure as adults (Ingels et al., 2011). It is imperative to consider the impact of the dominant culture on educational achievement, given the differences among different groups. Schools are not culturally neutral, and students from low socioeconomic backgrounds are disadvantaged by their lack of cultural capital. Therefore, this lack of cultural capital may impact their academic achievement, which may also play a role in their overrepresentation in special education. The concept of cultural capital was developed by Pierre Bourdieu (1977) as part of a larger framework that analyzed the reproduction of class based on power and privilege, and examined how culture impacts processes of inequality. In Bourdieu's schema, cultural capital was the focal point of cultural reproduction. This dynamic model emphasized the importance of three forms of capital: social, economic, and cultural. Cultural capital generally refers to cultural background, knowledge, and skills that are passed from one generation to the next (Bourdieu, 1977; Lareau, 2003). In mainstream institutions, cultural capital frequently reflects the values of the dominant class. As a result, students from privileged backgrounds enter school with advantages in these areas and are rewarded for this type of aptitude.

Three particular aspects of cultural capital, as originated by Bourdieu (1977) and modified by Lareau (2003), make it an appropriate and compelling framework for examining the mechanisms underlying group disparities in educational outcomes. First, cultural capital is noted as being passed from one generation to the next, which is a critical component. If students are not taught explicitly how to gain valuable cultural capital, they will lag behind. For example, Lareau found that working class students, both African American and White, lacked the linguistic cultural capital to navigate the educational system. This is in contrast to the students of the upper tier who knew how to navigate the educational system. Second, the school system systematically valorizes upper class cultural capital and depreciates the cultural capital of the lower class. Hence, children are rewarded for meeting institutional standards and proficiencies that are heavily influenced by class and race. Therefore, the success that CLD students have in this framework cannot be completely attributed to their quantifiable performance. For example, in Lee's (2005) study, standards for excellence and good citizenship that teachers and staff used to gauge students were closely related to whiteness. "Whiteness is associated with economic self-sufficiency, independence, and self-discipline, while blackness is associated with welfare, dependency, failure, and depravity" (Lee, 2005, p. 3). Consequently, CLD children, when striving for excellence, in essence were striving to obtain qualities of their white counterparts. Similarly, Obidah and Teel (2001) found that the lens in which individuals view others affects our perceptions of others. Specifically, when Teel (2001) reflected on her own beliefs and misconceptions, she found that she used the dominant culture as the standard for excellence and viewed cultural differences negatively. Hence, members of the dominant culture do not have to quantify their performance because they are the standard for excellence.

Delpit's (1988) *The Silenced Dialogue: Power and Pedagogy in Educating Other People's Children* proposed a solution, which is to understand the "silenced dialogue" of marginalized groups. She identified five complex themes that define "the culture of power" and she described how classrooms replicate the power structures of society. As she noted,

> These issues include the power of the teacher over the students; the power of the publishers of textbooks and of the developers of the curriculum to determine the view of the world presented; the power of the state in enforcing compulsory schooling; and the power of an individual or group to determine another's intelligence or "normalcy." Finally, if schooling prepares people for jobs, and the kind of job a person has determines her or his economic status and therefore, power, then schooling is ultimately related to power. (p. 283)

The rules of engagement are required for participation in the schooling realm and, in particular, in "...linguistic forms, communicative strategies, and presentation of self..." (Delpit, 1988, p. 283). Those that are able to navigate the culture tend to have more power than those that are unable. Delpit contended that the culture of power is based on those in power—upper and middle classes. Students sent to school in the upper and middle class neighborhoods carry codes of power with them. In her words, Delpit stated that:

> If you are not already a participant in the culture of power, being told explicitly the rules of the culture makes acquiring power easier. In my work within and between diverse cultures, I have come to conclude that members

of any culture transmit information implicitly to comembers. However, when implicit codes are attempted across cultures, communication frequently breaks down. Each cultural group is left saying, "Why don't those people say what they mean?", as well as, "What's wrong with them, why don't they understand?" (p. 283)

Finally, disenfranchised groups are often aware of the existence of power, whereas those with power are least willing or least aware of its reality. Delpit (1988) suggested that students be taught explicitly the codes necessary to participate in American social structures, in conjunction with the power structures that comprise these complex structures. Moreover, students should be helped to see their value and acknowledge their own "expertness" as well. A teacher may address cultural capital and supporting students in coming to understand the rules of the culture of power or a teacher may assign explicit value to the culture of the children—perhaps the use of culturally relevant pedagogy, multicultural education, and/or the encouragement of voice among children. Delpit concluded that reform efforts created for marginalized students should be created in collaboration with adults who share their culture.

DISPROPORTIONATE REPRESENTATION OF STUDENTS IN SPECIAL EDUCATION

Controversy over the rates at which certain demographic or socioeconomic categories are represented within the population of students with disabilities remains a prominent feature of public debates over special education. More specifically, concerns have been repeatedly raised about the overrepresentation of particular student groups in special education programs. In principle, the idea behind overrepresentation is that a given characteristic or condition appears within a particular group at a rate higher than it "should," relative to that group's inherent level of risk for experiencing the condition. The converse would hold true for underrepresentation. In practice, however, the factors that determine risk for a disability are numerous, complex, highly intertwined with one another, and often difficult to observe directly or measure empirically. As a result, researchers generally evaluate levels of group over- or underrepresentation solely on the basis of prevalence—that is, by comparing the rates at which disabilities are diagnosed for a particular group relative to other groups or the student population as a whole. From this perspective, the available evidence has consistently demonstrated disparities in the prevalence of special education placement rates across racial and ethnic groups and by gender.

With regard to disproportionality, Smith (2004) reported that African American students constitute 33% of students classified as cognitively disabled and placed in special education, despite the fact that African American students only comprise 15% of the general student population, ages 6 to 21 years. While, the overall percentage of African American students classified as cognitively disabled was less than two percent (1.7%) of all African American students attending school. About nine percent of all school-aged individuals are diagnosed with a disability and receive special education services. Relative to the national baseline, African American and Native American students are more likely (and Asians less likely) to receive special education services than the average student. Rates of special education among Hispanic and White students are close to the national average (Smith, 2004). Even within a group with a high prevalence of diagnosed disabilities, rates of identification for some disability categories may be dramatically higher than for others. For instance, overall, African American students receive special education services at a rate about 40% higher than the national average across racial and ethnic groups. However, rates of these with cognitive disability and emotional disturbance are extremely elevated within the African American population, roughly twice the national average. Generally, disproportionate representation has been noted in high-incidence categories that involve more subjective diagnoses (e.g., cognitive disability, specific learning disabilities, and emotional disturbance).

Gender disparities have become a significant concern in debates over special education placement. Males are diagnosed with disabilities nearly twice as often as female students. Data from the U.S. Department of Education's Office for Civil Rights (OCR) (2007) on specific learning disabilities, cognitive disability, and emotional disturbance show that males from every racial and ethnic group are more likely than females to be in special education. Considerable public attention has been concentrated on the high rates of disability diagnosed for CLD males, especially African Americans. The incidence of cognitive disability among African American males rises to 220 percent of the rate found in the general student population, with rates of emotional disturbance two and a half times the national average.

Despite the fact that males from some historically disadvantaged groups are much more likely to receive special education services, the differential rates of diagnosis for males versus females within CLD groups are rather similar. For instance, males from all racial and ethnic groups are about 80% to 90% more likely than females to be diagnosed with a disability. Male-female differentials are larger for some diagnoses, although comparable across groups. For example, males are about three times as likely to be labeled emotionally disturbed compared to the females in their respective racial-ethnic classification. That suggests that the high prevalence of special education placement among African American males may be largely attributable to the elevated baseline levels of disability diagnosed among all

African Americans, and then compounded by the elevated rates of diagnosis found among males of all racial and ethnic groups.

REDUCING DISPROPORTIONATE REPRESENTATION OF CLD IN SPECIAL EDUCATION

While the Civil Rights Movement propelled policies that contributed to significant increases in academic achievement, advancement in educational achievement of African American students since the early 1990s has declined. Educational activists and researchers have actively sought alternative approaches to spur academic excellence for students from diverse backgrounds. These approaches are discussed in the subsections below.

Multicultural Education Practices

The multicultural education movement in the United States grew out of the Civil Rights Movement of the 1960s, reflecting the recognition of all experiences of CLD students. Consequently, a number of theorists made the call for greater infusion of multicultural literature into the curriculum. Taylor (1995) emphasized that the literature can serve as a platform in which students can see positive reflections of themselves. An implementation of multicultural literature contributes to the understanding of how students perceive others as well as themselves. When students see themselves mirrored in books and literature, they gain an affirmation of themselves and their identities (see Taylor, 1995). Earlier, Yokota (1993) suggested that images that children glean from literature have a powerful impact on their sense of self and view of others. The literature can influence values and beliefs and can challenge existing thoughts that may prove destructive. Clearly, the literature that displays positive depictions has a positive influence on self-worth and identity, whereas the literature with negative depictions has an adverse effect.

Montgomery (2000) and Norton (1995) advocated for cultural congruency in instruction by stating that educators are often drawn to what is familiar. This is also true in the selection of reading materials (Vacca, Vacca, & Gove, 2000, p. 504). It is common for educators to select literature based on familiar themes, experiences, characters, and values. The literature choices and themes are often congruent with the dominant culture. Put another way, if educators select literature congruent to their culture and if Whites comprise the majority of the teacher population, then the literature tends to affirm the dominant culture. Therefore, the exclusion of other cultures inherently becomes a standard practice for the educator as well as for the student. Norton further agreed that goals of multicultural education could be ascertained through the inclusion of multicultural literature into the curriculum. Doni Kwolek Kobus (as cited by Norton, 1995, p. 1995) indicated that multicultural literature provides (a) understanding and respect for each child's cultural group identities; (b) respect for and tolerance of cultural differences, including differences in gender, language, race, ethnicity, religion, region, and disabilities; (c) understanding of and respect for universal human rights and fundamental freedoms; (d) preparation of children for a responsible life in a free society; and (e) knowledge of cross-cultural communication strategies, perspective taking, and conflict management skills to ensure understanding, peace, tolerance, and friendship among all peoples and groups.

Textbooks overwhelmingly perpetuate the beliefs of the dominant culture (Gay, 2000). In a study conducted by Sleeter and Grant (1991), the findings revealed that little attention is given to different CLD groups interacting with each other, in textbooks, in Grades 1–8, and in the areas of mathematics, social science, and reading. Additionally, Sleeter and Grant stated that, "...there is an imbalance across ethnic groups of color, with most attention given to African Americans and their experiences." The content educators provide on ethnic issues is conservative in nature. The disparities in gender and social class prevail, since the curriculum is closely aligned with mainstream culture. Concerns set forth by CLD people are not consistently featured in the elementary and secondary curricula. Although empirical research does not substantiate how biases of textbooks affect students of marginalized groups, the inadequacy of textbooks to represent culturally diverse groups is clearly problematic, and, in a variety of manners, does not help either. There are a number of accounts that express discontent, feelings of exclusion, and inaccuracies.

Culturally congruent teaching practices suggest that the infusion of ethnic content alone is not sufficient to meet the needs of non-White students. The notion of cultural relevance is greater than language; it encompasses other aspects of student and school cultures (Ladson-Billings, 1994). Tharp (1982) suggested that teachers use mechanisms and curriculum that integrate concepts with students' prior knowledge. According to Ladson-Billings (1994),

> Culturally relevant teaching is a term I have used to describe the kind of teaching that is designed not merely to fit the school culture to the students' culture but to use student culture as the basis for helping students understand themselves and others, structure social interactions, and conceptualize knowledge, thus, culturally relevant teaching requires the recognition of African American culture as an important strength upon which to construct the school experience. (p. 314)

Furthermore, Yamauchi (2005) contended that "the notion is that all students learn—but what and how they learn may differ across groups, depending on who students interact with and the kinds of expectations, beliefs, and knowledge that are emphasized in those interactions" (p. 105). The sociocultural perspective attributes the student's success, or lack of success, to the alignment between the home, community, and school. In addition, Yamauchi concluded that "when teachers and students come from different cultural backgrounds there tends to be less intersubjectivity between them and cultural clashes or misunderstandings are more likely to occur" (p. 105).

There have been a number of other significant studies that have contributed to the concept of culturally sensitive pedagogy. Au and Jordan (1981) conducted a case study of the Kamehameha Early Education Program (KEEP), a language arts development project. The project examined methods utilized to teach native Hawaiian children to read. The authors hypothesized that poor school achievement by many CLD children is related to the nature of teacher–pupil classroom interaction. In a related study, Tharp (1982) noted that decisions about instructional objectives and instructional style can have a direct impact on student performance. For example, Au and Jordan found that the lessons of the teacher with high student–teacher contact result in higher levels of achievement than those of the teacher with low student–teacher contact.

Banks (1994, 1995) has made a number of significant contributions to the concept of culturally sensitive pedagogy. For instance in 1994, he purposed three approaches to multicultural education, namely, curriculum reform, achievement strategies and intergroup education. In 1995, Banks formulated four practices to integrate cultural content into the school curriculum and ranked them in terms of dedication to ideals of multiculturalism. First is the contributions practice which focuses on "heroes and heroines, holidays, and discrete cultural elements" (p. 112). Second is the additive practice, which adds culture, content, concepts, and themes to the existing curriculum. Third is the transformational practice which "changes the paradigms which allows students to view concepts from different perspectives" (p. 112). Fourth is the social action practice (an extension of the transformational practice), which facilitates learning by completing projects as well as implementing solutions to resolve issues. Banks stressed this practice brings in an activist component to promote social justice for marginalized groups.

Another contribution was by Ladson-Billings (1992) who explained common themes of effective teaching practices for African American students after examining two educators individually and comparing and contrasting their teaching practices. Ladson-Billings concluded that "both teachers provide support for the students to 'be themselves' and choose academic excellence rather than allow academic achievement to seem alienating or foreign" (p. 317). The teachers saw value in their students' cultures and embraced their backgrounds while displaying the importance of academic excellence. Ladson-Billings suggested that teachers model both positive student-to-student as well as teacher-to-student relationships, empowering the students by sharing power. These positive interactions assist in creating a supportive classroom environment and in recreating a more familial structure. Ladson-Billings (1994) used the above information to extend the framework of culturally relevant teaching in her book *The Dreamkeepers*. She stated the following about this extension,

> The notion of "cultural relevance" moves beyond language to include other aspects of student and school culture. Thus culturally relevant teaching uses student culture in order to maintain it and to transcend the negative effects of the dominant culture. The negative effects are brought about, for example, by not seeing one's history, culture or background respected in the textbook or curriculum or by seeing that history, culture, or background are distorted. (p. 17)

Ladson-Billings suggested that using the culture of the students as the focal point assists in empowering the student. She noted, "culturally relevant teaching is a pedagogy that empowers students intellectually, socially, emotionally, and politically by using cultural referents to impart knowledge, skills and attitude" (pp. 17–18).

More recently, Gay (2000) provided illustrations of techniques for practicing "border" pedagogy and giving voice to culturally diverse groups. She posited two fundamental pedagogical principles:

1. Differences in how students assign meaning to learning stimuli and how this is affected by diverse social and cultural formations which give them voice, agency, and identity; and
2. The obligation of teachers to use the cultural frameworks of students to make knowledge more relevant and accessible.

Gay discussed how African Americans, Hispanic Americans, Native Americans, and other disenfranchised groups are communal in nature and tend to benefit from more participatory practices. As she indicated,

> African American, Latino, Native American, and poverty cultures tend to be highly communal, group based, and action oriented. Therefore, teaching and learning strategies that are participatory, cooperative, collaborative, and that use frequently varied formulas are likely to be more culturally compatible and successful for students from these backgrounds than the more traditional use of competitive, individualistic, passive and monotonous routines. Using a

variety of cultural pluralistic materials, experience and examples to illustrate
practice and demonstrate mastery of theoretical principles and intellectual
skills has significant potential for improving the academic success of culturally different students. (pp. 173–174)

By using culture as a framework, this makes knowledge more real, relevant,
and accessible to the students.

Using teacher voices to raise awareness, Obidah and Teel's (2001) study
focused on improving teaching practices and examined the impact of racial
and cultural differences on teaching and learning in the classroom. The
results of the study indicated that beliefs, intentions, and personalities of
individual teachers play a greater role in student success than materials or
text. Obidah and Teel purported that the unintended biases of "White"
teachers may interfere with the process of teaching and learning as experienced by CLD students. Teachers can have a significant influence on the
education of African American children; however, many teachers do not
feel adequately prepared to teach in urban classrooms. In the words of Obidah (2001), "the knowledge I was gaining from my experience as a public
school teacher was difficult to bring into the discussion in the university
classroom" (p. 25). Obidah and Teel learned that dialogue and critical
reflection assist in helping to put together the pieces of this complex illustration. As they indicated,

> Our story is a difficult and complex one to tell because it has been quite an
> emotional process for both of us singularly and simultaneously; we have ex-
> perienced such difficult emotions and frustration, confusion, pain, suspicion,
> disillusionment, fear, anxiety, and anger. On the other hand, we have each
> found the process to be encouraging, rewarding, moving, thought provoking
> and invaluable. (p. 103)

Their study accentuated the value of critically reflective practice. By reflecting on their roles as teachers, researchers, and writers, Obidah and Teel
discovered how to act with their evolving understanding of their role as
teachers and the influence of their racial backgrounds.

Teacher Expectations and Beliefs

Gay (2000) provided a review of teacher expectations that point to
trends that offer insight for improving instruction. A plethora of variables
influence teacher expectations, ranging from racial identity, gender, ethnicity, social class, and home language. All of these variables facilitate the
formulation of teacher expectations. Gay asserted that teacher expectations have a direct impact on student achievement. As she noted, "culture

also influences student and teacher expectations as well as how they engage in classroom interactions" (p. 54). In Western Caucasian cultures in particular, the rules of engagement deemed necessary for success in the classroom are typically incompatible with those of culturally diverse groups, which can create disequilibrium. The students may seem quiet or disengaged when they are overwhelmed or baffled. Expectations held by teachers from the dominant culture that exclude the historical context of students create an environment that could compromise the educational landscape for students (Obiakor, 1998). Often, students who do not comply with policies and procedures are labeled as noncompliant, and require constant redirection and reprimanding from the teacher or service provider. This gives the inaccurate perception that students lack the mainstream cultural competence. As Gay posited, "Before a genuine ethos of caring can be developed and implemented on a large scale, educators must identify and understand current noncaring attitudes and behaviors, and how they can obstruct student achievement. This understanding will help to locate places and spaces in classroom interactions that need to be changed and to determine which aspects of caring will be most appropriate to expedite student achievement" (p. 53). Trends in teacher expectations offer some insight for improving instruction. Specifically, teacher expectations influence the quality of instruction. For example, teachers who assert they believe all children can learn, but allow students to sit all day without insisting that they learn, fail to carry out their belief. Further, the assumptions teachers have about intellectual capabilities, ethnicity, and gender are directly related to their expectations for the students (see Obiakor, 1998). For instance, teachers tend to have higher expectations for European American students than for CLD students and their expectations for students are aligned to their beliefs.

In research that explores individuals who are effective with diverse students (e.g., Gay, 2000; Ladson-Billings, 1994), caring has been identified as a pillar of culturally responsive teaching that brings together the individual with the society, the community, and each other (Gay, 2000; Obiakor, 1998). Historically, common practice in Western cultures or in the school setting is to fix culturally "deprived" students and make them conform to Eurocentric norms. Educators who genuinely care for students have children who perform well academically, socially, morally, and culturally (Gay, 2000). In research conducted with students of all diverse backgrounds in the United States, Mercado (1993) indicated that students' memories of schools were characterized as "homes away from home" (Gay, 2000, p. 47). For teachers to implement an effective culturally responsive framework, they "... must have commitment, competence, confidence, and content about cultural pluralism" (Gay, 2000, p. 52). With this in mind, McAllister (2002) conducted a study with 34 practicing teachers examining their beliefs and perceptions about the role of empathy in their teaching practices. According to McAllister, empathy is necessary in helping educators become more effective teachers; however, it is not the only element that should be considered when working with diverse learners. In addition, McAllister stressed that educators should also utilize tenets of successful culturally responsive teachers in conjunction with empathy in the classroom.

In examining the basis on which teaching decisions are made, Sleeter (2005) agreed that beliefs partially come from prior experience. Marginalized groups tend to have a different ideology than the mainstream culture, which creates disequilibrium. The beliefs and assumptions of teachers dictate the lens through which students are examined (Guskey, 1993). This aspect was present in a study by Guskey (1984) who gathered data on 117 intermediate and high school teachers, 52 of whom participated in an in-service on Mastery Learning. The results of this study suggested that teachers who become more effective in their teaching tended to accept the increased responsibility for the learning outcomes of their students and tended to become more positive in their attitudes toward teaching (Guskey). The latter findings were also reported by Brookover and Lezotte (1979) who found that teachers in effective schools felt a strong sense of responsibility for the learning of their students. Guskey emphasized that teachers who believe they have less control of students consider these students to be low-ability, and, consequently, these teachers feel less able to influence the learning of these presumed low-ability students. Positively, Ferguson (2003) posited that improved skills on the part of some teachers participating in Guskey's study indicated that teachers could learn responsive teaching methods that weaken the link between the past and future performance.

CONCLUSION

Many would contend that there is an associated stigma with special education, which stems from certain societal assumptions. One assumption is that special education is a distinct and ineffective place—physically separating students rather than supplying a student with a specific set of services. The assumption is rooted in the discrepancy between special education programs in majority-minority schools versus those in majority white and Asian schools. Special education in the minority schools will often be a distinct learning environment with a separate curriculum that offers few opportunities. In majority white and Asian schools, however, special education services more successfully meet students' needs. This disparity in services may account for the reason parents in majority white and majority Asian districts push very hard for their children to receive special education services, while parents in majority–minority districts try very hard not to have their children placed in special education. Moreover, the stigma and disparity in services is confirmed by the continual dispro- portionate placement of African American (as well as Hispanic and Na- tive American) students in special education programs. This reverberates throughout their lifespan through higher incarceration rates, lower col- lege attendance, blunted employment opportunities, lower socioeconom- ic well-being, more dire health statistics, and lower life expectancies (Fra- zier, 2009; Garibaldi, 1992). Given that CLD students, particularly African American children, are less likely to make academic progress and exit special education placements than their White counterparts (Blanchett, 2006), they are more likely to suffer from these long-term consequences and become locked into a disempowering life context. With this under- standing, the magnitude of the crisis becomes clear. The overrepresenta- tion of African Americans in special education becomes not merely an educational dilemma; but it becomes a civil rights violation and a major culprit in the school-to-prison pipeline. While we cannot ignore the in- justices in many schools, we should respectfully acknowledge that schools and teachers could provide quality special education services to remedi- ate specific educational challenges. In the end, these challenges hamper students' ability to reintegrate and fully participate in mainstream classes.

REFERENCES

Au, K., & Jordan, C. (1981). Teaching reading to Hawaiian children: Finding a cul- turally appropriate solution. In H.T. Trueba, G.P. Guthrie, & K.H. Au (Eds.), *Culture and the bilingual classroom: Studies in classroom ethnography* (pp. 139– 152). Rowley, MA: Newbury House.

Banks, J. (1994). *Multiethnic education: Theory and practice.* Needham Heights, MA: Allyn & Bacon.

Banks, J. A. (1995). Multicultural education: Historical development, dimensions, and practice. In J. A. Banks & C. A. M. Banks (Eds.), *Handbook of research on multicultural education* (pp. 3–24). New York: Macmillan.

Blanchett, W. J. (2006). Disproportionate representation of African Americans in special education: Acknowledging the role of white privilege and racism. *Edu- cational Researcher, 35*(6), 24–28.

Bourdieu, P. (1977). *Outline of a theory of practice.* Cambridge; New York: Cambridge University Press.

Brookover, W. B., & Lezotte, L. W. (1979). *Changes in school characteristics coincident with changes in student achievement.* East Lansing, MI: Institute for Research on Teaching, Michigan State University.

Delpit, L. D. (1988). The silenced dialogue: Power and pedagogy in educating other people's children. *Harvard Educational Review, 58*(3), 280–289.

Donovan, M., & Cross, C. (2002). *Minority students in special and gifted education.* Washington, D.C.: National Academy Press.

Dunn, L. M. (1968). Special education for the mildly retarded: Is much of it justifiable? *Exceptional Children, 35*(1), 5–22.

Ferguson, R. F. (2003). Teachers' perception and expectations and the Black–White test score gap. *Urban Education, 38*(4), 460–507.

Frazier, G. B. (2009). *Voices of success: African American male school leaders.* Ann Arbor, MI: University of Michigan Press.

Garibaldi, A. (1992). Preparing teachers for culturally diverse classrooms. In M.E. Dilworth (Ed.), *Diversity in teacher education: New expectations* (pp.101–129). San Francisco: Jossey-Bass.

Gay, G. (2000). *Culturally responsive teaching: Theory, research, and practice.* New York: Teachers College Press.

Guskey, T. R. (1984). The influence of change in instructional effectiveness upon the affective characteristics of teachers. *American Educational Research Journal, 21*(2), 245–259.

Guskey, T. R. (1993). Policy issues and options when states take over local school districts. *International Journal of Educational Reform, 2*(1), 68–71.

Hobson v. Hansen, 265 F. Supp. 902 (D.D.C. 1967).

Hollingworth, L. (1923). *Special talents and defects: Their significance for education.* Ithaca, NY: Cornell University Library.

Ingels, S. J., Pratt, D. J., Herget, D. R., Burns, L. J., Dever, J. A., Ottem, R., ... LoGerfo, L. (2011). *High school longitudinal study of 2009 (HSLS:09): Base-year data file documentation (NCES 2011-328).* Washington, DC: U.S. Department of Education, National Center for Education Statistics.

Ladson-Billings, G. (1992). Reading between the lines and beyond the pages: A culturally relevant approach to literacy teaching. *Theory into Practice, 31*(4), 312–320.

Ladson-Billings, G. (1994). *The dreamkeepers: Successful teachers for African-American children.* San Francisco: Jossey-Bass.

Lareau, A. (2003). *Unequal childhoods: Class, race, and family life.* Berkeley, CA: University of California Press.

Larry P. v. Riles, 495 F. Supp. 926 (N.D. Cal. 1979) aff'd, 793 F.2d 969 (9th Cir. 1984).

Lee, C. D. (2005). The state of knowledge about the education of African Americans. In J. King (Ed.), *Black education: A transformative research and action agenda for the new century* (pp. 45-72). Mahwah, NJ: Lawrence Erlbaum Associates.

Losen, D.J., & Orfield, G. (2002). *Racial inequity in special education.* Cambridge, MA: Harvard Education Press.

McAllister, G. (2002). The role of empathy in teaching culturally diverse students: A qualitative study of teachers' beliefs. *Journal of Teacher Education, 53*(5), 433–443.

Mercado, C. I. (1993). Caring as empowerment: School collaboration and community agency. *Urban Review, 25*(1), 79–104.

Montgomery, W. (2000). Literature discussion in the elementary school classroom: Developing cultural understanding. *Multicultural Education, 8*(1), 33–36.

Norton, D. (1995). *Through the eyes of a child: An introduction to children's literature* (4th ed.). New York: Merrill/Macmillan Publishing Co.

Obiakor, F. E. (1998). Teacher expectations of minority exceptional learners: Impact on "accuracy" of self-concepts. *Exceptional Children, 66*(1), 39–53.

Obidah, J. (2001). Mediating boundaries of race, class, and professional authority as critical multiculturalists. *Teachers College Record, 102*(6), 1035–1060.

Obidah, J. E., & Teel, K. M. (2001). *Because of the kids: Facing racial and cultural differences in schools.* New York: Teachers College Press.

Sleeter, C. E. (2005). *Un-standardizing curriculum: Multicultural teaching in standards-based classrooms.* New York: Teachers College Press.

Sleeter, C. E., & Grant, C. A. (1991). Race, class, gender, and disability in current textbooks. In M. Apple & L. Christian Smith (Eds.), *The politics of the textbook* (pp. 78–110). New York: Routledge Publications.

Smith, D. D. (2004). *Introduction to special education: Teaching in an age of opportunity* (5th ed.). Needham Heights, MA: Allyn & Bacon.

Taylor, J. C. (1995). Distance education technologies: The fourth generation. *Australian Journal of Education Technology, 11*(2), 1–7.

Teel, K. M. (2001). *Making school count: Promoting urban student motivation and success.* New York: Routledge.

Tharp, R. G. (1982). The effective instruction of comprehension: Results and description of the Kamehameha Early Education Program. *Reading Research Quarterly, 17*(4), 503–527.

Underwood, J., & Mead, J. F. (1995). *Legal aspects of special education and pupil services.* Boston: Allyn & Bacon.

U.S. Department of Education. (2010). *IDEA data.* Retrieved September 1, 2011 from https://www.ideadata.org/PartBReport.asp

U.S. Department of Education, Office of Civil Rights (2007). *Annual Report to Congress of the Office for Civil Rights: Fiscal Year 2006.* Washington, DC: U.S. Government Printing Office.

Vacca, J. L., Vacca, R. T., & Gove, M. K. (2000). *Reading and learning to read* (4th ed.). New York: Pearson Longman. Yamauchi, F. (2005). Why do schooling returns differ? Screening, private schools, and labor markets in the Philippines and Thailand. *Economic Development and Cultural Change, 53*(4), 959–981.

Yokota, J. (1993). Issues in selecting multicultural children's literature. *Language Arts, 70*(3), 156–167.

CHAPTER 6

EDUCATING ASIAN AMERICAN STUDENTS WITH EXCEPTIONAL NEEDS

Ying Hui-Michael

The Asian American population is the fastest growing racial group in the 21st century. The population increased by 43%, from 10.2 million to 14.7 million between 2000 and 2010, more than any other major racial group. The population moved up from about 4% of total population in 2000 to about 5% in 2010 (Humes, Jones, & Ramirez, 2011). As the general Asian American population has increased, the Asian American student population has also grown with a similar rate across the United States. For example, in the 2000–2001 academic year, the Asian/Pacific Islander (API) population had about a 4.2% enrollment in public schools, and reached a 4.8% enrollment in the 2007–2008 school year. While this population had about a 2% growth rate in the Midwest and South regions, their enrollments in the Northeast and West were significantly higher, namely, 5.6% and 9.4%, respectively in the 2007–2008 school year (National Center for Education Statistics, 2010).

Asian American students have not been given much attention in national and state discussions on special education for culturally and linguistically

Multicultural Education for Learners with Special Needs in the Twenty-First Century, pages 85–104
Copyright © 2014 by Information Age Publishing

85

diverse (CLD) students. Two possible factors could attribute to this lack of attention. First, statistically, Asian American students have been reported as a "doing well" group. Many national achievement reports have noted these students outperform their counterparts from other racial groups. For example, according to the National Center for Education Statistics (2010), Asian American 4th- and 8th-graders had higher scores than did other CLD groups on the 2005 National Assessment of Educational Progress (NAEP) reading and mathematics assessments. In addition to this positive statistical achievement data, Asian American students are often depicted as "model minority" students. The above factors have lead to a stereotypical assumption that Asian American students (a) are high academic achievers, (b) outperform other racial group students in academics, (c) are good at math, (d) are well-behaved and disciplined, and (e) are from families that highly value education. However, both the positive statistical achievement data and stereotypical assumptions can be detrimental to Asian American students because they obscure the fact that these students have diverse characteristics. Furthermore, statistical data provided by schools, districts, states, and the federal government often lump the diversity range of Asian American subgroups into a single "Asian" category. Unfortunately, Asian American students with limited English skills, low achievement, and special needs are often masked by this aggregation data. This can lead to educators being influenced by the positive statistical data and stereotypes resulting in their overlooking many academically struggling Asian American students who may have special education needs (Doan, 2006; Hui-Michael & Garcia, 2009). Such positive data and stereotypes may also impact research about Asian American students. While there are many studies about achieving Asian American students, there is a limited research on Asian American students who struggle and have special education needs.

DEMOGRAPHICAL DIVERSITY AMONG ASIAN AMERICANS

Asian American is a term that refers to people who come from families having origins of Far East, Southeast Asia, or Indian subcontinent, including, for example, Cambodia, China, India, Japan, Korea, Malaysia, Pakistan, the Philippine Island, Thailand, and Vietnam (U.S. Department of Commerce, 2010). The term, Asian/Pacific Islander (API) has been and is still used in many national-level documents and research-based literature. Therefore, although the focus of this chapter is on Asian American students, many statistical reports cited in this chapter combine the categories of Asian with Pacific Islander. Asian American students represent a wide range of diversity in language, culture, nationality, religion, family practice, socioeconomic status (SES), and academic achievement. The distinct characteristics of Asian American students must be examined by subgroup, to avoid the common obfuscation, which places all Asian American students into one category.

Immigration Experiences

Great complexity and differences in immigration histories exist among Asian Americans. They have more than a 150-year history of immigration to this country. Prior to 1965, most Asian immigrants were Chinese, Filipino, Japanese, and Korean. Many Chinese came to the United States to build railroads and to work in the gold mines in the 1800s. The Japanese went to the Hawaiian Islands to work on the pineapple and sugar cane farms. The Filipinos also went to the Pacific and Hawaiian Islands for agricultural work. The majority of them arrived after the 1965 Immigration Act (Chan, 1991). Immigrants from China and India have been coming to the United States at a steady pace in recent years. Due to this immigration pattern, there are high percentages of Chinese and Indian students in the United States who are foreign born. For instance, in 2007, about 19% of all students born outside the United States were Asian, with students in the following subgroups: 5% Chinese, 4% Asian Indian, 3% Filipino, 3% Korean, 2% Vietnamese, and 1% Japanese (National Center for Education Statistics, 2010).

The recent immigrant Asian Americans include two groups, namely, those who left their home countries voluntarily and those who were forced to leave as refugees. The first group is composed of mostly middle- and upper-class immigrants who left their homelands for educational and professional opportunities. The second group is composed of Southeast Asians refugees who left their homelands due to war and/or political persecutions. The term, Southeast Asian refugees is used to describe people who immigrated from Cambodia, Laos, and Vietnam while excluding individuals from Thailand, Malaysia, and other surrounding Southeast Asian countries. Since the U.S. involvement in the Vietnam War, millions of Southeast Asian refugees have come to this country. Vietnamese immigrants are the largest group among Southeast Asian refugees in the United States. There have been three waves of Vietnamese refugees in the last three decades. In 1975, the first large group of Vietnamese refugees fled to the United States with the collapse of the Thieu regime—they were mostly young, well-educated and English-speaking Vietnamese from urban areas. Between 1977 and 1983, the second wave of refugees came to the United States mostly by escaping via boat. This group was more diverse, representing various ethnicities, nationalities, religions, and languages. As a group, these people were less educated, less literate, and less familiar with Western cultures, and more rural than those in the first wave. A third wave of refugees arrived after 1985 in small numbers—most the third wave of people came to the United States through family reunification programs (Campi, 2005; Weinberg, 1997).

It has been reported that school performance of many of Southeast Asian refugee students has been negatively affected by their traumatic immigration experiences (Dao, 2001). These students are more likely to have fewer years of education and higher drop rates while being perceived negatively by their teachers as students unable to learn (Dao, 2001; Ima, 1998; Lee & Kumashiro, 2005). Today, the majority of young Southeast Asian refugee students are members of the second and third generations (Wright & Boun, 2011). Although they may not share the characteristics of the original Southeast Asian refugees, many U.S.-born Southeast Asian students still face many educational challenges. For instance, some Southeast Asian American groups (i.e., Cambodian and Laotian) demonstrate a lower level of improvement on English language tests than English language learners from other racial/ethnic groups (Hill, 2004). Also, in a survey of 467 Southeast Asian American young adults in California, the participants reported that they experienced many educational and social obstacles such as limited English proficiency, a lack of appropriate English language instruction, an inadequate culturally relative curriculum, and limited educational and financial supports from parents for college education. However, it has also been documented that many Southeast Asian refugee students have benefitted from their educational opportunities in U.S. schools which allowed them to succeed and enroll in college (Vang, 1999; Weinberg, 1997; Wright & Boun, 2011). For example, in Wrigth and Boun's (2011) study, Southeast Asian refugee students reported that despite obstacles (e.g., a lack of information about college and parent support), the majority of them, more than 72% were enrolled in college.

Socioeconomic Status

Poverty has negative effects on a child's well-being, cognitive development, and academic achievement (Brooks-Gunn & Duncan, 1997). Although statistics on poverty often reflect Asian Americans' well-being, there are significant socioeconomic differences among this population. For example, the National Center for Education Statistics (2010) reported that API children represented a lower poverty rate at 11% than the 2007 national poverty rate of 17.5%. In addition, Asian Indian, Filipino, and Japanese children had an average poverty rate of 7.5%, compared to that of White children at 10.1% while Vietnamese children had a 17.5% poverty rate and those children belonging to other APA groups had a 11% poverty rate (see The National Center for Education Statistics, 2010).

Similar to students in the United States, a student socioeconomic status in their home countries is as important factor in achieving successful academic achievement. Immigrant students from higher-income families often have formal schooling and home literacy experience in their home countries that are allow them to transfer easily to English and their new cultural environment. The socioeconomic backgrounds that Asian Americans bring to this country range widely, from relative success and well-being, to risk characteristics, all of which impact the students' school performance. For instance, many recent Chinese immigrants include those who are well-educated professionals coming from China's prosperous urban areas, and ones who have little formal education and have suffered poverty in China (Zhou & Lee, 2012).

Educational Attainment and Achievement

Many education statistical reports indicate that Asian Americans have high education attainment, high achievement scores and low representation in special education. For example, the National Center for Education Statistics' (2010) report showed that in 2007, a higher percentage of API 4th and 8th graders scored at or above proficient on both reading and math assessments compared to their peers of other racial groups. Compared to the entire student population, Asian American students are more likely to complete their schooling and have higher grade-point averages while being overrepresented in gifted programs (Donovan & Cross, 2002).

It is important to analyze the disparities among Asian subgroups. Some analysis of state level data has indicated consistently that many Asian American students have achieved much lower verbal scores than the average (e.g., Cheng, Ima, & Labovitz, 1994; Hill, 2004). Also, Cheng et al.'s (1994) analysis of subgroups in gifted program in California revealed that Asian American students with limited English proficiency were seriously underrepresented in the gifted category as compared to Asian American students who were fluent English speakers. In addition, Niedzwiecki and Duong's (2004) analysis of the 2000 U.S. Census data revealed that 42% of Asian Americans aged 25 years and over had a bachelor's degree or higher in comparison to 24% of the entire U.S. population. The rate for Asian Indian, Chinese, Filipino, Japanese, and Korean individuals ranged from 43 to 61%. On the other hand, the rates for Southeast Asians were lower than the average of the U.S. population, at 20% for Vietnamese, 9% for Cambodian, and only 7% for Hmong and Laotian Americans. In addition, when compared to 85.3% of the U.S. population, 2009 disaggregated data showed that only 61.5% of Cambodian, 61.7% of Hmong, 62.5% of Laotian, and 70% of Vietnamese Americans aged 25 years and over held a high school degree or higher (Southeast Asia Resource Action Center, 2011). Knowing this data, it is unrealistic to assume that all Asian American students are superior students and excel academically. In actuality, there are many Asian American students who perform poorly in the academic areas and complete only a few years of education. Further, there is another critical educational issues confronting Asian American students, namely, the underrepresentation of Asian American students in special education (see Doan, 2006; Hui-Michael & Garcia, 2009). This underrepresentation of API students in special education should not be perceived as a positive educational statistic because API students with disabilities are unidentified and their academic, behavioral and emotional needs are not being appropriately addressed.

THE UNDERREPRESENTATION IN SPECIAL EDUCATION

Asian American students are placed in special education programs at considerably lower rates than their non-Asian American peers. According to the 28th Annual Report to Congress on the Implementation of the Individuals with Disabilities Education Act (U.S. Department of Education, 2009), 4.57% of API students ages 6 through 21 years received special education and related services, while other racial groups had higher rates: American Indian/Alaskan students 13.67%, Black students 12.44%, White students 8.65%, and Hispanic students 8.33%. The risk ratios for different disabilities indicated that Asian American students were almost 50% less likely to be identified with high incidence disability categories (i.e., specific learning disabilities, speech or language impairments, intellectual impairments, and emotional disturbance) than their peers from other racial groups combined. Among the four categories, speech or language impairments had the highest risk ratio while emotional disturbance had the least. For the largest disability category, specific learning disabilities, only 1.73% of the total API student population received special education services while the placement rates for other groups were much higher, at 3.86% for White students, 4.74% for Hispanic students, 5.65% for Black students, and 7.5% for American Indian/Alaska Native students. This underrepresentation data reflects the need to increase appropriate educational services to Asian American students, especially those who are English language learners and those who have special needs. Further, the data suggest that a contributing factor to this underrepresentation is teachers' inaccurate special education referral decision making (Doan, 2006; Hui-Michael & Garcia, 2009; Poon-McBrayer & Garcia, 2000).

Overlooking Low Performing Students

Influenced by positive statistics and stereotypes as well as Asia American students' "good" behavior, teachers and service providers might fail to notice some students' academic problems and neglect to refer those with potential disabilities for special education evaluation. In general, teachers and service providers hold positive perceptions of Asian American students about their academic and behavioral performance; they often perceive them as being better prepared academically than other students (e.g., Tenenbaum & Ruck, 2007), and being well behaved and well adjusted to the mainstream (e.g., Chang & Sue, 2003). Hui-Michael and Garcia (2009) found that as a group elementary teachers had positive stereotyped perceptions about Asian American students. In fact, before examining their own individual students' performance, the se elementary teachers believed as a group Asian American students have value education highly, are intelligent, and exhibit a strong work ethic. Hui-Michael and Gracia found that the teachers often overlooked the struggles of the low performing Asian American students who demonstrated good learning attitudes and behavior (e.g., completing home work and following directions). Although these low performing students showed difficulties in their academics, the elementary teachers still held optimistic expectations for them. For example, although one teacher recognized her student's academic struggles and failure on the state tests in the past, she believed that this student would pass an upcoming state tests.

Behavior can significantly influence teachers' special education referral decision making. Synthesizing the research evidence and literature (e.g., Doan 2006; Hui-Michael & Garcia, 2009; Kaufman, 2005; Lane, Mahdavi, & Borthwick-DutTy, 2003), one can conclude that (a) teachers highly value some positive behavior related to academic performance, such as, work habits, compliance, and motivation; (b) certain types of behavior (e.g., distractive classroom behavior and lack of focus) lead to students' school failure; (c) there is a tendency to refer students whose academic underachievement is accompanied by disturbing behavior; and (d) there is the less likelihood to provide instructional intervention and/or consider special education referral for low performing students when they demonstrate good school behavior. Because Asian parents often encourage their children to show good school-related behavior, such as respecting teachers and completing assignments (Zhao & Qiu, 2008), it is possible that many low performing Asian American students who are perceived as well-behaved might not be considered as having learning disabilities. Furthermore, there is concern that Asian American students who have an emotional disability and good school behavior are not referred by teachers because they are not viewed as being exceptional or atypical due to positive stereotyped perceptions.

Using Limited English Proficiency to Explain Academic Difficulties

In 2007, an estimated 1.3 million Asian American students spoke a language other than English at home. About 17% of these students had limited English proficiency (National Center for Education Statistics, 2010). Due to the number of Asian language groups involved, it is more likely that Asian American English language learners (ELLs) are placed in general education classrooms with English as a second language support. Like any ELLs, Asian American ELLs have a similar journey in acquiring English as a second language. Many Asian American ELLs who have only been in English instructional settings for few years may only demonstrate minimum-level Basic Interpersonal Communication Skills (BICS), and even less competency in Cognitive Academic Language Proficiency (CALP). BICS that involve conversational skills often require less complex language competencies than CALP, which refers to language skills associated with literacy and cognitive development (Cummins, 2006). There are similar characteristics represented by students who are not proficient in cognitive academic English and those who have disabilities (Hamayan, Marler, Sanchez-Lopez, & Damico, 2007). For example, both students with learning disabilities and ELLs might show similar academic difficulties (e.g., poor reading comprehension and writing and inability to complete written assignments) and behavior problems (e.g., hyperactive and disruptive behaviors). If teachers and service providers do not have adequate knowledge of how etiological and linguistic/cultural factors in learning and teaching influence these students' learning, they might have difficulty in determining the sources of the problems. Some researchers (e.g., Artiles & Ortiz, 2002; McNamara, 1998) indicated that many ELLs, especially Hispanic ELLs were often misdiagnosed for disabilities due to teachers' misinterpretation of a disability as the cause of learning problems.

The research has shown that teachers are more likely to perceive Asian American students' academic problems as due to a lack of English proficiency, and less likely to struggles caused by disabilities (Hui-Michael & García, 2009; Poon-McBrayer & García, 2000). This was supported in a study by Hui-Michael and Garcia's (2009) who found that elementary general education classroom teachers tended to rule out disabilities as a possible cause for their low performing ELLs, especially for those students who were quiet and demonstrated good school behavior. Hui-Michael and Gracia pointed out that teachers frequently explained that their ELLs' academic struggles were due to limited English proficiency which lead them to recommend that these students receive more ESL assistance from the ESL teacher rather than referring them for special education related assistance. Because Asian American students are often encouraged by their parents to show self-control and reserve their behavior (Chan & Lee, 2004; Leung, 1998), it is possible that teachers might not observe distractive behaviors among these students who have academic struggles. Since many Asian American parents often provide educational support at home to help with their children's homework and to learn English (Parette, Chuang, & Huer, 2004; Zhao & Qiu, 2008), teachers may be forced to believe Asian American ELLs will make progress without special education or other service support.

Apparently, teachers' inadequate preparation in teaching Asian American students is a factor in their inaccurate instructional decision making (Chang, 1995; Doan, 2006; Hui-Michael & Garcia, 2009). Specifically, teachers' misperceptions about Asian American students, coupled with a lack of knowledge about particular disabilities and the language and culture of Asian American students are factors that may influence their false referrals and inadequate instructional practices. These findings are not unique many researchers (e.g., Doan, 2006; Hui-Michael & Garcia, 2009; Obiakor, 2008; Ortiz, Wilkinson, Robertson-Courtney, & Kushner, 2006) have continued to emphasize that teachers and related educational professionals must be prepared to ultimately examine students' learning and their own teaching in sociocultural contexts.

EXAMINING DISABILITY RELATED ISSUES FROM A SOCIOCULTURAL PERSPECTIVE

To effectively deal with stereotypes of students from different cultural groups, general cultural practices of a particular group must be accurately understood; and factors such as variation in individual differences must also be taken into considerations (Gudykunst & Kim, 2003). Acculturation is another essential factor that must be addressed when understanding Asian American students. "Acculturation is the process of adaptation to a new cultural environment" (Collier, 2004, p. 240). A person's cognition and behavior are shaped by the integration of the new and the first culture. For example, a U.S.-born Asian American mother might have a different view about disabilities and special education services from a new immigrant mother due to their different levels of acculturation. Collier (2004) also pinpointed that many students' responses to the acculturation experience may reflect similar characteristics of a disability, such as high anxiety and confusion. In the following section, general sociocultural practices and educational issues that affect Asian American students are delineated.

Educational Values and Practices

Formal education is highly valued by Asian Americans; and Asian parents often encourage their children to attain the highest educational degree possible (Hwa-Froelich & Westby, 2003). They believe hard work is important for success in their lives; and Asian American children are encouraged to attend school, finish their homework, and do their best on their academic assignments and tests (e.g., Chan & Lee, 2004; Cheng & Chang, 1995). Clearly, many Asian immigrants emphasize education at home, such as helping their children with homework or hiring tutors for their children's academic needs (Paratte et al., 2004; Wang, 2009). According to Wang (2009), these immigrants strive to find the best education for their children even if it involves relocating to a better school community. Their desire to get the best education for their children is exemplified by the comments of a parent in Wang's study who stated that "my education experience and success story prove that without sound knowledge, excellent skills, and communication abilities, I couldn't survive in this so competitive environment. I think I have the responsibility to let my children know the competitive reality and life in front of them" (p. 17). In addition, this statement reflects that cultural identity cannot be solely attributed to understanding the importance of formal education. Rather, educational values based on ones status in society (i.e., as an immigrant professional parent) profoundly influences schooling of Asian Americans students in the United States (Sue & Okazaki, 1990).

Asian parents who practice traditional values believe the importance of obeying those in authority and respecting elders. These values have a significant influence on Asian American students' school performance. When these values are compared with Western parents, Asian parents have a high respect for teachers and administrators, and tend to encourage their children to respect their teachers by following teachers' direction, being quiet in the classroom, and showing good behavior (Chan & Lee, 2004; Shen & Mao, 1990). Many Asian American children are also taught to be reserved and modest in verbal and nonverbal behaviors. Such behavioral practices may lead to Asian American students' disguising their emotional stress and suffering internally (Chan & Lee, 2004; Leung, 1998).

Perceptions of Disabilities

Cultural practices influence a person's belief about disabilities (Parette et al., 2004; Roseberry-McKibbin, 2008). In many Asian cultures, disabilities are perceived differently from Westerners. The most common belief in many Asian cultures is that a disability is a sign from God that parents are being punished for their sins; for example, some believe cerebral palsy could be caused by a father's extramarital affair during pregnancy (Chan & Lee, 2004). As a result, disabilities can be perceived as a source of shame. Parents might not openly share the information about their child's disability with people outside the family circle (Jegatheesan, 2009; Lo, 2010). In her study about parent and professional interactions, Jegatheesan (2009) found that many Asian American parents who had a child with a disability were hesitant to share information about their child' disability with professionals and some even lived in secrecy to prevent friends and neighbors from finding out.

It must be noted that not all Asian parents have negative perceptions about disabilities. For example, in a parental attitude study about disabilities, Parette et al. (2004) found that a group of Chinese American parents did not share any perception of disability as a source of shame. Parette et al. (2004) concluded that the parents' realistic and healthy attitude was significantly impacted by their educational backgrounds and acculturation.

In many Asian countries, students who do not show physical/sensory impairment and significant cognitive disabilities are not considered as having disabilities (personal observation). Because hard work is highly valued, for example, the academic difficulties of children with learning disabilities who do not have a physical/sensory impairment might be misperceived as a lack of work ethic rather than a disability. As a result, Asian parents might not share their child's needs nor seek out special education services from his/her schools. Instead these parent might seek out outside services such as home tutoring and community/church support for their struggling children.

Asian Parents' Experiences in Special Education

It is evident from a number of studies (e.g., Chang, 1995; Hwa-Froelich & Westby, 2003; Jegatheesan, 2009; Lin, 2002; Lo, 2008) that Asian Americans, especially first-generation immigrants, have experienced difficulty communicating with professionals which has resulted in a lack of successful access to existing services. All the studies reported that limited English ability is a barrier to parent–teacher communication on the part of both Asian American parents and school professionals. In Jegatheesan's (2009) study, parents reported their frustration for not being able to communicate with the professionals due to limited English proficiency. Also, although interpreters were used at the IEP meetings, the quality of the translation was perceived questionable by the parents. For example, one parent reported that the interpreter in the IEP meeting did not even know the basic special education terms. Similar findings were also presented in Lo's (2008) study about Chinese parents' participation in IEP meetings. Lo reported that the interpreters often did not understand specific educational terms, did not know how to translate and frequently only summarized the main points of the large information that was shared by the professionals.

It is common knowledge that there are different communication styles between Asian cultures and the U.S. mainstream culture. Asian cultures are high-context cultures, while the U.S. mainstream culture is a low-context culture (Gudykunst & Kim, 2003). In high-context culture communication, people may not rely only on clear and explicit verbal expression but rely on presumptions based on nonverbal signals. To preserve harmony, Asian Americans have a tendency to use indirect styles to avoid confrontation. Jegatheesan (2009) found that even for the well-acculturated, Asian parents who understood the importance of speaking up for the benefit of their children, they often felt it difficult to do so due to their Asian cultural upbringing. Asian parents might be unlike the parents of the mainstream culture in expressing their dissatisfactions directly to school professionals. Also, Lin (2002) observed that some Asian parents were viewed as lacking proper communication skills, inclined to talk behind the teachers' back and were too timid to communicate directly with teachers. Limited understanding of the American mainstream school culture is another barrier that may restrict Asian American parents' communication with schools. This was noted in Chang's (1995) and Lo's (2008) research with Chinese parents who exhibited considerably confusion about the special education service process. Similarly, parents in Lin's (2002) and Jegatheesan's (2009) studies reported their lack of knowledge of special education. In these studies, parents freely described their unpleasant experiences with school professionals related to their child's special referral and placement, which the researchers stressed was a correlate of the parents need to better understand the special education system in the United States.

In many cases, teachers and school professionals view Asian American parents as less concerned and involved with their child's school situation than mainstream American parents (Shen & Mao, 1990). Linguistic and cultural factors may explain this phenomenon. Often, Asian parents are less able to be highly involved in their child's school simply due to a language barrier. For example, it is unlikely that parents with limited English proficiency feel comfortable going to their children's classrooms for instructional involvement, inquire about curriculum aspects at an open house, and/or discuss their child's academic progress at a parent–teacher conference without translation support. In addition, Asian American parents might have a different understanding of parent–school roles due to Asian American parent's tendency to respect school professionals' expertise and authority (Jegatheesan, 2009; Shen & Mao, 1990). In fact, visiting their children's classrooms may be viewed as interfering with the school's academic practice.

Asian American Students in Special Education Programs

The U.S. Department of Education's (2009) indicated that Asian American ELLs are more likely to receive speech related services than other special education services. Typically, these services start early in childhood as API have the largest proportion of infants and toddlers receiving home intervention services (e.g., speech, nursing, psychological, counseling, family training, social work) when compared to other races (Dyches & Prater, 2010). Also, more Asian American students are referred for language deficits rather than mathematical and logical difficulties (Chang, 1995; Niu & Luo, 1999). Interestingly, they often referred to speech-related services by their classroom teachers because of their slowness in English acquisition, poor oral expression, and/or poor comprehension (Chang, 1995). Also, a number of Studies (Chang, 1995, Niu & Luo, 1999; Hui, 2005) revealed that academic delay in the areas of writing and reading were the main reason for special education referrals while the students referred are typically described as having poor reading comprehension and not understanding English sound/symbol relationships. Asian American students are not typically referred for mathematical deficits. For example, in Chang's (1995) study, only one of these sixteen Chinese students was referred because of math difficulties. Similar findings were reported by in Niu and Luo's (1999) study which matched the characteristics described in Chang's study and examined 14 elementary and middle Chinese American ELLs with learning disabilities. They found that though the academic difficulty pattern of these students was similar to the general pattern of all students with learning disabilities, the Chinese American students in this study demonstrated average ability in mathematics, even with mathematics verbal problems. Finally, Niu and Luo emphasized that while these students showed mastery of computation and problem-solving skills, reading skill was their primary weakness.

CULTURALLY AND LINGUISTICALLY RESPONSIVE
PRACTICE: FUTURE IMPERATIVE

Although Asian American students represent a considerably small population in many districts, and they are often perceived as a "doing well" group, schools must make the commitment to meet the needs of Asian American students. As it has been discussed in this chapter, Asian Americans are diverse in many cultural, social and educational issues, and not all Asian American students are "super" students without struggles. To meet individual students' needs, educators must make learning more personal and meaningful by considering cultural and linguistic characteristics as well as experiences and perspectives of these students and their families (Gay, 2000). Culturally and linguistically responsive teachers appreciate their cultural heritages as well as their students. Such teachers must recognize that cultural and linguistic experiences their students bring to school are essential to their learning (Obiakor, 2008; Ortiz et al., 2006; Roseberry-McKibbin, 2008).

Many teachers have limited cross-cultural experience and knowledge, and are not adequately prepared in educating children from diverse backgrounds (Sleeter & Grant, 2009). Also, they might be even less familiar with Asian American cultures compared to their knowledge of other CLD groups (Doan, 2006). It is possible that teachers' stereotypes about a particular group may be reinforced by the general trait of the group provided by some of this training (personal observations). Teachers and service providers would do well to recognize that cultural assumptions and stereotypes influence their work. Teachers and service providers must realize that even positive stereotypes gained from a variety of resources are not necessarily accurate, nor are the consequences of these positive stereotypes necessarily positive when applied to students' education. Teachers must ultimately be prepared to look at cultural and linguistic implications to everyday learning and teaching in their classroom. Adopting a culturally and linguistically responsive teaching framework can be helpful. With this framework in mind, the following practical suggestions for educating Asian American students are recommended:

- Teachers and service providers must be encouraged to gather information about Asian cultures regarding educational values, perception of disabilities/special education, family practices, nationalities/ethnicities/languages, immigration backgrounds, and the interrelations among these factors in learning and teaching contexts. Districts/schools can use parents and professionals in the community who come from a particular Asian culture to help facilitate the faculty's greater understanding of specific cultural values and practices.

- Teachers and service providers must increase their competence in the special education knowledge base and teaching of ELLs because the two are often interrelated. Their general knowledge about second language acquisition and characteristics of disabilities can increase their skills in distinguishing language difference from disabilities.

- English language development is a major component in educating Asian American students. Understanding the characteristics of a particular Asian language and its influence on English language acquisition will assist teachers and service providers with providing effective language instruction. It is impossible to generalize an Asian speaker's English language patterns due to the variety of Asian languages/dialects (Roseberry-McKibbin, 2008). Teachers and service providers can gain such knowledge from gathering information from Asian American students, parents, and professionals, as well as examining the existing literature (e.g., Cheng, 1991; Swan & Smith, 2006).

- Teachers and service providers need to evaluate students' proficiency in both their first language and English (Haager, Klingner, & Aceves, 2010). While there is a limited number of written assessments in Asian languages, teachers and service providers can collect comprehensive assessment data by interviewing Asian parents, and asking ESL/bilingual teachers to translate and/or conduct assessments to understand students' first language proficiency. Additionally, teachers and service providers need to determine student's social and academic language proficiencies to ensure appropriate instructional decisions. Some screening tools, for example, Collier's Classroom Language Interaction Checklist (2009) can be adapted and used to assess ELLs' first and English language proficiencies at different social and instructional settings.

- Behavioral support is essential for Asian American students, although some of them do not show distractive behavior. For Asian American students who seem to fit the "expected" Asian American students' behavioral trait (e.g., quiet, not talking back, and completing homework), teachers and service providers need to be aware of possible negative effects of positive stereotypes. In addition, teachers and service providers must ensure that these students comprehend classroom instruction. Techniques such as spending one-on-one time with students/parents and asking questions might give these professionals some ideas about students' learning. Not every Asian American student demonstrates good behavior. For those who show problematic behavior, teachers and service providers need to evaluate the cause of the behavior (e.g., student's limited English proficiency, a disability, or teacher's ineffective instruction), and provide behavioral intervention.

- Culturally and linguistically responsive instruction must focus on the strengths of students. For Asian ELLs who have language/literacy skills in their native language, using native language instruction can assist them in activating prior knowledge and transferring of the knowledge to English (Genesee, Lindholm-Leary, Saunders, & Christian, 2006). Meaningful learning begins with allowing students to view the curriculum and instruction from their cultural perspective. Some specific strategies include (a) purposely infusing history and cultures related to Asian American students into curriculum, (b) applying instructional activities that connect with Asian American students' cultural experience, and (c) extending learning experience to home and community.

- Asian parents' school involvement can be improved by various school supports. Schools and teachers need to be resourceful and thoughtful for selecting interpreters. Asian American community organizations and translation services can provide the information for trained or qualified interpreters. Asian American parents can be invited to participate in school professional development related to cross-cultural communication. To a large degree, professionals and parents can learn from each other about different communication styles.

CONCLUSION

As the Asian American student population continues to grow, schools will continue to face the need to provide culturally and linguistically responsive practices for this population. For professionals, the first and most important issue is to acknowledge the distinct characteristics among Asian American population in their immigration, social, and education experiences. The underrepresentation of Asian American students in special education has been and still is a pronouncing issue in the field. The attribution of the underrepresentation reflects (a) the negative effect of the model minority syndrome, (b) teachers' inadequate knowledge/skills in special education, and (c) the lack of preparation of professionals in teaching English as a second language. Examining various educational issues from a sociocultural perspective is essential to understanding how linguistic and cultural factors influence Asian American students' school performance. It is important to use culturally and linguistically responsive practices that meet the specific needs of Asian American students. Teachers and service providers must be trained and supported in the areas of (a) overcoming stereotypes, (b) understanding particular Asian cultures/languages, (c) increasing knowledge/skills in assessment and instruction, and (d) enhancing school and home collaboration.

REFERENCES

Artiles, A. J., & Ortiz, A. A. (2002). *English language learners with special education needs: Identification, assessment and instruction.* McHenry, IL: Delta Systems.

Brooks-Gunn, J., & Duncan, G. J. (1997). The effects of poverty on children. *The Future of Children, 7*(2), 55–51.

Campi, A. (2005). *From refugees to Americans: Thirty years of Vietnamese immigration to the United States.* Washington DC: American Immigrant Council. Retrieved from http://www.immigrationpolicy.org/sites/default/files/docs/RefugeestoAmericans.pdf

Chan, S., & Lee, E. (2004). Families with Asian roots. In E. W. Lynch & M. J. Hanson (Eds.), *Developing cross-cultural competence: A guide for working with children with their families* (3rd ed.) (pp. 219–98). Baltimore: Paul H. Brookes.

Chan, S. C. (1991). *The Asian Americans: An interpretive history.* Boston: Twayne Publishers.

Chang, D. F., & Sue, S. (2003). The effects of race and problem type on teachers' assessments of students behavior. *Journal of Consulting and Clinical Psychology, 17*, 235–242.

Chang, J. M. (1995). LEP, LD, poor, and missed learning opportunities: A case of inner-city Chinese American children. In L. L. Cheng (Ed.), *Integrating language and learning for inclusion: An Asian/Pacific focus* (pp. 31–59). San Diego, CA: Singular.

Cheng, L. L. (1991). *Assessing Asian language performance: Guidelines for evaluating limited-English proficient students* (2nd ed.) Oceanside, CA: Academic Communication Associates.

Cheng, L. L., & Chang, J. M. (1995). Asian/Pacific Islanders students in need of effective services. In L. L. Cheng (Ed.), *Integrating language and learning for inclusion* (pp. 3–27). San Degio, CA: Singular.

Cheng, L. L., Ima, K., & Labovitz, G. (1994). Assessment of Asian and Pacific Islander students for gifted programs. In S. B. Garcia (Ed.), *Addressing cultural and linguistic diversity in special education: Issues and trends* (pp. 30–45). Reston, VA: The Council for Exceptional Children.

Collier, C. (2004). Developing instructional plans and curricula for bilingual special educationstudents. In L. M. Baca & H. T. Cervantes (Eds.), *The bilingual special education interface* (pp. 230–73). Upper Saddle River, NJ: Pearson Education.

Collier, C. (2009). *Classroom language interaction checklist (CLIC).* Vancouver, WA: Cross Cultural Developmental Education Services.

Cummins, J. (2006). How long does it take for an English language learner to become proficient in a second language? In E. Hamayan & R. Freeman (Eds.), *English language learners at school: A guide for administrators* (pp. 59–61). Philadelphia, PA: Caslon.

Dao, M. (2001). The effectiveness of reciprocal teaching with Vietnamese American students. In C. C. Park, A. L. Goodwin & S. J. Lee (Eds.), *Research on the education of Asian and Pacific Americans* (pp. 21–40). Greenwich, CT: Information Age Publishing.

Doan, K. (2006). A sociocultural perspective on at-risk Asian-American students. *Teacher Education and Special Education, 29*, 157–167.

Donovan, M. S., & Cross, C. T. (2002). *Minority students in special and gifted education*. Washington, DC: National Academy Press.

Dyches T. T., & Prater, M. A. (2010). Disproportionate representation in special education: Overrepresentation of selected groups. In F. E. Obiakor, J. P. Bakken, & A. F. Rotatori (Eds.), *Current issues and trends in special education: Identification, assessment, and instruction* (Vol. 19, pp. 53–71). Bingley, UK: Emerald Group Publishing Limited.

Gay, G. (2000). *Culturally responsive teaching: Theory, research, and practice*. New York: Teacher College, Columbia University.

Genesee, F., Lindholm-Leary, K. J., Saunders, W., & Christian, D. (2006). *Educating English language learners: A synthesis of empirical evidence*. New York: Cambridge University Press.

Gudykunst, W. B., & Kim, Y. Y. (2003). *Communicating with strangers: An approach to intercultural communication*. New York: McGraw-Hill.

Hagger, D., Klingner, J. K., & Aceves, T. C. (2010). *How to teach English language learners: Effective strategies from outstanding educators*. San Francisco: Jossey-Bass.

Hamayan, E., Marler, B., Sanchez-Lopez, C., & Damico, J. (2007). *Special education considerations for English language learners: Delivering a continuum of services*. Philadelphia, PA: Calson.

Hill, E. G. (2004). *A look at the progress of English learner students*. Sacramento, CA: Legislative Analyst's Office.

Hui, Y. (2005). *General education teachers' perceptions: Implications for special education*. Unpublished doctoral dissertation. Austin, TX: University of Texas.

Hui-Michael, Y., & Garcia, S. B. (2009). Teachers' perceptions and attributions of Asian American students. *Multiple Voices, 12*(1), 21–37.

Humes, K. R., Jones, N. A., & Ramirez, R. R. (2011). *Overview of race and Hispanic origin: 2010, 2010*. Washington DC: U. S. Census Bureau.

Hwa-Froelich, D. D., & Westby, C. E. (2003). A Vietnamese Head Start interpreter: A case study. *Communication Quarterly, 2*(4).

Ima, K. (1998). Education Asian newcomer secondary students: Four case studies of schools. In V. O. Pang & L. L. Cheng (Eds.), *Struggling to be heard: The unmet needs of Asian Pacific American children* (pp. 243–264). Albany, NY: State University of New York.

Jegatheesan, B. (2009). Cross-cultural issues in parent-professional interactions: A qualitative study of perceptions of Asian American mothers of children with developmental disabilities. *Research & Practice for Persons with Severe Disabilities, 34*, 123–136

Kauffman, J. M. (2005). *Characteristics of emotional and behavioral disorders of children and youth*. Upper Saddle River, NJ: Pearson.

Lane, K. L., Mahdavi, J. N., & Borthwick-DutTy, S. A. (2003). Teacher perceptions of the prereferral intervention process: A call for assistance with school-based interventions. *Preventing School Failure, 47,* 148–155.

Lee, S. J., & Kumashiro, K. K. (2005). *A report on the status of Asian Americans and Pacific Islanders in education: Beyond the "model minority" myth.* Washington, DC: National Education Association.

Leung, B. (1998). Who are Chinese American, Japanese American, and Korean American children: Cultural profiles. In V. O. Pang & L.L. Cheng, L. (Eds.), *Struggling to be heard: The unmet needs of Asian Pacific American children* (pp. 11–26). Albany, NY: State University Plaza.

Lin, H. C. (2002). *Perspectives on communication from teachers and Chinese American families of exceptional students.* Unpublished doctoral dissertation. Austin, TX: University of Texas.

Lo, L. (2008). Level of participation and experiences of Chinese families in IEP meetings. *Preventing School Failure, 53,* 21–27

Lo, L. (2010). Perceived benefits experienced in support groups for Chinese families of children with disabilities. *Early Child Development and Care, 180*(3), 405–415.

McNamara, B. E. (1998). *Learning disabilities: Appropriate practices for a diverse population.* Albany, NY: State University of New York Press.

National Center for Education Statistics, Institute of Education Science (2010). *Status and trends in the education of racial and ethnic minorities.* Retrieved from http://nces.ed.gov/pubs2010/2010015/index.asp

Niedzwiecki, M., & Duong, T. C. (2004). *Southeast Asian American statistical profile.* Washington DC: Southeast Asia Resource Action Center.

Niu, X., & Luo, W. (1999). Patterns of performance of Chinese-American students with learning disabilities: A pilot study. *International Journal of Disabilities, Development and Education, 46*(1), 117–129.

Obiakor, F. E. (2008). *The eight-step approach to multicultural learning and teaching* (3rd ed.). Dubuque, IA: Kendall/Hunt.

Ortiz, A. A., Wilkinson, C. Y., Robertson-Courtney, P., & Kushner, M. I. (2006). Considerations in implementing intervention assistance teams to support English language learners. *Remedial and Special Education, 27*(1) 53–63.

Parette, P., Chuang, S. L., & Huer, M. B. (2004). First generation Chinese American families' attitudes regarding disabilities and educational interventions. *Focus on Autism and Other Developmental Disabilities, 19*(2), 114–123.

Poon-McBrayer, K. F., & García, S. B. (2000). Profiles of Asian American students with LD at initial referral, assessment, and placement in special education. *Journal of Learning Disabilities, 33,* 61–71.

Roseberry-McKibbin, C. (2008). *Multicultural students with special needs: Practical strategies for assessment and intervention* (3rd ed.). Oceanside, CA: Academic Communication Associates.

Shen, W. J., & Mao, W. M. (1990). *Reaching out to their cultures: Building communication with Asian-American families.* ERIC Clearinghouse on Urban Education.

Sleeter, C.E. & Grant, C.A. 2009. *Making choices for multicultural education: Five approaches to race, class and gender* (6th ed.). New York: John Wiley & Sons.

Southeast Asia Resource Action Center, Asian American Legal Defense (2011). *Re: Comments on the U.S. Department of Education interagency working group action plan on Asian Americans and Pacific Islanders. A letter to secretary Arne Duncan.* Washington, DC.

Sue, S., & Okazaki, S. (1990). Asian American educational achievements: A phenomenon in search of an explanation. In D. T. Nakanishi & T. Y. Nishida (Eds.), *The Asian American educational experience: A source book for teachers and students* (pp. 133–145). New York: Routledge.

Swan, M., & Smith, B. (2006). *Learner English: A teacher's guide to interference and other problems* (2nd ed.). New York: Cambridge.

Tenenbaum, H. R., & Ruck, M. D. (2007). Are teachers' expectations different for racial minority than for European American students? A meta-analysis. *Journal of Educational Psychology, 99,* 253–273.

U.S. Department of Commerce, Bureau of the Census (2010). *2010 Census questionnaire reference book.* Washington DC: U.S. Department of Commerce.

U.S. Department of Education, Office of Special Education and Rehabilitative Services, Office of Special Education Programs (2009). *The 28th annual report to congress on the implementation of the individuals with disabilities education act, 2006* (vol. 1). Washington, DC: U.S. Department of Education.

Vang, A. T. (1999). Hmong-American students: Challenges and opportunities. In C. C. Park & M. Y. Chi (Eds.), *Asian-American education: Perspectives and challenges (pp.56–78).* Westport, CT: Greenwood.

Wang, W. X. (2009). Language, parents' involvement, and social justice: The fight for maintaining minority home language: A Chinese-language case study. *Multicultural Education, 16*(4), 13–18.

Weinberg, M. (1997). *Asian-American education: Historical background and current realities.* Mahwah, NJ: L. Erlbaum.

Wright, W. E., & Boun, S. (2011). Southeast Asian American education 35 years after initial resettlement: Research report and policy recommendation. *Journal of Southeast Asian American Education & Advancement, 6,* 1–77.

Zhao, Y., & Qiu, W. (2008). Policy implications of model minority education research. In G. Li & L. Wang (Eds.), *Model minority myth revisited: An interdisciplinary approach to demystifying Asian American educational experiences* (pp. 315–330). Greenwich, CT: Information Age Publishing.

Zhou, M., & Lee, R. (2012): *Traversing ancestral and new homelands: Chinese immigrant transitional organizations in the United States.* Retrieved from http://www.princeton.edu/cmd/working-papers/2012TransnationalMeeting/2012-China.pdf.

CHAPTER 7

EDUCATING NATIVE AMERICAN LEARNERS WITH EXCEPTIONALITIES

Scott Sparks and Abdullah Al Odail

Children from Native American communities are more likely to be identified as having a disability than any other culturally and linguistically diverse group (U.S. Department of Education, Office of Special Education Programs, 2004). Native Americans have a 22% disability prevalence rate and American Indians and Alaska Natives have the highest rate of disabilities and lowest opportunity for access to culturally sensitive programs and services of all races (National Education Association, 2003). For American Indians and Alaska Natives children, their difficulty starts earlier in life. For example, Dyches and Prater (2010) noted that these infants and toddlers proportionally receive more services such as audiology, health, nutrition, specialized instruction, vision, and other preschool educational intervention than young children from other races. Morrison (2009) noted that Native Americans with disabilities are vastly underserved nationwide. Most Native American youth attend public schools rather than their own tribal schools which accounts for much of the lack of cultural practice in school. This occurs primarily as a result of federal funding reductions for Bureau

Multicultural Education for Learners with Special Needs in the Twenty-First Century, pages 105–123
Copyright © 2014 by Information Age Publishing

of Indian Affairs (BIA) supported schools. In the public school identification process, assessment procedures are not often modified to take into consideration the unique cultural aspects of Indian students and overlooks the learning and thinking processes that they have acquired in their Native American cultures. The idea of overrepresentation of students from native populations in special education is not new. These students have been disproportionately diagnosed as having language disorders and learning disabilities for many years (U.S. Department of Education, Office of Special Education Programs, 2004)). Further, the Office of Special Education Programs (OSEP) reported that 14.1% of Native Americans have disability labels in school. This compares with 8.4% and 12.6% for Hispanic and African American students, respectively. Of course, Native American students only account for 1% of minority groups whereas Hispanic and African Americans are 14% and 12% (National Center for Education Statistics, 2007). As a group Native American children with identified disabilities aged 6–21 years have "the highest risk ratio for being eligible for special education services than other races combined" (Dyches & Prater, p. 63). Clearly, an overidentification of students who are Native Americans needing special education services is a reality in public schools. How can this reality be reversed? This chapter will attempt to answer this critical question.

THE ISSUE OF ASSESSMENT IN SPECIAL EDUCATION

McMillan (2007) noted that assessment is a systematic process of asking educationally relevant questions about a student's learning behavior for the purpose of service provision and instruction. For assessment to be relevant, the teacher or evaluator must try to know:

1. Whether the child has a particular category of disability or, in case of a reevaluation of a child, whether the child continues to have such a disability.
2. The present levels of performance and the educational needs of the child.
3. Whether the child needs special education and related services, or in the case of a reevaluation, whether the child continues to need special education and related services.
4. In the case of a reevaluation, whether any additions or modifications to the special education and related services are needed to enable the child to meet the measurable annual goals set out in the IEP and to participate, as appropriate, in the general curriculum, or in the case of a preschool child, developmentally appropriate environments and learning activities.

McMillan stressed that assessments should be used by teachers to assess their students in the classroom. According to McMillan, an elementary teacher should apply several kinds of assessments tools that will inform him/her of students' progress. Assessment is useful in the class because it does assess students' learning and teachers' instruction. Since students have different abilities, teachers need to know how to meet students' needs. For example, students with disabilities have different needs and it would be incomprehensible to use an overhead projector lessons to a student with visual impairment (McMillan).

There are significant relationships between assessment and instruction (see Brigham & Bakken, 2013; Obi, 2010; Plotts, 2012). Teachers choose the instruction plans that fit with students' needs or abilities. Assessment helps to observe the movement of learners and learning and addresses the learning problems directly. Also, assessment involves evaluating instruction, school programs, curriculum, and students. The first major component of assessment is its purpose. The purpose of classroom assessment is to improve students' performance and abilities. Secondly, the measurement of assessment is to find out how much of a trait, attribute, or characteristic an individual possesses. Thirdly, evaluation requires judgments about quality which necessitates critically utilizing test scores and other information to plan an appropriate curriculum intervention. In essence, classroom assessment helps teachers find the context of the realities of teaching and teacher decision-making in standards-based education. There is considerable emphasis on the nature of learning and how different assessments are most appropriate for different targets (McMillan, 2007). For example, portfolio assessment allows a teacher to create a portfolio of students' work. It allows teachers to make assignments for students to complete and also allows students to add the assignments they would like to include. Portfolios help students show their improvements on specific learning goals. There are different types of portfolios, namely; platform, records, development, and assessment. They help students to step forward in their learning and adapt with it. By capturing important pieces of a student's work in each academic area, an informal picture of that student emerges. From this information, teachers and other professionals in conjunction with families may make more appropriate curriculum decisions for a child.

The idea of an assessment strategy is to identify interest areas that may represent strengths and use these areas to improve progress in those subjects that are not so interesting or easy. However, using only one assessment strategy is not appropriate and teachers and parents need to work together to develop a plan for finding important information about the student that will help in developing a curriculum based on the general education curriculum that will not be frustrating to the student.

Students from Native American communities enrolled in public schools are more likely to have low reading achievement test scores, substance abuse problems, and live in poverty. For example, the dropout rate for Native American students is higher than the dominant White culture. Further, greater numbers of Native American children consume alcohol, cigarettes, and marijuana than other Culturally Linguistically Diverse (CLD) groups. Also, when they are compared to other races, they have "the highest percentage of students who are removed to an interim alternative educational setting due to possession of guns or weapons (Dyches & Prater, 2010). Finally, poverty figures are higher among Native Americans than their white counterparts (National Center for Education Statistics, 2007). Given the above challenging characteristics for Native American students, how can schools modify the identification and assessment process to more fairly serve students from Native American cultures? One primary initiative is to establish school support teams that focus on the challenging problems that these students face. Such a team could meet and help modify identification and assessment procedures for special education for individual students. Once the assessment is complete, the team could function in a way that utilizes Native American cultural standards as a guide. If a student is determined to require special education services, school support teams can provide valuable assistance in Individualized Education Program (IEP) and/or 504 plan development. This is especially true in view of the requirement in the 2004 Individuals with Disabilities Education Act (IDEA) that the annual goals and objectives must be tied directly to the general education curriculum. Since teams are probably comprised of both special and nonspecial educators, general and special education perspectives are well represented.

On the whole, identification and assessment procedures are supposed to be modified to reflect the unique culture of the student. During such consideration of individual culture, one should consider that there is no such thing as one unified Indian "reality" (Gross, 1995). Native American communities are not monolithic, but represent extremely diverse viewpoints and beliefs. In 1492, Christopher Columbus labeled the inhabitant of the Bahamas "Indians" thinking he was in India. By this act, he put a very diverse group of people under one label and started a poor tradition that has led to many stereotypical ideas of who Native Americans are and how they act (Lynch & Hanson, 1992). Traditional education for Native Americans has always been ecologically based on how each tribe adapted to specific environments in unique ways. In the Northeast, Indians revered the trees and integrated them into their everyday life. Likewise, the Plains Indians had a spiritual relationship with the buffalo while the Northwest Indians had a spiritual connection with salmon. This process of adapting to the specific environments of Native Americans is a central variable in understanding the true diversity that exists between Native American Tribes. In contrast, an overgeneralization of what an Indian is prevents alternative views from being heard and tried. By depicting a fairer representation of this diversity, more accurate strategies can be used with students from Native American cultures.

PLACEMENT OPTIONS

As noted earlier, many students from Native American backgrounds are over identified in disabilities particularly, emotional disorders and learning disabilities (U.S. Department of Education, Office of Special Education Programs, 2004). However, when one examines the causes of such behavior, three major factors emerge as reasons for academic and behavioral problems, they are; (a) low self-esteem related to group identity, (b) achievement motivation, and (c) culture conflict. These factors are discussed in detail below.

Self-Esteem Related Problems

The child welfare system itself has been a cause of social breakdown by taking Indian children away from their culture and placing them in non-native settings. This was seen as necessary given the reluctance on the part of native adults to become foster or adoptive parents. Once in non-native living situations, many Indian youth suffer from an identity crisis and have difficulty defining their cultural being. Research has shown that becoming disconnected from one's culture leads to a lack of motivation among Native American students which then leads to being left behind academically (Clark, 2009). Families play crucial roles in socializing their youngsters. They also help them to define their eventual place in the social order and shape and mediate family members' definitions of themselves as individuals. It should not come as a surprise that separating large numbers of Native American children from their respective families serves to increase self-concept difficulties, poor motivation, and poor achievement for them which may lead to placement into a special education setting.

Due to the above negative effects of being separated from ones family, the Indian Child Welfare Act (ICWA) was passed in 1978. The ICWA established a number of procedural directives and standards aimed at strengthening tribal sovereignty and stopping transracial placement practices. Unfortunately, tribally based child welfare programs have responded to their increasing caseloads by acting as other jurisdictional units have historically behaved—they are breaking up native families, separating children from their parents, and making extensive use of out-of-home care. This perpetuation of bad practice of foster placement alienates Native American youth further from their indigenous culture. Positively, recent court rulings have begun to offer protections to Indian families to decrease this practice (Nativetimes, 2009).

Motivational Problems

Motivation to achieve requires a great deal of encouragement from family members and school personnel. However, the sociological factors related to Native Americans do not help the case for achievement motivation. Children need role models within their families that will help to encourage their achievement and recognize it appropriately in cultural ways. Children with disabilities often have difficulties with both academic and social aspects of school and need external motivation to help them develop their own internal motivation. However, when a child's family is very poor and living on a small reservation, and when the family has alcohol and/or drug problems, achievement motivation is compromised significantly. This has forced child welfare programs to deal with the critical issue of out-of-home placement. This vicious cycle of troubled families must be addressed before any significant motivation can be achieved in the child's own native culture. The family preservation approach calls for creating a service continuum, delivering services concerned with basic life skills and environmental problems to children and parents in normalized settings such as the home, rendering services that support and strengthen families, and employing the person-in-environment perspective. Cultural conflict can also lead to poor school achievement and placement in special education settings. It should be noted that while negative aspects are being discussed about native families above, there are many more positive aspects of native families that enhance their children's life such as superior cultural mores, positive role modeling, love, and emotional and nurturing support.

Cultural Conflict

Teachers need to make a deliberate effort to familiarize CLD students with mainstream culture and school practices. Students from Native American backgrounds need to know how mainstream Americans view the world. The idea of empowerment of Native American students does not suggest that they change their cultural beliefs and behaviors but that they learn to adapt to specific situations and acquire necessary coping skills. For instance, health and physical disabilities may create placement problems for students from Native American backgrounds. Available data indicate that the prevalence of overweight and obesity in American Indian/Alaskan native preschoolers, school-aged children, and adults is higher than the respective United States rates for all races combined (Halpern, 2007). Halpern (2007) reported several emerging trends that were apparent in reviewing intervention studies *currently* being implemented by federal agencies, although many of these projects have not yet completed a formal evaluation. First, in addition to behavioral approaches, several studies have focused on environmental interventions (e.g., walking trails and diet sodas in vending machines). Next, many current studies are multilevel and/or multicomponent interventions that involve more than one level of the socioecological model (e.g., community, school, individual, and family) as well as more than one key strategy (e.g., physical activity, nutrition education, and breastfeeding). Another major implication of obesity research is that Native American students are at risk of chronic heart disease and diabetes. Schools that teach Native Americans must address the issue of obesity prevention in order to prevent related disabilities from emerging.

A few years ago, Hawkins, Cummins, and Marlatt (2004) conducted a study to prevent drug addiction among Indian youth. Drug users have had health and well-being effects from their drug usage on their bodies. This study indicated that there are a variety of intervention procedures that have been used to avoid or stem the increase of drug usage such as tobacco, inhalants, alcohol, and marijuana in Indian youth. According to this study, males have a higher rate than females with substance abuse. In addition, the number of drug programs should be increased to cover the issues of substance usage by American Indian and Alaska Native adolescents (Hawkins et al.). A few years ago, Manson (2000) conducted a study to explore and clarify the information about mental health needs of American Indians and Alaska Natives. The study highlighted the limits of psychiatric nomenclature and conceptual frameworks for enlightening native constructions of mental health and mental problems. The experience and appearance of psychopathology can be both different and identical across cultures. More importantly for Native Americans, psychological problems occur as tribes and other native community-based organizations seek to balance self-determination, resource management, fiscal responsibility, and culturally informed prevention, treatment, and aftercare options for their members.

Another health concern for Native Americans is related to social problems experienced within their own communities. Researchers have suggested that poverty and drug abuse, and lack of parental involvement are serious problems in Indian households (Dillinger, 2012). Each of these factors can lead to significant disabling conditions and the placement of children in special education settings. For instance, Fetal Alcohol Syndrome (FAS) and its less serious cousin Fetal Alcohol Effects (FAE) are both prevalent in native cultures. Alcoholism is one of the most significant public health problems among Native Americans. They are five times likely than Whites to die of alcohol-related causes; they also have higher rates of drunken driving related deaths than the general population (U.S. Department of Health and Human Services, 2007). Children with FAS and FAE conditions sometimes show significant cognitive, physical, behavioral, and developmental delays. This becomes vary serious as the incidence rate of FAS in the United States is .2 to 1.0 per 1,000 live births, but the rate among Native Americans is 1.5 to 2.5 per 1,000 live births.

Clearly, children who live in poverty often suffer nutritionally which leads to a variety of disabling conditions including obesity. Poverty is an acute problem among Native Americans (Dillinger, 2012). While poverty itself is not a disabling condition, many of the sociological factors related to poverty may result in special education placement. It is vital to recognize that Native American communities lack good sanitary conditions and stimulating academic experiences. Further, parents who cannot find jobs often become overly stressed and take their frustrations out on family members causing a variety of emotional problems in children. Too few opportunities, poor living conditions, and being separated from the dominant society can lead to poor school achievement. While schools can help to prevent some of these problems by providing nutritious meals, emotional support, and extended classroom opportunities, the family must be a part of an overall program of wellness. Positively, Native American families bring much strength to the table including positive traditional cultural practices.

CURRICULUM CONSIDERATIONS

The curriculum of Native American learners should reflect common standards that guide the education of all children. Culturally sensitive education is not a way to side-step the core curriculum but rather a way to enhance the learning of that curriculum. As Wilder, Jackson, and Smith (2001) noted, culture is more than race or ethnicity, it encompasses all aspects of life and guides crucial decision making. Given this level of importance, it seems obvious that cultural factors would be considered in developing a curriculum for culturally diverse learners. Of course, the age of the child should govern the curriculum to some extent, and that starts with early intervention. Infants and toddlers are served with the goal of minimizing the impact of disabilities on future development. Native American youth have a significant need for health care services in early intervention (Faircloth, 2006). These health needs include speech and language needs, monitoring of diabetes, counter acting the effects of fetal alcohol syndrome, and reducing obesity among Native American students.

The IEP guides the curriculum for children older than 3 years of age and is a part of the Individuals with Disabilities Education Improvement Act of

2004 (IDEIA, 2004). Under the Act, goals and objectives must be tied to the general curriculum. This does not mean that there is one way to deliver the curriculum, just that it should occur with all learners present and not separated. Within the general curriculum, native cultural values and beliefs can be incorporated to enhance the curriculum for all learners. The individualization of the child's curriculum should take into consideration cultural issues that will need to be addressed within the IEP such as technology accommodations, and learning environment adjustments. A small percentage of Native American learners attend tribal schools while most attend local public schools that may or may not reflect the native culture. A small accommodation of using local native imagery to present curriculum content like mathematics problems shows an appreciation for the native culture. Similarly, sharing stories during story time about native customs and traditions can expand the curriculum for all learners and enhance the status of native children. Faircloth (2006) suggested that the target hiring of Native American teachers and para-educators can create a much more relevant modeling experience for Native American students. Lastly, the curriculum needs to reflect the local native culture. This aspect was highlighted by Sparks (1999).

> The Native American community is extremely diverse and that diversity must be considered when presenting information to children in school. Otherwise, the teacher runs the risk of stereotyping Native American children into one homogeneous group and perpetuating the myth of one single "Indian Reality." It should not be forgotten that cultural education in public schools is aimed as much at changing ideas of children from the dominant culture as it is in providing a relevant learning environment for children from culturally and linguistically different backgrounds. (p. 14–15)

This knowledge of the reality of native students is something that teachers must obtain as well as the skill to infuse it into the curriculum. Ingalls, Hammond, Dupoux, and Baeze (2006) point out that culturally responsive teaching is a critical skill for special education teachers of Native American students given that they are disproportionately identified with a disability that requires special education services.

How a student learns the curriculum should also be a part of curriculum adaptations. Determining whether a student is a highly visual learner or an auditory learner, etc. are relevant curriculum determinations that should be considered within a cultural context. With this in mind, Ingalls et al. (2006) reported on a number of previous studies about native learners that seem to fit particular learning modalities. They suggested that native learners prefer visual demonstrations and private practice to other forms of curriculum engagement. This is consistent with the notion of concrete learning that is well used in special education whereby one does something rather than talk about doing that task. They also note that many native learners prefer to reflect on a problem before talking and may take some additional time to respond to a question from teachers or others.

Instructional Modifications

How the curriculum is delivered is within the realm of teachers and other educators and, like the curriculum, modifications to instruction that reflect cultural and linguistically diverse learners are critical. One unique aspect of Native American languages is not simply their diversity but also the alarming drop in fluent speakers in a majority of tribes. Thornton (2009) reports that of 300 indigenous languages, only 175 remain. This linguistic loss for Native Americans will only serve to exacerbate their identity crisis and may result in even more dropouts and more children entering special education. While it is important for Native American students to learn English, it is equally important for them to learn and/or maintain their native language in order to be able to pass on their culture to another generation. Schools need to provide accurate information to teachers regarding using native languages. One commonly cited answer to the dilemma of providing Native American and other students with information about specific indigenous languages and traditions is to include Elders as instructors in schools. Elders often bring knowledge of traditional language and culture to the learning environment. In tribal schools, Elders are an everyday experience and the tribal culture permeates throughout the curriculum. Children learn about their heritage in the traditional oral manner using symbolism, metaphor, stories, and music. However, unless a public school is in an area that has a high number of Native Americans, this practice of including Elders in the instructional program is not as prevalent. In such situations, teachers need to go out of their way to find Elders and other native speakers and to incorporate them into their cultural instruction of all children. In this way, students are exposed to the Native American heritage in a very real way that lends itself well to the learning styles of Native American youngsters. By being sensitive to the specific learning styles of Native American youth, the teacher can provide them with a meaningful education and prepare them to live in "multiple realities" within society.

Understanding a child's family life and the values that guide them is an important consideration in development instructional strategies. Keltner, Crowell, and Taylor (2005) point out that most native families define disability by the level of functional limitation it presents and suggests that this leads to the type of services that families seek for the child. Knowing about specific rituals, traditions, and customs will help the educators develop instructional techniques that utilize these family values. Some things that educators might observe about family members are their level of involvement with their child's education. For example, while it is critical that family members actively participate in IEP, it is important for the educator to take care that personal judgments about the families lifestyle does not get in the way of serving children. However, soliciting family assistance isn't always a simple process as documented by human services professionals who have shared their frustrations related to working with families for many years (Rowley & Rehfeldt, 2002).

THE ROLE OF TECHNOLOGY

The vast array of assistive and learning technologies has changed the playing field for people with disabilities and allows them opportunities to succeed (see Bouck, 2010; Parette & Peterson-Karlan, 2010). More importantly, technology is playing a very significant role in the education of Native American learners with exceptionalities. For instance, Goins, Spencer, Goll, and Rogers (2010) reported that 22% to 26% of elder Native Americans use assistive technology. This would indicate a general acceptance of assistive technology among all tribal members since tribal elders are seen as role models. A good example of assistive technology helping the learner is from the human–computer interaction (HCI) perspective that is used with deaf learners. This field is about more than just the technology of CALL (Computer Assisted Language Learning). According to Hemard (2004), teachers and service providers take into account the individual dimension when working with deaf students, their assistive technologies and learning environments. Since students have differing interests, abilities, and tastes, they have their own preference for one type of technology over another. Knowing the students' preference will greatly assist teachers and students in learning. Being flexible and offering choices lead to a satisfactory comfort level with technology. Practice is also a key aspect in the relationship between assistive technology and its users; and it is a routine that helps students to acquire skills in areas such as writing. Also, the development of technology has greatly assisted students in language learning. An example of such a device is the Universal Serial Bus (USB), memory sticks for saving large numbers of texts and videos (Levy & Stockwell, 2006).

Assistive Technology is a device or service that helps to improve the learning environment for Native American students with disabilities that bypass the effects of a disability on learning. It can be classified as either high tech that requires electrical support or low tech that does not require electricity. Examples of high-tech tools are calculators, word prediction software, and voice recognition software. Low-tech examples are cassette recorders, pencil grips, and head pointers. Assistive educational technology as a tool makes information accessible to students who have disabilities. This tool provides a support method between the teacher and Native American student in a learning environment and helps students learn effectively in a classroom with other students. Technology is a tool for the teacher or service provider to use in the classroom to help improve and provide effective instruction for Native American students with or without disabilities in learning environments (see Courtad & Bouck, 2013). Assistive technology can assist Native American students with disabilities in organizing their thoughts and outlining their ideas. A good example of an assistive technology tool is the word processor on a computer that (a) provides many types of fonts and styles; (b) allows students to customize their work; (c) use graphic images, drawing, and video to learning tasks; and (d) gives students the means and motivation to spread new and difficult ideas. Visual assistive technology devices like graphic organizers can do this and outlined note taking can also work. Writing assistance devices such as word processing programs and computers can help Native American students with disabilities put ideas on paper without needing a pencil. Examples of assistive technology devices that help students organize their thought and outline their ideas are spellcheckers, dictionaries, and thesaurus programs. Teachers and service providers can utilize the editing capabilities of the word processor by asking students to revise other students' papers or work. Assistive technology that can help in Native American students' productivity includes hardware-based and software-based tools. Some of these tools are calculators, spreadsheets, databases, and graphics software; and they enable students to work on math or other subjects that may require calculating, categorizing, grouping, and predicting events (see Courtad & Bouck, 2012). Productivity tools also can be found in small, portable devices called personal digital assistants (PDAs) and in the more current technology in Smartphones. Access to reference materials can assist Native American students with disabilities in gathering and synthesizing knowledge for their academic work. Applications on smart phones and tablet computers are offering a world of tools for Native American students with disabilities and can be life changing.

Telecommunications and multimedia provides new learning tools for Native American students. Cognitive assistance is a collection of software for instructing students through the use of tutorials, drill and practice, problem-solving, and simulations. Multimedia CD-ROM-based application programs are a tool for reading improvement. Talking word processors and CD-based books read each page of the story, highlighting the words on the computer screen as they are read. Students can click on the pictures to see the definition and hear the pronunciation. These books are available in all languages, so Native American students can read in their native language while being exposed to a second language. A study titled *Native American Family Technology Journey* (2006) examined opportunities available to Native Americans to discover what technology and innovation can mean for their families. *The Journey*, which was supported by the International Business Machines Corporation and Career Communications Group, played host to computer and Internet workshops, educational and career seminars, and interactive demonstrations. It provided technology access and training to Native Americans residing in urban centers, rural areas, and on tribal lands. At the same time, a forum was created in which Native People learned more about the technology's possibility in assisting their unique languages, stories, and customs from one generation to another (Native American Family Technology Journey, 2006).

Brescia and Daily (2007) discussed the essentials of having economic improvement and technology skills on American Indian reservation. They studied the benefits of having a leader that understands and supports the wide array of information technology for the tribe and other available resources. The results found a number of concerns including awareness of the use of technology, off-the-shelf programs, and applications for business issues that were noted by respondents (Brescia & Daily). In the same vein, Varma (2009) conducted a study to examine the students' precollege familiarity with computers along gender lines. The result showed that the interest in using computers at home and in schools for female students was less than for male students (Varma, 2009). De Mars (2010) conducted a study to evaluate access to electronic resources among Native Americans. The subjects of the study were 708 Native Americans with disabilities who live on Great Plains reservations. The results showed that the 66% of the 708 participants had a computer, and approximately half had Internet access. Given this primacy of social networks, De Mars recommended an increase in electronic information targeted toward Native Americans with disabilities with an emphasis on Web 2.0 technologies. However, fewer Native American's families utilize the internet at home and even fewer still access information about their child's Individualized Education Program (IEP) or Individualized Family Service Plan (IFSP). It was noted that a substantial number of Native Americans with disabilities who live on Indian reservations on the great plains access the internet and email frequently even though it is below the national average. It seems obvious that some attention to using the internet to benefit Native American students in school is needed among Native American communities.

GOING BEYOND THE TRADITION

Native families with children who have disabilities must face the decision of labeling their child in order to receive special education services and an Individualized Education Program or refuse the label and not be eligible for and IEP. However, more and more families are learning about 504 Accommodation plans and using them to individualize a program without a disability label. A 504 plan serve Native American students who do not qualify for special education but may benefit from educational intervention accommodations. A 504 plan prohibits discrimination on the basis of a person's disability in all programs receiving federal funds. The 504 plan is written by general education teachers in consultation with a team of professionals that includes the parents and or child, if he/she is of age. Many Native American families are suspicious of disability labels and do not want them applied to their children. For these families, a 504 plan might be a satisfactory option to help their child receive individualized educational accommodations which can assist in their learning and achievement. Interestingly, children who do not qualify for special education can utilize the 504 plans as a civil right. deBettencourt (2002) conducted a study to examine differences between the Individuals With Disabilities Education Act (IDEA) and Section 504 of the Rehabilitation Act of 1973. Table 7.1 highlights these differences.

CONCLUSION

This chapter examined the status of Native American students with disabilities who are diverse, unique, and complex in their educational needs. Their educational needs are made more challenging due to their connection to the federal government and sovereign status of living on reservations. Some Native American students are educated in BIA supported schools that are affiliated with tribes while 90% are educated in public schools across the country. Meaningful educational programming for these students requires an understanding that they come from an indigenous population of people with diverse tribal language issues. Unfortunately, their diverse ethnic aspects have lead to Native American students being overidentified as requiring special education services. Some of this overidentification has been due to inadequate assessment practices that fail to recognize how their cultural status may affect evaluation results. When these students are placed into special education programs, the students do not always value the relevance of American education which leads to excessive dropouts and prolonged absences. Correction for this high drop out rate may necessitate the need for educators to utilize 504 Accommodation plans to make their education more relevant.

It is common knowledge that the adjustment and quality of life of Native American students is complicated but family problems related to high poverty rates, excessive alcoholism incidents, psychological and psychiatric dysfunction, family breakdown, and health problems such as obesity. As a

TABLE 7.1 Differences Between the Individual With Disabilities Education Act (IDEA) and Section 504 of the Rehabilitation Act of 1973

IDEA	Section 504
Identification Differences	
All school-age children that fit within particular categories of suitable environment. For example, "autism, learning disabilities, speech or language impairment, emotional disturbance, traumatic brain injury, visual impairment, hearing impairment, deafness, mental retardation, deaf–blindness, multiple disabilities, orthopedic impairment, and other heath problems"(deBettencourt, p. 18).	Persons who fit the definition of qualified handicapped person, has a "physical or mental impairment that obstacle the life activity. For example: walking, seeing, hearing, speaking, breathing, learning, working, caring for oneself, and performance manual tasks" (deBettencourt, p. 18).
Differences in Evaluation	
• Full comprehensive evaluation required by multidisciplinary team.	• Evolution draws on information from a variety of sources and is documented
• Requires informed and written consent	• Decision made by knowledgeable group—Does not require consent of parents, only notice
• Requires a reevaluation of each child, if conditions warrant a reevaluation, or if the child's parent or teacher requests a reevaluation, but at least once every 3 years	• Periodic reevaluation required
• Provides for independent evaluation at district expense if parents disagree with first evaluation	• No provision for independent evaluation at school's expense
• Reevaluation not required before significant change in placement	• Reevaluation required before a significant change in placement
Differences in Responsibility to Provide Free Appropriate Public Education	
• Requires an individualized education program	• Does not require an IEP, but does require a plan
• Appropriate education means a program designed to provide educational benefit for a person with disabilities	• Appropriate means an education comparable to the education provided to those students who are not disabled
• Placement may be any combination of special education and general education classrooms	• Placement usually in general education classroom
• Related services, if required	• Related services, if needed
Differences in Due Process Procedures	
• Must provide impartial hearings for parents who disagree with the identification, evaluation, or placement of the student	• Must provide impartial hearing for parents who disagree with the identification, evaluation, or placement of the student
• Requires written consent	• No consent requirement

(continued)

TABLE 7.1 Differences Between the Individual With Disabilities Education Act (IDEA) and Section 504 of the Rehabilitation Act of 1973 (continued)

IDEA	Section 504
• Delineates specific procedures	• Requires that parent have an opportunity to participate and be represented by counsel—other details left to the discretion of the school
• Hearing officer appointed by impartial appointee	• Hearing Officer usually is appointed by school
• Provides stay put provision until all proceedings are resolved	• No stay put provisions
• Parents must receive 10 days notice prior to any change in placement	• No requirement of days notice prior to change of placement
• Enforced by U.S. Department of Education, Office of Special Education	• Enforced by U.S. Department of Education, Office of Civil Rights.

Suggestion for Teachers

Awareness of personnel: Teachers should know who serves as the school based Chairperson for IDEA and who serves as the Section 504 Compliance Officer

Awareness of forms: Teachers should know what school district forms are used to document the process of identifying and serving students under IDEA and Section 5054

Teacher documentation: Examples of students' inability to stay on task, emotional outbursts, and completed work should be kept on a daily basis (IEPs) and completed forms should be available for review by the teacher on a regular basis. A record of all telephone calls and meetings with parents should be kept in a secure place.

Awareness of school policies: Teachers should keep a copy of school district requirements for Section 504 and IDEA

Confidentiality: Teachers should keep all materials confidential, including names of children.

Source: deBettencourt (2002)

way to eliminate these problems, dominant and native social service systems have placed Native American children into non-native foster homes. This practice has caused more difficulties for the children as it separates them from native families and slowly disintegrates the traditional heritage of tribal life. To correct these aspects, school systems must plan accordingly for adequate mental, disease, and nutritional health intervention. Another consideration is a requirement to keep tribal cultures (languages, identity, and healthy self-concepts) alive. Interventions such as the Elder involvement have been found to be effective. Finally, technology offers a significant potential for serving Native American learners on a number of different levels. It helps in health, language, and the academic interventions. Another powerful intervention is the incorporation of technologies into the Native American students with disabilities curriculum to help level the playing field for them. In addition, Native American families are encouraged to use the internet to provide a pathway to sharing information without distance barriers to assist their children in knowledge acquisition. Only when we take all the above variables into consideration will we truly help Native American students with and without disabilities to maximize their fullest potential.

REFERENCES

Bouck, E. C. (2010).technology and students with disabilities: Does it solve all the problems. In F. E. Obiakor, J. P. Bakken, & A. F. Rotatori (Eds.), *Current issues and trends in special education: Research, technology and teacher preparation* (Vol. 20, pp.91–104). Bingley, UK: Emerald Group Publishing Limited.

Brescia, W., & Daily, T. (2007). Economic development and technology-skill needs on American Indian reservations. *American Indian Quarterly, 31*(1), 23–43.

Brigham, F. J., & Bakken, J. P. (2013). Assessment and LD: Determining eligibility, selecting services and guiding instruction. In J. P. Bakken, F. E. Obiakor, & A. F. Rotatori (Eds.), *Learning disabilities: Identification, assessment, and instruction of students with LD* (Vol. 24, pp. 55–74). Bingley, UK: Emerald Group Publishing Limited.

Clark, H. (2009). *Classes aim to preserve urban Indian heritage.* Retrieved from Nativetimes.com.

Courtad, C. A., & Bouck, E. C. (2012). Technology and students with emotional and behavioral disorders. In J. P. Bakken, F. E. Obiakor, & A. F. Rotatori (Eds.), *Behavioral disorders: Practice concerns and students with EBD* (Vol. 23, pp. 179–205). Bingley, UK: Emerald Group Publishing Limited.

Courtad, C. A., & Bouck, E. C. (2013). Assistive technology for students with learning disabilities. In J. P. Bakken, F. E. Obiakor, & A. F. Rotatori (Eds.), *Learning disabilities: Practice concerns and students with LD* (Vol. 25, pp. 153–173). Bingley, UK: Emerald Group Publishing Limited.

deBettencourt, L. U. (2002). Understanding the differences between IDEA and Section 504. *Teaching Exceptional Children, 34*(3), 16.

DeMars A. (2010). Internet usage by Native Americans with disabilities living on American Indian reservations in the Great Plains. *Rural Special Education Quarterly, 29*(2), 34–43.

Dillinger Z. (2012). *Native American poverty. Voices.* Retrieved fromYahoo.com.

Dyches, T., & Prater, M. A. (2010). Disproportionate representation in special education: Overrepresentation of selected subgroups. In F. E. Obiakor, J. P. Bakken, & A. F. Rotatori(Eds.), *Current issues and trends in special education: Identification, assessment, and instruction* (Vol. 19, pp. 53–71). Bingley, UK: Emerald Group Publishing Limited.

Faircloth, S. C. (2006). Early childhood education among American Indian/Alaskan Native children with disabilities: Implications for research and practice. *Rural Special Education Quarterly, 25*(1), 56–62.

Goins, R. T., Spencer, S. M., Goli, S., & Rogers, J. C. (2010). Assistive Technology use with older American Indians in a southeastern tribe: The native elder care study. *The American Geriatrics Society, 23,* 89–92.

Gross, E. R. (1995). Deconstructing politically correct practice literature: The American Indian case. *Social Work, 40,* 206–213.

Halpern, P. (2007). *Obesity and American Indians/Alaska Natives.* Washington, DC: Healthand Human Services.

Hawkins, E. H., Cummins, L. H., & Marlatt, G. (2004). Preventing substance abuse in American Indian and Alaska Native youth: Promising strategies for healthier communities. *Psychological Bulletin, 130*(2), 304–323.

Hemard, D. (2004). Enhancing online CALL design: The case for evaluation. New York: Cambridge University Press.

Individuals with Disabilities Education Act (IDEA) of 2004, 20 U.S.C. & 1401 et seq.

Individuals with Disabilities Individual Improvement Act (IDEIA) of 2004, P.L. 108–466: U.S.C. & 603(30) (A)(B).

Ingalls, L., Hammond, H., Dupoux, E., & Baeza, R. (2006). Teacher's cultural knowledge and understanding of American Indian students and their families: Impact of culture on a child's learning. *Rural Special Education Quarterly, 25,* 16–24.

Kelter, B. R., Crowell, N. A., & Taylor, W. (2005). Attitudes about disabilities in a southeastern American Indian tribe. *American Indian Culture & Research Journal, 29,* 57–74.

Levy, M., & Stockwell, G. (2006). CALL. *Dimensions options and issues in computer-assisted language learning,* 1–310.

Lynch, E. W., & Hanson, M. J. (1992). Developing *cross-cultural competence: A guide for working with young children and their families.* Baltimore: Paul H. Brookes.

Manson, S. (2000). Mental health services for American Indians and Alaska Natives: Need, use and barriers to effective care. *Canadian Journal of Psychiatry, 45*(7), 617–626.

McMillan, J. H. (2007). *Classroom assessment: Principles and practice for effective standards based instruction.* Boston: Pearson.

Morrison, D. (2009). *Disabilities: Native Americans are people too.* Retrieved from Starnewsonline.com.

National Center for Educational Statistics (2007). *Status and trends in the education of racial and ethnic minorities.* Washington, DC.

National Education Association (2003). *Native Americans with Disabilities don't get services.* NEA Online Newsletter, August, 2003.

Native American Family Technology Journey. (2006). *TechTrends: Linking Research & Practice to Improve Learning, 50* (1), 46.

Nativetimes (2009). *Kansas ruling protects tribal children.* Retrieved from Nativetimes.com.

Obi, S. (2010). Curriculum-based assessment: The most effective way to assess students with disabilities. In F. E. Obiakor, J. P. Bakken, & A. F. Rotatori (Eds.), *Current issues and trends in special education: Identification, assessment, and instruction* (Vol. 19, 87–97). Bingley, UK: Emerald Group Publishing Limited.

Parette, H. P., & Peterson-Karlan, G. R. (2010). Using assistive technology to support the instructional process of students with disabilities. In F. E. Obiakor, J. P. Bakken, & A. F. Rotatori (Eds.), *Current issues and trends in special education:*

Research, technology, and teacher preparation (Vol. 20, pp. 73–89). Bingley, UK: Emerald Group Publishing Limited.

Plotts, C. A. (2012). Assessment of students with emotional and behavioral disorders. In J. P. Bakken, F. E. Obiakor, & A. F. Rotatori (Eds.), *Behavioral disorders: Identification, assessment, and instruction of students with EBD* (Vol. 22, pp. 54–85). Bingley, UK: Emerald Group Publishing Limited.

Rowley, D., & Rehfeldt, R. A. (2002). Delivering human services to Native Americans with disabilities: Cultural variables and service recommendations. *North American Journal of Psychology, 4*(2), 309.

Sparks, S. (1999). Educating the Native American exceptional learner. In F. E. Obiakor, J. O. Schwenn, & A. F. Rotatori (Eds.), *Multicultural education for learners with exceptionalities* (Vol. 12, pp. 73–89). Stamford, CT: JAI Press.

Thornton, D. (2009). *The link between language and sovereignty.* Indian Gaming, October U.S. Department of Education, Washington, DC: Office of Special Education Programs.

U.S. Department of Education (2004) *Individuals with Disabilities Education Improvement Act* (2004). Washington, DC: U.S. Government Printing Office.

U.S. Department of Health and Human Services. (2007). Fetal *alcohol spectrum disorders among Native Americans.* Washington, DC: U.S. Government Printing Office.

Varma, R. (2009). Gender differences in factors influencing students towards computing. *Computer Science Education, 19*(1), 37–49.

Wilder, L. K. J., Jackson, A. P., & Smith, T. B. (2001). Secondary transition of multicultural learners: Lessons from the Navajo Native American experience. *Preventing School Failure, 45,* 119–124.

CHAPTER 8

EDUCATING FOREIGN-BORN IMMIGRANTS

Today's "Special" Learners in Schools

Festus E. Obiakor,
Cheryl A. Utley, and Sean Warner

The 2010 American Community Survey (ACS) (U.S. Census Bureau) estimated the number of foreign-born immigrants in the United States (U.S.) to be nearly 40 million or 13% of the total population. More than 90% of these immigrants came from Cuba, the Dominican Republic, Jamaica, Haiti, and Trinidad and Tobago, and Cuban immigrants in particular have been among the top ten foreign-born groups in the United States each decade since 1970. The foreign-born immigrant population from Latin America was the largest region-of-birth group, accounting for over half (53%) of all foreign-born immigrants. By comparison, 28% of the foreign-born immigrants were born in Asia, 12% in Europe, 4% in Africa, 2% in Northern America, and less than 1% in Oceania. Among the 21.2 million foreign-born immigrants from Latin America, 11.7 million, or over half (55%), were born in Mexico. Of the total foreign-born immigrant population, 29% were born in Mexico.

Multicultural Education for Learners with Special Needs in the Twenty-First Century, pages 125–136
Copyright © 2014 by Information Age Publishing
All rights of reproduction in any form reserved.

Foreign-born immigrant children, also referred to as limited English proficient and English-Language Learners (ELLs), are a fast-growing segment of the school-age population in the United States, representing multiple countries, linguistic differences, and ethnic diversity (Glick & Hohmann-Marriott, 2007). These children are astonishing in their diversity, hailing from nearly 200 different countries and speaking a wide array of languages and dialects. Among the regions of birth, the poverty rate was highest for the foreign-born immigrant population from Latin America (24%) and Africa (21%). Within Latin America, the poverty rate was highest for the foreign-born immigrant population born in Mexico (28%). About 31% of foreign-born immigrant children (under the age of 18) were living below the poverty level, compared with about 21% of native born. About 39% of foreign-born immigrant children born in Latin America and 37% born in Africa were living in poverty. Of foreign-born immigrant children born in Mexico, more than 2 in every 5 (46%) were living below the poverty level. About 30% of foreign-born immigrant children from the Caribbean or Other Central America lived in poverty. At the current pace, by the year 2040 one in three children will grow up in a household with at least one foreign-born immigrant parent (Suarez-Orozco, Suarez-Orozco, & Todorova, 2008). Today, one in five children in primary and secondary schools have at least one foreign-born immigrant parent.

SCHOOLING CHALLENGES
OF FOREIGN-BORN IMMIGRANT STUDENTS

Current research on foreign-born immigrant students in the United States is very complex. The majority of foreign-born immigrant youth arrive in this country with academic deficiencies that impact their schooling. This situation is further aggravated by their lack of familiarity with academic norms and standards, customs, and societal institutions. Also, their families often lack U.S. citizenship, access to public benefits, and a fluent command of the English language. They are also more likely to be racial minorities, to come from poor families, and to live in large urban areas where school systems are under-resourced and achievement falls below national norms (Van Hook, Brown, & Kwenda, 2004). Naturally, then, when newly-arrived foreign-born immigrant children are compared to white, nonpoor, fully English proficient, native-born youth who attend highly-resourced schools, the majority earn lower test scores, have lower grades and fewer years of schooling (Crosnoe, 2005). These situations place them at risk of being misidentified, misassessed, mislabeled, misplaced, and misinstructed (Obiakor, 1999, 2001, 2007, 2008).

At the same time, several studies have shown that foreign-born youth fare relatively well when compared to native-born who have similar racial/ethnic and socioeconomic profiles (Conger, Schwartz, & Stiefel, 2007; Glick & White, 2003). With the exception of some Central American children, much of this research points to a general advantage of being a native-born immigrant or at least having an immigrant parent, despite the challenges associated with learning a foreign language and new customs (Conger et al., 2007; Glick & White, 2003; Perreira, Chapman, & Stein, 2006; Perreira, Harris, & Lee, 2006). Foreign-born immigration scholars often attribute this finding to selective migration on unobserved characteristics. That is, though many foreign-born immigrants arrive in the United States with low levels of human capital that inhibit their upward mobility, they may possess a unique mindset or skill (e.g., strong attachment to school, work, family, and community) that puts them ahead of native-born with similar human capital inputs (Obiakor & Afolayan, 2007; Obiakor, Grant, & Obi, 2010).

Foreign-born parents' income level partially determines their ability to intervene or provide better resources for their children's academic attainment (Obiakor & Afolayan, 2007). For example, some immigrant parents lack transportation to take their sons and daughters to extracurricular and community activities (Perreira, Harris et al., 2006; Perreira, Harris, & Lee, 2007). In contrast with their middle-class peers, many low income children of immigrants lack computers and internet access (Suarez-Orozco et al., 2008). In particular, because many immigrant parents work long hours in inflexible low-wage jobs, they are often unavailable to attend school meetings during the day or help their children after school with homework (Suarez-Orozco et al., 2008). According to the Longitudinal Immigration Student Adaptation Study (LISA), the vast majority of immigrant parents— regardless of income, children's gender or regional nativity—would like their children to do well in school and go on to college (Suarez-Orozco & Qin, 2006; Suarez-Orozco et al., 2008). Immigrant parents are at times unable to help with their children's homework due to their own limited education and unfamiliarity with English. In fact, only 38% of the LISA students could ask someone in their family to help with their homework (Suarez-Orozco et al., 2008). Because of their limited English skills, knowledge of the U.S. educational system, and access to bilingual institutional support for their children's schooling, some immigrant parents—especially those who are low income—must rely entirely on their children's school boards and teachers to make decisions about what is best in the education of their children. However, when located in poor urban communities, schools are more limited in institutional resources (Lew, 2007). Alternative resources to compensate for parents with lower levels of English, such as tutoring or after school programs, are less available to students with low-income families (Lew, 2007). Teacher perceptions—and student effort—appear to be correlated with, and may explain, the increased likelihood of attaining higher levels of education for third generation immigrant peers. Unfortunately, some foreign-born parents' lack trust in the U.S. public school system and exhibit lower levels of classroom involvement (Kao & Thompson, 2003), thus potentially decreasing the motivation of their children and negatively affecting teachers' perceptions of their efforts.

SPECIAL EDUCATION AND ENGLISH LANGUAGE LEARNERS

The sociopolitical, historically rooted issue of disproportionate representation of ELL students in high incidence special education categories (e.g., LD) has been a source of debate for educators, policymakers, researchers, parents, and community stakeholders (Artiles, Harry, Reschly, & Chinn, 2002; Obiakor, 2001). Many years ago, Dunn (1968) documented the problem of overrepresentation when he questioned the feasibility and impartiality of special-education placements for culturally and linguistically diverse (CLD) and economically disadvantaged students in high incidence disability categories of mental retardation, LD, and emotional disturbance. Almost forty years after the 1975 passage of the Education of All Handicapped Children Act (P.L. 94-142), the issue of disproportionate representation of foreign-born ELLs backgrounds is still a wide-ranging and reoccurring problem throughout the nation. At the core of ELL disproportionate representation are traditional referral and assessment procedures. Many questions have been raised about the efficacy of teacher referrals, particularly how they relate to teacher bias and subjectivity in evaluating student performance and behavior (National Research Council, 2002; Obiakor, 1999).

In urban schools, foreign-born ELLs children develop within a broad set of environments and circumstances: families, neighborhoods, communities, classrooms and schools, and societies. There is evidence of influence from each of these levels of environmental organization on psychological development, learning, and schooling. For foreign-born ELLs, contextual issues include (a) poverty, (b) attendance in underfunded schools, (c) low social status according to ethnic and immigrant membership, (d) familial stress, (e) teacher expectations, and (f) incompatibility between home and school environments as related to first language, knowledge, skills, behavior, and ways of learning (National Academy Council, Institute of Medicine, 1997).

Despite discussions by researchers and scholars, ELLs have consistently encountered multidimensional problems that range from earning lower test scores, lower grades, and fewer years of schooling. Rather than focus on innovative intervention techniques that are not culturally responsive and that could help them maximize their fullest potential, the focus has been on unidimensional techniques that highlight a history of inequality in school resources, teachers blaming parents, and parents mistrusting teachers (Obiakor, Utley, & Smith, 2002). Clearly, all of these situations and circumstances make it easier for these foreign-born ELLs to be misidentified, misassessed, mislabeled, misplaced, and misinstructed in general education and special education (Obiakor, 1999).

TOWARDS SOLUTIONS:
USING THE COMPREHENSIVE SUPPORT MODEL

The implementation of the Comprehensive Support Model (CSM) (Obiakor, Grant, & Dooley, 2002) combines collaborative strategies with multi-faceted interventions. To educate foreign-born learners who we identify as foreign-born ELLs, the CSM must be functionalized and goal-directed. The components of the CSM are inextricably interwoven and each component of the CSM (i.e., the self, family, school, community, and government) collaboratively plays a role in the education of these learners who are at risk of being placed in special education programs.

Valuing the Self

Educational systems are designed to intellectually and socially develop all students into tomorrow's leaders (Obiakor, 2007). The self, in this case, represents foreign-born who are also ELLs. These students have to learn to survive and thrive in ill-equipped schools, dilapidated neighborhoods, and in spite of seemingly uncaring governments. It is unrealistic to expect these children to flourish when they are deprived of the basic necessities of life. Those who thrive in such adverse conditions are classified as resilient because they have the ability to successfully adapt to life in the face of social disadvantages. These students have to be resilient to make it through biased methods of identification, assessment, placement, and instruction. As a consequence, changes in assessment, curriculum, instruction, and preservice training are needed to increase outcomes of these students in general and special education programs (Obiakor & Utley, 1997).

Many laws have been passed to open doors that were previously closed to foreign-born ELLs. While these laws have failed in their quest to produce a perfect system, the role that these students play can help to further the full intent of these laws. These students must be helped to be responsive to the environment and take proactive steps to maximize their learning potential. The CSM encourages foreign-born students to be active, motivated, and responsible members of the support system if they in tend to benefit from the process. Additionally, they must demonstrate self-efficacious and self-empowerment attitudes. No intervention technique will be successful unless students are involved in the process. Even with a great support system, students must be self-knowledgeable, self-loving, and self-responsible. As a consequence, teachers, families, and community members must believe in them, create success-oriented environments, and give them opportunities to grow.

Valuing the Family

Although the student is the centerpiece of the CSM, families act as the cornerstone of this model. Families are responsible for the care, love, support, and development of the child (Obiakor, Grant et al., 2002). The CSM elucidates the importance of the foreign-born ELL family in creating a solid foundation for the child. The substantial contributions of the family both genetically and environmentally aid and assist in shaping foreign-born ELLs. It is common knowledge that the family serves as the bridge that connects the foreign-born ELLs with the school. Clearly, it can never be divorced from educational and social duties and responsibilities after the foreign-born ELL reaches compulsory age.

It is essential that the family members of foreign-born ELLs participate in schools, classrooms, sporting events, field trips, school performances, and Parent Teacher Association (PTA) meetings to maximize the potential of all students. When the family is actively involved in school, potential behavioral or learning problems are handled expeditiously; and comprehensive preventive and proactive techniques can be designed to create more culturally responsive general and special education classrooms for foreign-born ELLs. Family empowerment extends a family atmosphere into the school and creates a home away from home for those foreign-born ELLs. In general and special education programs, no intervention technique will succeed without parental support and involvement.

Valuing the School

The choice of curriculum, instruction, and discipline styles can be the difference between success and failure of foreign-born ELLs. These learners are forced to endure teaching styles that are Eurocentric and that do not maximize their educational potential. Consequently, some scholars and educators have argued that some of these learners are often misunderstood, misidentified, misassessed, miscategorized, and misinstructed (Obiakor, 1999, 2001, 2007; Obiakor & Beachum, 2005; Utley & Obiakor, 2001). It is no surprise that they are overrepresented in special education programs and underrepresented in programs for students with gifts and talents. These disproportionate numbers are attributed to Eurocentric interpretations and sometimes illusory conclusions by educational professionals.

Many colleges and universities have failed to satisfactorily prepare educators for today's classrooms. More than two decades ago, Haberman (1995) asserted that upon completion of traditional teaching programs, teachers are as prepared for urban classrooms as a swimmer who prepared for the English Channel by training in the university swimming pool. As Guillaume, Zuniga-Hill, and Yee (1995) emphasized, teachers of diverse students should "commit to professional growth regarding issues of diversity" (p. 70). To correct current school problems confronting foreign-born ELLs, efforts must be made to proactively promote progressive multicultural thinking. It is essential that institutions of higher learning design more classes to respect the growing demographic shifts of the United States and equip teachers with multicultural pedagogical techniques. General and special educators must be willing to leave their comfort zones and learn to reach out to foreign-born ELL families and communities (McAllister & Irvine, 2000; Obiakor, Harris-Obiakor, Obi, & Eskay, 2000). The school must keep its pulse on community and family activities, especially as they become increasingly diverse. By using resource persons from the home and community, the school reduces cultural ignorance, fosters a working relationship between the two entities, and provides learning environments that facilitate success for all children. Teachers and service providers can take advantage of resource persons in the community to advance their classroom instructions (see Obiakor, 2008; Obiakor & Afolayan, 2007; Obiakor et al., 2010)).

Valuing the Community

The community is a macrocosm of the family. This relationship has been described not only as intertwined but also as reciprocal (Ford & Reynolds, 2001; Obiakor, Harris-Obiakor, & Smith, 2002). A neighborhood without a positive foundational support is without expectations, obligations, and moral codes. The connection between the environment and school generally is ignored in most discussions about reform and improvement (see Ford & Reynolds, 2001). In fact, improvements in schools are not possible unless improvements in the environment are designed. We believe general and special education reform and restructuring programs have failed because they have not fully used the resources within the environment of foreign-born ELLs. Resources such as clergy and community members should be incorporated into reform plans. Neighborhoods and communities have proven to have great impacts on determining the academic achievement, depression level, emotional development, social behavior, and self-esteem of foreign-born ELLs (Ford & Reynolds, 2001; Obiakor, 2008).

Clearly, the whole village must be responsible to raise a responsible child. This is especially critical for foreign-born ELLs who are at risk of being placed in special education programs. Peterson (1992) noted that "community in itself is more important to learning than any method or technique. When community exists, learning is strengthened—everyone is smarter, more ambitious, and productive. Well-formed ideas and intentions amount to little without a community to bring them to life" (p. 2). General and special educators can ill afford to divorce themselves from the community, and vice versa. Obstacles that face communities will continually manifest themselves in schools, and the way educators address them will have life-lasting implications (Larrivee, 1992; Lovitt, 2000). The impetus behind the CSM is to remove fraudulent multicultural paradigms employed in many schools and the society as a whole. Fraudulent multiculturalism creates a fraudulent sense of community where problems are swept under the rug. For interventions to succeed in general and special education programs for foreign-born ELLs, communities must be involved in schools and vice versa (Ford & Reynolds, 2001).

Valuing the Government

The landmark Supreme Court case of *Plessey v. Ferguson* in 1896 mandated that races could be separated as long as facilities for each group were commensurate. This era, known by many as the Jim Crow era, blatantly disregarded the law because institutions were separate but unequal. The critical question is, "How much has the government done to change these injustices over the past years for foreign-born ELLs in general and special education programs?" In 1954, *Plessey v. Ferguson* was ruled unconstitutional with the *Brown v. Board of Education of Topeka* decision that led the initiative to desegregate public schools. The legislative branch of the government has sometimes stepped in to prevent foreign-born ELLs from being disproportionately placed in special education classes based on the use of intelligence tests alone. For example, through important legislative mandates (e.g., the 1975 Education for All Handicapped Children Act, the 1990 Individuals with Disabilities Education Act, the 1997 reauthorization of the Individuals with Disabilities Education Act, and the 2004 Individuals with Disabilities Education Improvement Act), the government has tried to enhance possibilities for a free and appropriate education for foreign-born ELLs. Although these legislative efforts are progressive and helpful, they are not in themselves the cure-all. The spirit of these laws has sometimes been missed, and as a consequence, savage inequalities as described by Kozol in 1991 continue to exist in many schools today. In addition, many of these government laws have guaranteed school funding for foreign-born ELLs on local, state, and federal levels; ironically though, inadequate funding continues to be a problem.

It is essential to note that government initiatives, such as Goals 2000, have allowed school districts to receive resources at local and state levels to implement divergent educational programs for all students. In addition, governments have funded and awarded grants to various institutions of higher learning and community organizations that aspire to design innovative programs for foreign-born ELLs. For instance, to help bridge economic and social gaps between people, notable efforts such as Charter and Choice Schools have been supported to create opportunities for all students. Clearly, governmental agencies can hold institutions accountable and mandate subsequent allocation or nonallocation to foster the compliance of rules, regulations, and positive outcomes for foreign-born ELLs. Local, state, and federal governments must be involved in upholding the laws. There should be accountability at all educational levels for all students; and the government must respect and enforce the legislation passed to ensure equality for all its citizenry. The CSM acknowledges the government as an inevitable force to fight injustices and enhance educational equality and quality for all learners (see Obiakor, Grant, & et al., 2002; Obiakor, Harris-Obiakor et al., 2002).

CONCLUSION

In this chapter, we have addressed the role of the CSM as a culturally sensitive intervention model for foreign-born ELLs. This model integrates efforts of the self (i.e., learner), family, school, community, and government in responding to the needs of all students. We believe the student has a role to play. In addition, families, both traditional and nontraditional, must continue to be central stakeholders in planning educational services to maximize the potential of foreign-born ELLs. General and special educators and other service providers must employ foreign-born ELL family advocates whose primary work would be to forge educational partnerships with foreign-born ELLs and the greater community. Local, state, and federal governments should be utilized for continual funding and for holding institutions accountable to ensure that foreign-born ELLs receive an appropriate education that meets their needs. In the end, educational services must be provided in an atmosphere of respect for the foreign-born ELLs family and an environment where communication is an ongoing priority.

The CSM has global implications for general and special education (Obiakor & McCollin, 2011). We need to know what others are doing to help foreign-born ELLs. If we can work together in our classrooms, families, communities, and governments, we can then work together in our global world. Shifting paradigms and powers can be a painstaking process; and as educators, we must be willing to step outside of our comfort zones to discover new intervention techniques for foreign-born ELLs. In a school where the CSM is implemented with integrity and fidelity, "learning" becomes a noncontroversial phenomenon that increases the goodness and quality of classroom activities for all students with learning problems. Our mission must be clear—We cannot help foreign-born ELLs in educational settings without taking advantage of their "selves," families, schools, communities, and governments.

REFERENCES

Artiles, A. J., Harry, B., Reschly, D. J., & Chinn, P. C. (2002). Over-identification of students of color in special education: A critical overview. *Multicultural Perspectives, 4,* 3–10.

Brown v. Board of Education, 347 U.S. 483 (1954).

Conger, D., Schwartz, A. E., & Stiefel, L. (2007). Immigrant and native born differences in school stability and special education: Evidence from New York City. *International Migration Review, 41*(2), 403–432.

Crosnoe, R. (2005). Double disadvantage or sins of resilience: The elementary school contexts of children from Mexican immigrant families. *American Educational Research Journal, 42,* 269–303.

Dunn, L. (1968). Special education for the mildly retarded: Is much of it justifiable? *Exceptional Children, 35,* 5–22.

Education for All Handicapped Children Act of 1975, 20 U.S.C. § 1400 et seq. (1975).

Ford, B. A., & Reynolds, C. (2001). Connecting with community resources: Optimizing the potential of multicultural learners with mild disabilities. In C. A. Utley & F. E. Obiakor (Eds.), *Special education, multicultural education, and school reform: Components of quality education for learners with mild disabilities* (pp. 208–227). Springfield, IL: Charles C. Thomas.

Glick, J. E., & Hohmann-Marriott, B. (2007). Academic performance of young children in immigrant families: The significance of race, ethnicity, and national origins. *The International Migration Review, 41*(2), 371–403.

Glick, J. E., & White, M. J. (2003). The academic trajectories of immigrant youths: Analysis within and across cohorts. *Demography, 40*(4), 759–783.

Guillaume, A. M., Zuniga-Hill, C., & Yee, I. (1995). Prospective teachers' use of diversity issues in a case study analysis. *Journal of Research and Development in Education, 28,* 69–78.

Haberman, M. (1995). *Star teachers of children in poverty.* West Lafayette, IN: Kappa Delta Pi.

Individuals with Disabilities Education Act (1990, 1991, 1997, 1999). 20 USC §1400 *et. seq.* (statute); 34 CFR 300 (regulations), Regulations Implementing IDEA (1997) (*Federal Register,* 1999, March 12, 1999, vol. 64, no. 48).

Individuals with Disabilities Education Improvement Act (2004). 20 USC § 1400 et seq. (2004).

Kao, G., & Thompson, J. S. (2003). Racial and ethnic stratification in educational achievement and attainment. *Annual Review of Sociology, 29,* 417–442.

Kozol, J. (1991). *Savage inequalities: Children in American schools.* New York: Crown.

Larrivee, B. (1992). *Strategies for effective classroom management: Creating a collaborative climate. Leader's guide to facilitate learning experiences.* Boston: Allyn & Bacon.

Lew, J. (2007). A structural analysis of success and failure of Asian Americans: A case of Korean Americans in urban schools. *Teachers College Record, 109(2),* 369–390.

Lovitt, T. (2000). *Preventing school failure: Tactics for teaching adolescents* (2nd ed.). Austin, TX: Pro-Ed.

McAllister, G., & Irvine, J. (2000). Cultural competency and multicultural teacher education. *Review of Educational Research, 70*(1), 3–24.

National Academy Council, Institute of Medicine (1997). *Improving schooling for language-minority children: A research agenda.* Washington, DC: Author.

National Research Council. (2002). *Minority students in special and gifted education.* Washington, DC: National Academic Press.

Obiakor, F. E. (1999, Fall). Teacher expectations of minority exceptional learners: Impact on accuracy of self-concepts. *Exceptional Children, 66,* 39–53.

Obiakor, F. E. (2001). *It even happens in "good" schools: Responding to cultural diversity in today's classrooms.* Thousand Oaks, CA: Corwin Press.

Obiakor, F. E. (2007). Multicultural special education: Effective intervention for today's schools. *Intervention in School and Clinic, 42,* 148–155.

Obiakor, F. E. (2008). *The eight-step approach to multicultural learning and teaching* (3rd ed.). Dubuque, IA: Kendall/Hunt.

Obiakor, F. E., & Afolayan, M. O., (2007, July). African immigrant families in the United States: Surviving the sociocultural tide. *The Family Journal: Counseling and Therapy for Couples and Families, 15,* 265–270.

Obiakor, F. E., & Beachum, F. D. (2005). *Urban education for the 21st century: Research, issues, and perspectives.* Springfield, IL: Charles C. Thomas.

Obiakor, F. E., Grant, P. A., & Dooley, E. A. (2002). *Educating all learners: The comprehensive support model.* Springfield, IL: Charles C. Thomas.

Obiakor, F. E., Grant, P., & Obi, S.O. (2010). *Voices of foreign-born teacher educators in the United States.* New York: Nova Science Publishers.

Obiakor, F. E., Harris-Obiakor, P., Obi, S. O., & Eskay, M. (2000). Urban learners in general and special education programs: Revisiting assessment and intervention issues. In F. E. Obiakor, S. A. Burkhardt, A. F. Rotatori, & T. Wahlberg (Eds.), *Advances in special education: Intervention techniques for individuals with exceptionalities in inclusive settings* (pp. 115–131). Stamford, CT: JAI Press.

Obiakor, F. E., Harris-Obiakor, P., & Smith, R. (2002). The comprehensive support model for all learners: Conceptualization and meaning. In F. E. Obiakor, P. A. Grant, & E. A. Dooley (Eds.), *Educating all learners: Refocusing the comprehensive support model* (pp. 3–17). Springfield, IL: Charles C. Thomas.

Obiakor, F. E., & McCollin, M. (2011). Using the comprehensive support model to work with culturally and linguistically diverse students with learning disabilities. *Learning Disabilities: A Contemporary Journal, 9*(1), 19–32.

Obiakor, F. E., & Utley, C. A. (1997). Rethinking preservice preparation for teachers in the learning disabilities field: Workable multicultural strategies. *Learning Disabilities Research & Practice, 12*(2), 100–106.

Obiakor, F. E., Utley, C. A., & Smith, R. (2002). The comprehensive support model for culturally diverse exceptional learners: Intervention in an age of change. *Intervention in School and Clinic, 38*(1), 14–27.

Perreira, K. M., Chapman, M. V., & Stein, G. L. (2006). Overcoming challenges and finding strength in a new immigrant Latino community. *Journal of Family Issues, 27*(10), 1383–1414.

Perreira, K. M., Harris, K. M., & Lee, D. (2006). Making it in America: High school completion by immigrant and native immigrant youth. *Demography, 43*(3), 511–536.

Perreira, K. M., Harris, K. M., & Lee, D. (2007). Immigrant youth in the labor market. *Work Publications, 34*(1). Sage.

Peterson, R. (1992). *Life in a crowded place: Making a learning community.* Portsmouth, NH: Heinenman.

Plessy v. Ferguson, 163 U.S. 537 (1896).

Suarez-Orozco, C., & Qin, D. B., (2006). Gendered perspectives in psychology: Immigrant origin youth. *International Migration Review, 40,* 165–198.

Suarez-Orozco, C., Suarez-Orozco, M. M., & Todorova, T. (2008). *Learning a new land: Immigrant students in American society.* Cambridge, MA: Harvard University Press.

U.S. Census Bureau. (2010). *American community survey.* Washington, DC: Author.

Utley, C. A., & Obiakor, F. E. (2001). Learning problems or learning disabilities of multicultural learners: Contemporary perspectives. In C. A. Utley & F. E. Obiakor (Eds.), *Special education, multicultural education, and school reform: Components of quality education for learners with mild disabilities* (pp. 90–117). Springfield, IL: Charles C. Thomas.

Van Hook, J., Brown, S. L., & Kwenda, M. (2004). A decomposition of trends in poverty among children of immigrants. *Demography, 41,* 649–670.

CHAPTER 9

PREPARING TEACHERS AND ADMINISTRATORS TO EDUCATE MULTICULTURAL LEARNERS WITH SPECIAL NEEDS

Floyd D. Beachum and Carlos R. McCray

The claim that we are living in a post-racial world and we are past civil-rights move-ment, it seems to me to be a cover for the problems that have reasserted themselves. We are quite a long, long, long, way from right racial reconciliation, racial justice, or participatory democracy or a fair and democratic society.

Ayers as cited in Brooks, 2012

This troubling quote underscores the ongoing social problems we face in today's society. Not only do the problems of racism, sexism, income in-equality, ableism, and others manifest themselves in society in general, they also manifest themselves in K–12 education, in particular. Moreover, this quote reminds us of the difficult and ongoing balance between educational excellence and equity. The purpose of this chapter is to advocate for cul-turally relevant teaching and leadership approaches and provide practical recommendations for teachers and administrators.

Multicultural Education for Learners with Special Needs in the Twenty-First Century, pages 137–147

DEMOGRAPHIC DIVERSITY IN K–12 SCHOOLS

The student population of K–12 schools in the United States has become more diverse in terms of race/ethnicity. This has direct and indirect implications for curricula, teaching strategies, resource allocation, and leadership approaches. "While children of color constituted about one-third of the student population in 1995, they are expected to become the numerical majority by 2035. This change will render the expression 'minority students' statistically inaccurate. By 2050, so-called minorities will collectively account for nearly 57 percent of the population" (Villegas & Lucas, 2002, p. 3). In places such as California, Hawaii, Mississippi, New Mexico, Texas, and the District of Columbia, culturally and linguistically diverse (CLD) students have become the majority with regard to K–12 student enrollments (National Center for Educational Statistics, 1998). Part of the issue here is that while the student population is becoming more diverse, the current cadre of teachers (Mizialko, 2005) and administrators (Tillman, 2003) in schools are overwhelmingly white. The result could be more cultural insensitivity, underteaching, and apathetic leadership. This is not to propose that only CLD teachers can teach CLD students or that white teachers can only teach white students. CLD teachers too, can have low expectations of CLD students (Kunjufu, 2002). This is why the expectations, attitudes, and beliefs of teachers and administrators are so important. Some schools have dealt with these issues for so long that "cultures of failure" have developed. Similarly, these same defeatist attitudes have hindered the progress of students with special needs.

THE INCLUSION OF STUDENTS WITH SPECIAL NEEDS

Modern inclusive practices in special education have a long history rooted in civil rights and educational legislation. The need to include students with special needs in schools was first highlighted in *Brown v. the Board of Education* in 1954 where the Supreme Court ruled that separate education was not equal. Although originally focused on segregation of schools between Black and white students, this ruling ignited families of students with special needs to advocate legally for the education of their children. As a result, in 1971 the *Pennsylvania Association for Retarded Children (PARC) v. Pennsylvania* case resulted in a declaration that a free and appropriate public education (FAPE) must be made available to all students regardless of academic or intellectual differences. Success continued for individuals with special needs with the passing of the Education for all Handicapped Children Act in 1975. This law (PL 94–142) has evolved over the years to become the Individuals with Disabilities Education Act (IDEA) of 1990; now the Individuals with Disabilities Education Improvement Act (IDEIA) of 2004. Today, IDEIA focuses on six core principles, namely: (a) to provide a FAPE to all students, (b) to implement a zero-reject framework for special education where no student can be turned away from a public education, (c) to educate students in the least restrictive environment (LRE) where they can succeed, (d) to provide multiple modes of assessment when classifying students to receive special education services, (e) to develop and individualize education plan (IEP) for all students in special education that meets their unique needs, and (f) to allow for due process when parents or students do not believe they are receiving the best education available. Together these principles provide students with special needs a fair, inclusive, and quality education. Furthermore, IDEIA provides specific categories of disabilities recognized federally and ensures that parents and students both have rights to be involved in the educational process. With IDEA, students with special needs are educated in public schools and receive the same valuable education as their nondisabled peers.

The historical context above allows educators and service providers to gain insight into how special educational originated. The next step is to examine its evolution. Special education students, much like CLD students, are many times alienated for being different because of ability status (Kunjufu, 2005; Obiakor, 2001). The result is a hierarchical system, in which students with special needs students get segregated from their peers. For CLD students with special needs students of color (especially in urban areas), this becomes double jeopardy as they pay the penalty for their race/ethnicity and ability status. In the words of Frattura and Topinka (2006):

> We educators consistently facilitate societal oppression through educational practices in support of separateness and then mystify it in nondiscriminatory acts that often discriminate through the very application of their regulations; that is, in school systems across our country, we have constructed a normed group of students whom we label "general education students." By the very nature of the title, we also have defaulted to another group of students, loosely labeled as nongeneral education students. Nongeneral education students are those students who do not meet the criteria of academic, physical, emotional, social, or behavioral success of the normed or dominant group, the general education students. (p. 327)

Scholarship supports the idea that CLD students are disproportionately placed in special education. Urban CLD students are many times misidentified, misassessed, mislabeled, miscategorized, misplaced, and misinstructed (Obiakor, Obiakor, Garza-Nelson, & Randall, 2005). Kunjufu (2005) noted that "African American males make up only 8% of the public school student population but constitute almost 30% of the students placed in special education" (p. vi). In general, these students are placed into special education more often than their white peers, especially within specific disability classifications (Harry, 1992; Kunjufu, 2001). Furthermore, the instrumentation and assessment tools utilized to measure many of these students' intelligence are sometimes used as a mechanism for misidentification and misplacement (Obiakor & Ford, 2002). The subjective impressions and perceptions which lead to overidentification are evident in negative teacher attitudes and low expectations for these students (Obiakor, Harris, & Beachum, 2009). Thus, as public education pushes for greater inclusion and accountability, it sometimes sacrifices many schools in urban communities, overlooking or stigmatizing vulnerable student populations.

CULTURALLY RELEVANT PEDAGOGY/TEACHING

There was a time in most U.S. schools when the delivery of instruction was only based on the discretion of the teacher. In many cases, the approach to teaching became boring, rudimentary, predictable, and in some cases, biased, intolerant, and racist (Beachum & McCray, 2012; Singleton & Linton, 2006; Tatum, 1997; Wagner, 2001). As a result scholars began to advocate for teaching approaches that are more aligned with the experiences and backgrounds of the students being taught. In its earlier stages, educators simply tried to integrate multicultural content into the existing curriculum, but this turned out to be ineffective (Cuban, 1972). It became evident that specific teaching approaches were needed to address the needs of racially and ethnically diverse student populations.

The notion of "culturally relevant pedagogy" came from the work of Gloria Ladson-Billings (1994). While studying highly effective African American teachers, she found that they fostered strong equity-based relationships with students, encouraged student's to take responsibility for their education, and had a passion for teaching. Ladson-Billings (1995) indicated a culturally relevant pedagogy had features such as:

1. Students must experience academic success.
2. Students must develop and/or maintain cultural competence.
3. Students must develop a critical consciousness through which they challenge the status quo of the current social order. (p. 160)

Thus, culturally relevant pedagogy should be integrated into the curriculum by "empowering students intellectually, socially, emotionally, and politically" (Ladson-Billings, 1994, p. 18).

Culturally Relevant Leadership

Leadership in today's schools requires innovative thinking, an understanding of sociocultural context, and the ability to interact with diverse communities, at the same time dealing with mandates and ambiguity; while this is not an easy task, school leaders cannot just keep on "doing things the way we have always done them." Therefore, we suggest what is known as culturally relevant leadership (see Beachum, 2011; Beachum & McCray, 2012). Specifically, it is founded on three tenets: liberatory consciousness, pluralistic insight, and reflexive practice.

Liberatory Consciousness

Liberatory consciousness is similar to critical consciousness which focuses on raising levels of awareness and knowledge toward the goal of liberty and equity for all people. The consciousness element shows that all educators are not conscious of the inequities in the American educational system. According to Villegas and Lucas (2002) "awareness of the pervasiveness and longevity of the inequities in schools and of the structures and practices that perpetuate them can be disheartening for prospective teachers [and administrators]. But it is essential that they recognize these realities. If they see schools through the rose-colored glasses of the meritocratic myth, they will unwittingly perpetuate inequities" (p. 58). Teachers and administrators should seriously work on raising consciousness levels to recognize the need for excellence and equity in education (Beachum & Obiakor, 2005). Furthermore, educators should find opportunities to expand their ideological, intellectual, and practical horizons with regard to educational equity and racial/ethnic diversity.

Pluralistic Insight

Pluralistic insight emphasizes a school leader's attitudes toward students. "It leans toward an affirming and positive notion of students (especially CLD students) that acknowledges the uniqueness of their experiences and their rich diversity" (McCray & Beachum, 2011, p. 92). The reality is that educators' (teachers and school leaders) expectations, attitudes, and dispositions are important components of the educational process (Irvine, 1990; Kunjufu, 2002; Obiakor, 2001; Tatum, 2007). This is extremely important because

> Regardless of our own racial or ethnic backgrounds, we have all been exposed to racial stereotypes and flawed educational psychology, and unless we are consciously working to counter their influence on our behavior, it is likely that they will shape (subtly perhaps) our interactions with those who have been so stereotyped. (Tatum, 2007, p. 52)

Ergo, school leaders must be willing to examine their own biases and attitudes to make sure they are making decisions that will be for the best of all students. Beachum (2011) stated that, "Culturally relevant leaders should assist people in the organization to understand themselves and their students. This requires not only the appropriate knowledge base, but also the proper attitude especially when working with students of color and/or of different cultures/backgrounds" (p. 32).

Reflexive Practice

The last tenet of Culturally Relevant Leadership is Reflexive Practice. It positions school leaders as "change agents who engage in ongoing praxis (reflection and action) for increased student success" (McCray & Beachum, 2011, p. 92). This third concept highlights leadership actions. Consequently, "the work of the educator is not viewed as strictly objective, but rather educators' work is connected to the surrounding community of the school and the external society at large" (Beachum, 2011, p. 33). Earlier, Singleton and Linton (2006) explained that educators should make sure that "the administration leads the effort to reach out to all parents and members of the community" (p. 227). In addition, a diversity-conscious school is a place where

> Parents and other community members do not feel disfranchised nor do they feel intimidated due to their own personal educational attainment, English language skills, racial description, economic status, dress, or perceptions of school derived from their own personal experiences. Families know that their voice matters in school affairs. (Singleton & Linton, 2006, p. 227)

Moreover, leaders model ethical behavior, collaboration, and self-assessment in an effort to attract others into a process of "self-exploration, commitment, and growth" (Quinn & Snyder, 1999, p. 169).

LEADERSHIP FOR THE FUTURE

Leadership in the future must be culturally relevant. School leaders must start with themselves, by opening and freeing their minds through liberatory consciousness. Next, they must address negative images, stereotypes, and messages which should result in a change in attitude as discussed in pluralistic insight. Finally, they must begin to carry out daily tasks differently according to reflexive practice. Following are some suggestions/ideas for using culturally relevant leadership in practice as suggested in Beachum and McCray (2012, pp. 241–242):

Teachers and leaders should:

- *Encourage and support diverse teaching methods.* Leaders must challenge teachers to explore multiple ways of teaching and learning. This would require school leaders to allow room for experimentation and possible *implementation dips.* An implementation dip is a temporary drop in performance when a new innovation is used (Fullan, 2004). School leaders must play more of a supportive role in instructional leadership and not just evaluative. In this kind of environment, teachers must be allowed to investigate, inspire, experiment, reflect, revise, relearn, and change with the approval of administration. At the same time, they must be held accountable because their goal is student success.

- *Create thoughtful learning communities that focus on student learning.* The notion of teachers sharing teaching strategies, having collaborative planning time, and collectively looking at student data is a relatively new phenomenon. For many years, teachers operated in silos within their own classrooms, fostering a closed culture marked by isolation and autonomy (Wagner, 2001). The duty to educate all students according to empirical evidence means that the old ways of operating must be revisited. School leaders must work to create the time and space for teachers to collaborate as well as organize professional development activities around student learning (Hord & Sommers, 2008). A practice-based activity for teachers is a concept called *lesson study* (see http://www.tc.edu/lessonstudy/index.html), where teachers work together in planning a lesson.

- *Share leadership opportunities and value multiple voices.* Culturally relevant leaders must look for opportunities to build leadership capacity among teachers. More specifically, this means identifying and encouraging others to take on more responsibilities, speak to broader audiences, and think beyond their immediate classrooms. Similarly, it is important that school leaders value the voices of all in the organization. "The administration and faculty together set the standards that the teachers work to achieve. Through their collaboration, they experience the freedom, ownership, and accountability they need to accomplish the job" (Singleton & Linton, 2006, p. 227). This requires the leader to make space even for dissent (not disrespect).

Fullan (2004) reminded us that skeptics can be valuable in the organization because they remind us of things we may have overlooked. Skeptics are different from cynics who, on the other hand, tend to be negative and undermine the organization's mission.

- *Connect the school with the community.* Schools are often intricately connected to the communities in which they reside. Thus, educational leaders must support efforts to involve the community-at-large in the life of the school. "Schools can never divorce themselves from the communities where they exist" (Swaminathan, 2005, p. 195). Educational leaders must create opportunities for dialogue, invite speakers, host events, and build coalitions with the external community.

CONCLUSION

Culturally relevant leadership has the potential to impact educational theory and practice. In reference to theory, it builds on a well-grounded literature base in culturally relevant pedagogy (Ladson-Billings, 1994, 1995; Howard, 2003) and culturally responsive teaching (Gay, 2000). With regard to practice, it has implications for both teachers and administrators. For teacher leaders, it encourages continuous personal/professional development in raising ones levels of consciousness and awareness with regard to working with CLD students. It also recognizes the fundamental humanity of all students and the fact that they should be affirmed, supported, and included despite race/ethnicity and ability status (English, 2002; Obiakor, Harris, & Beachum, 2009). Finally, it suggests that these educators identify and address instances of individual and institutional bias in the school. For educational administrators, the lessons from culturally relevant leadership include creating a school culture/climate of inclusion where all students feel welcomed and affirmed. Cox (2001) suggested that leaders who are serious about diversity seek to create multicultural organizations. This type of organization has well-managed diversity that results in improved problem solving, increased creativity and innovation, increased organizational flexibility, and better recruitment and retention.

Finally, culturally relevant leadership is informed by liberatory consciousness, pluralistic insight, and reflexive practice. It builds upon a long line of multicultural and diversity-related research but yet expands into new pedagogical landscapes to inform the work of teacher leaders and administrators to improve the entire school. Culturally relevant leadership can be a useful way to involve and engage CLD students and support and accept students with disabilities. In the end, we must be guided by the insightful words of Landsman and Lewis (2011) when they wrote:

In 10 years, the majority of our students will be of color. Our job then, as educators and change makers, is no less important than the healthy future of our young people and our world. And let it be forgotten, White students, as well as those students of color have a great amount to gain from equity for all. For the sake of all of our children we must follow up our reading with action and our contemplation with change. (pp. 7–8)

REFERENCES

Beachum, F. D. (2011). Culturally relevant leadership for complex 21st century school contexts. In F. W. English (Ed.), *Sage encyclopedia of educational leadership and administration* (2nd ed.). Thousand Oaks, CA: SAGE.

Beachum, F. D., & McCray, C. R. (2012). The fast and the serious: Exploring the notion of culturally relevant leadership. In J. Moore & C. W. Lewis (Eds.). *Urban school contexts for African American students: Crisis and prospects for improvement* (pp. 231–247). New York, NY: Peter Lang.

Beachum, F. D., & Obiakor, F. E. (2005). Educational leadership in urban schools. In F. E. Obiakor & F. D. Beachum (Eds.), *Urban education for the 21st century: Research, issues, and perspectives* (pp. 83–99). Springfield, IL: Charles C. Thomas.

Brooks, J. S. (2012). *Black school. White school: Racism and educational (mis)leadership.* New York, NY: Teachers College Press.

Brown v. Board of Education, Topeka, 347 U.S. 483,74S, Ct.686, 91 L. Ed.873 (1954).

Cox, T., Jr. (2001). *Creating the multicultural organization: A strategy for capturing the power of diversity.* San Francisco: Jossey-Bass.

Cuban, L. (1972). Ethnic content and "white" instruction. *Phi Delta Kappan, 53,* 270–273.

Education of All Handicapped Children Act (P.L. 94–142) (1975).

English, F. W. (2002). On the intractability of the achievement gap in urban schools and the discursive practice of continuing racial discrimination. *Education and Urban Society, 34*(3), 298–311.

Frattura, E. M., & Topinka, C. (2006). Theoretical underpinnings of separate educational programs: The social justice challenge continues. *Education & Urban Society, 38*(3), 327–344.

Fullan, M. (2004). *Leading in a culture of change: Personal action guide and workbook.* San Francisco: Jossey-Bass.

Gay, G. (2000). *Culturally responsive teaching: Theory, research, and practice.* New York, NY: Teachers College Press.

Harry, B. (1992). *Cultural diversity, families, and the special education system: Communication and empowerment.* New York, NY: Teachers College Press.

Hord, S. M., & Sommers, W. A. (2008). *Leading professional learning communities: Voices from research and practice.* Thousand Oakes, CA: Corwin Press.

Howard, T. C. (2003). Telling their side of the story: African American students' perceptions of culturally relevant teaching. *The Urban Review, 33*(2), 131–149.

Individuals with Disabilities Education Act of 1990 (Pub. L. No. 101–476, 104 Stat. 1142).

Individuals with Disabilities Education Improvement Act of 2004, 20 U.S. C. & 1400 et seq. (2005).

Irvine, J. J. (1990). *Black students and school failure.* New York, NY: Greenwood Press.

Kunjufu, J. (2001). *State of emergency: We must save African American males.* Chicago: African American Images.

Kunjufu, J. (2002). *Black students–Middle class teachers.* Chicago: African American Images.

Kunjufu, J. (2005). *Keeping black boys out of special education.* Chicago: African American Images.

Ladson-Billings, G. (1994). *The dreamkeepers: Successful teachers of African-American students.* San Francisco: Jossey-Bass.

Ladson-Billings, G. (1995). But that's just good teaching! The case for culturally relevant pedagogy. *Theory into Practice, 34,* 159–165.

Landsman, J., & Lewis, C. W. (Eds.) (2011). A call to action and self-reflection for White teachers in diverse classrooms. In J. L. Landsman & C. W. Lewis (Eds.), *White teachers/diverse classrooms: Creating inclusive schools, building on students' diversity, and providing true educational equity.* (2nd ed.), (pp. 1–8). Sterling, VA: Stylus.

McCray, C. R., & Beachum, F. D. (2011). Capital matters: A pedagogy of self-development: Making room for alternative forms of capital. In R. Bartee (Ed.). *Contemporary perspectives on capital in educational context* (pp. 79–100). Charlotte, NC: Information Age Publishing.

Mizialko, A. (2005). Reducing the power of 'whiteness' in urban schools. In F. E. Obiakor & F. D. Beachum (Eds.), *Urban education for the 21st century: Research, issues, and perspectives* (pp. 176–186). Springfield, IL: Charles C. Thomas.

National Center for Education Statistics (1998). *Data file:1996–97 common core of data public elementary and secondary school universe.* Washington, DC: U. S. Government Printing Office.

Obiakor, F. E. (2001). *It even happens in "good" schools: Responding to cultural diversity in today's classrooms.* Thousand Oaks, CA: Corwin Press.

Obiakor, F. E., & Ford, B. A. (2002). *Creating successful learning environments for African American learners with exceptionalities.* Thousand Oaks, CA: Corwin Press.

Obiakor, F. E., Harris, M. K., & Beachum, F. D. (2009). The state of special education for African American learners in Milwaukee. In G. L. Williams & F. E. Obiakor (Eds.), *The state of education of urban learners and possible solutions: The Milwaukee experience* (pp. 31–48). Dubuque, IA: Kendall Hunt.

Obiakor, F. E., Obiakor, P. H., Garza-Nelson, C., & Randall, P. (2005). Educating urban learners with and without special needs: Life after the *Brown* case. In F. E. Obiakor & F. D. Beachum (Eds.), *Urban education for the 21st century: Research, issues, and perspectives* (pp. 20–33). Springfield, IL: Charles C. Thomas.

Pennsylvania Association for Retarded Children v. Commonwealth 334 F. Supp. 1257 (E.D. PA 1971) and 343 F. Supp. 279 (E.D. PA. 1972).

Quinn, R. E., & Snyder, N. T. (1999). Advanced Change Theory: Culture Change at Whirlpool Corporation. In J.A. Conger, G.M. Speitzer, & E.E. Lawler III (Eds.), *The leader's change handbook: An essential guide to setting direction & taking action* (pp. 162–194). San Francisco: Jossey-Bass.

Singleton, G. E., & Linton, C. (2006). *Courageous conversations about race: A field guide or achieving equity in schools.* Thousand Oaks, CA: Corwin Press.

Swaminathan, R. (2005). Building community in urban schools: Promises and challenges. In F. E. Obiakor, & F. D. Beachum (Eds.), *Urban education for the 21st century: Research, issues, and perspectives* (pp. 187–198). Springfield, IL: Charles C. Thomas.

Tatum, B. D. (1997). *Why are all the Black kids sitting together in the cafeteria? And other conversations about race.* New York, NY: Basic Books.

Tatum, B. D. (2007). *Can we talk about race? And other conversations in an era of school resegregation.* Boston, MA: Beacon Press.

Tillman, L. C. (2003, Fall). From rhetoric to reality? Educational administration and the lack of racial and ethnic diversity within the profession. *University Council for Educational Review, 14*(3), 1–4.

Villegas, A. M., & Lucas, T. (2002). *Educating culturally responsive teachers: A coherent approach.* Albany: State University of New York Press.

Wagner, T. (2001). Leadership for learning: An action theory of school change. *Phi Delta Kappan, 82,* 378–383.

CHAPTER 10

USING TECHNOLOGY TO EDUCATE MULTICULTURAL LEARNERS WITH SPECIAL NEEDS

Howard P. Parette, Jr. and Jeffrey P. Bakken

Multicultural education has been described as "equal educational opportunities" afforded students from diverse racial, ethnic, social class, and cultural groups (Banks, 1997). Considerable variation in the values, preferences, and learning styles of students from such groups, particularly those with disabilities, has been reported (Kalyanpur & Harry, 1999; Parette, 1998; Parette, Huer, & Peterson-Karlan, 2008). Based on a continually evolving understanding of these students, multicultural educational practices have also been described to provide guidance to education professionals (Banks & Banks, 2001; Grant & Ray, 2010; Obiakor, 2007; Trumbull, Rothstein-Fisch, Greenfield, & Quiroz, 2001). These practices should create opportunities for active, interactive, and engaging learning, and emphasize critical and creative thinking, learning skills, and social awareness as well as facts and figures (Gorski, 2001).

Multicultural Education for Learners with Special Needs in the Twenty-First Century, pages 149–174

TECHNOLOGY AND MULTICULTURAL EDUCATION

Important in the delivery of 21st century curricula to multicultural students with disabilities is the use of varying technologies (Bakken & Parette, 2007; Clark, 2008; Parette & Peterson-Karlan, 2010a; Peterson-Karlan & Parette, 2005; Torres, 2009). Depending on the purpose of the technologies and how they are used by or with multicultural students with disabilities, they generally fall into three distinct categories: (a) information and communication technology (ICT), (b) instructional technology (IT), and (c) assistive technology (AT).

ICT technologies are enablers of core 21st century learning skills (International ICT Literacy Panel, 2007), and students increasingly use them to communicate and collaborate with others, problem solve, find information, and manage their lives more effectively or efficiently (Parette & Peterson-Karlan, 2010a). Examples include photocopy machines, word processing and graphics software, Microsoft® PowerPoint™, cell phones, text messaging, blogs, Wikis, and the Internet. Instructional technology (IT) includes tools that increase instructional (a) effectiveness (i.e., learning in a better way than without the technology-supported experience), (b) efficiency (i.e., learning faster), and (c) appeal (i.e., increases possibility that students will devote time and energy to the learning task, Peterson-Karlan & Parette, 2005). Examples of IT include computers, DVDs, LCD projectors, digital audio and video recording or editing devices or software used by teachers to prepare or present information, interactive whiteboards, educational software, and hand-held devices (e.g., iPods).

Many of the ICT and IT tools used in today's classrooms have been described as being readily available (Blum, Parette, & Travers, 2011; Parette, 2011a, b). That is, these technologies reflect Web 2.0 features (e.g., interactivity with users, provide means to add and edit content), that are accessible as free and downloadable software or available as a premade activity at a Web site (e.g., Cambium Learning, 2006; Crick Software, Inc., 2011; South Carolina ETV Commission, 2011), or can be purchased locally (e.g., digital cameras, iPad, iPod, Smartphone, apps; Blum, Parette et al., 2011; Parette, 2011a, b). Both ICT and IT tools enable the education professional to more effectively and efficiently design and deliver individual, small-, and large-group instruction, though multicultural students with disabilities will often need additional supports, or AT, to participate in these classroom activities. AT devices include an array of technologies that can help a multicultural student perform tasks he or she could not do otherwise at some expected level of performance (Parette, Peterson-Karlan, Wojcik, & Bardi, 2007). Examples of AT devices include visual schedules, graphic organizers, electronic communication systems, wheelchairs, hearing devices, text-to-speech software, talking word processors, and seating and positioning systems. Bakken and Parette (2007) discussed issues related to both IT and AT use with multicultural students, with an emphasis on family involvement in decision-making, understanding a family's value system, and recognizing important cultural background variables that might influence children and families (e.g., cooperation vs. personal achievement–the importance of holidays). While ICT and IT have their role in supporting the learning experiences of all students—both typical and those from multicultural backgrounds who have disabilities—AT is of particular importance since it helps to "level the playing field" regarding educational opportunity.

AT AND FLOOR OF OPPORTUNITY

Almost three decades ago, the concept of an educational "floor of opportunity" for students with disabilities was established in the landmark Supreme Court case, *Hedrick Hudson School District v. Rowley* (1982). This case clarified that schools must provide services ensuring that all children with disabilities have the opportunity to participate in the curriculum (Parette & Peterson-Karlan, 2010b; Sullivan & Thorius, 2010). Parette and Peterson-Karlan (2010b) observed that, by definition, students with disabilities must have compensatory supports for such a floor of opportunity to be present, thus enabling them to participate effectively in the curriculum. The No Child Left Behind Act of 2001 certainly articulated the need for such opportunity, given the importance of narrowing the achievement gap between "high and low performing children, especially the achievement gap between minority and nonminority students, and between disadvantaged children and their more advantaged peers" [20 U.S.C. § 6301(3)]. Similarly, the Individuals with Disabilities Education Improvement Act Amendments (IDEIA) of 2004 mirrored this concern for a floor of educational opportunity (i.e., an "equal educational opportunity"; 20 U.S.C. § 1400(c) (7))].

To create such a floor for educational opportunity, an assumption is that education professionals have an "understanding" of environments in which educational services are provided (Bakken & Parette, 2007; Grant & Ray, 2010; Parette & Peterson-Karlan, 2010a). This theoretically assumes some degree of understanding regarding differences that exist among students across cultural groups. If such an understanding were in place, education professionals could then make educational decisions regarding curricula delivery based on sensitivity to all learners. In the process of developing an individual education program (IEP) for any student with disabilities, collaboration among an array of team members is required. The IEP process culminates in a plan that guides the delivery of special education services for the student having a disability. Consideration is also given to the student's participation in the general education curriculum [20 U.S.C. § 1400(c) (5) (a)].

The very nature of the IEP process and team members' involvement with families from multicultural backgrounds reflects an intersection of cultures, and thus an intersection of *difference* (Sullivan & Thorius, 2010). Such an intersection also creates the potential for "dissonance," or divergence of individuals along lines of values, experiences, and expectations (Kemp & Parette, 2000; Parette, Huer, & VanBiervliet, 2005). This may be further compounded by intergenerational differences between parents and family members and their children with disabilities as a result of acculturation (i.e., the degree to which values and behaviors change in response to changes in society; Parette, Huer, & Scherer, 2004; Parette et al., 2005). For example, one has but to use the example of technology changes in our society to understand the marked generational differences in preferences for and use of technology in 21st century settings. Peterson-Karlan and Parette (2005) provided a succinct description of how students with disabilities have been broadly acculturated to the presence of both IT and ICT in our society, as well AT availability and its use in home and educational settings. Multicultural students with disabilities also have increasingly had both access to and preferences for a range of technologies in their daily lives, including Smartphones, iPods, iPads, and computers (Griffiths, 2010; Mesch, 2011; Wilson, 2011). These technologies, however, cannot be fully understood and decisions made from a multicultural perspective without understanding the nature of "activities" in children's classrooms and the "demands" placed on students (Parette & Peterson-Karlan, 2010a). Any activity within a classroom places physical, cognitive, and/or social/linguistic demands of students. How these demands are met will be contingent upon the multicultural perspective of the student (i.e., the degree to which technology acculturation has occurred, the nature of ICT and IT supports provided in the classroom, and preferences for learning) and the AT supports needed to ensure that specific tasks can be completed in classrooms (see Bray, Brown, & Green, 2004; Cools, Evans, & Redmond, 2009).

Assistive Technology Decision-Making

In the process of developing an IEP, all team members have the additional responsibility of "considering" assistive technology (AT) devices for each student with a disability [20 U.S.C. § 1401 § 614(B)(v)]. AT devices include an array of technologies that can help a student perform tasks he or she could not do otherwise at some expected level of performance (Parette et al., 2007). AT services, such as evaluations, student and/or family training, and professional development, are also a required consideration when appropriate [20 U.S.C. 1401 § 602(2)]. Numerous resources are available to assist education professionals in the AT consideration process to more effectively identify and integrate assistive technology devices and services into the curricula for students with disabilities (Center for Technology in Education, Johns Hopkins University; and Technology & Media Division [TAM] of the Council for Exceptional Children, 2005; Cook & Hussey, 2002; Dell, Newton, & Petroff, 2008; King, 1999; Parette & Peterson-Karlan, 2010a; Sadao & Robinson, 2010).

As with the IEP process more broadly, AT consideration is couched in an operational assumption that team members understand each multicultural student's (a) educational environment, and (b) his or her abilities and challenges in meeting the demands of activities within the classroom (Bakken & Parette, 2007; Parette et al., 2005). Sensitivity to the preferences and needs expressed by family members across cultural groups are certainly critical components of AT consideration (Parette et al., 2005), and finds support in the language of the IDEIA (2004). For example, the language of the IDEIA states that AT services may include "evaluation of the child's needs, including a functional evaluation of the child in his or her customary environment [emphasis added]" [20 U.S.C. 1401 § 602(2) (A)]. This language could be interpreted to broadly include a wide range of culturally-relevant values, preferences, and child/family characteristics. Understanding of any student's abilities and the subsequent identification of appropriate AT devices and services cannot be made absent some awareness of important cultural influences on the student and family (Bakken & Parette, 2007; Kemp & Parette, 2000; Parette, Huer et al., 2004). For example, some AT tools, such as electronic augmentative and alternative communication devices, may draw attention to themselves when used in public settings. From the family perspective of some multicultural groups, "fitting in" and not being perceived as being "different" would be more important than the perceived benefits held by education professionals regarding use of a particular device (Wilson, 2011). Noted in Table 10.1 are family values which may potentially assist education professionals during AT decision making when working with students from varying multicultural backgrounds. Such cultural group preferences must be viewed with caution, as articulated differences in perceptions of and needs for assistive technology previously reported were based on cultural focus group research conducted more than a decade ago (cf. Parette, Brotherson, & Huer, 2000; Parette, Huer, & Brotherson, 2001).

Given what we know about the ubiquitous nature of technology in 21st century settings, the relevance of some of this earlier thinking is questionable. What may be even more important than comparing differences among students across cultural groups is recognition that all students with disabilities in 21st century classroom settings have grown up with a vast

TABLE 10.1   Cultural Group Preferences Potentially Affecting Technology Decision-Making for Students With Disabilities

Euro-American	African-American	Asian-American	Hispanic-American	Native American
Families may: • Prefer technology that does not make children look different to extended family members • Want to minimize stress of integrating devices into home life, forcing them to choose between quality of life issues and technology usage • Want to be taught how to teach their children to use devices • Desire specific and ongoing training to ensure that they can use technologies with children effectively • Want community to use technologies with their children • Want technologies that make children more independent and socially accepted • Change their perceptions of technologies after receipt and implementation in home and community	Families may: • Prefer technologies that do not draw undue attention in social settings • Prefer electronic speech devices that use dialect of culture • Prefer technologies that allow for rapid use during communication with multiple partners • Prefer technologies that allow children choices or independence across environmental settings • Prefer simple-to-use technologies • Prefer technologies that are easy to transport and maintain • Prefer technologies that enable children to be accepted by others	Families may: • Want technologies that do not increase child independence, which are functional, and do not replace traditional family care giving roles • Want technologies that do not draw undue attention in social settings • Prefer technologies that provide direct, immediate benefits vs. long-term benefits • Prefer that professionals assume responsibility for training in use of, maintenance, and support of technologies • Desire ongoing support for family usage of technologies • Desire to see technologies used by other children and families before accepting their utility	Families may: • Prefer electronic speech devices which use dialect of culture • Have high expectations for children to be able to use the technologies at important family celebrations • Desire to have training provided to siblings who may assume responsibility for maintenance of certain technologies • Prefer not to use technologies in home setting if children's basic needs are being met • Prefer technologies that allow some degree of independence at home • Prefer not to have training/ support services provided in home settings • Prefer collaborative implementation of technologies	Families may: • Prefer technologies that are easily transportable and facilitate interactions with extended family members • Prefer technologies that use colors and symbols reflective of children's culture • Prefer electronic speech devices that use language of family's culture • Prefer technologies that allow children's personalities and social needs to emerge, thus allowing families to "know children as persons" • Be fearful of using sophisticated technologies • Prefer technologies that support children's identification and interaction with members of clan

Source: © 2011 Howard P. Parette. Adapted with permission

array of technologies. These students, particularly those from multicultural backgrounds who are second and third generation, have been acculturated to use and expect technologies in their daily lives (cf. Parette et al., 2004; Peterson-Karlan & Parette, 2005). The technology use patterns and preferences of these children, even those with disabilities, may be quite different from those of children a decade ago. Consequently, more recent thinking in the field of special education is that classroom planning take into consideration both the cultural values held by students and their families and differences among students "on the front end" when planning for and integrating technology into classroom learning experiences (Courtad, Watts, Parette, & Kelly, 2010; Parette, Watts, & Courtad, 2010). Many resources are available regarding specific AT applications that can support multicultural students with disabilities (see Table 10.2).

UNIVERSAL DESIGN FOR LEARNING AND MULTICULTURAL STUDENTS WITH DISABILITIES

Given that there may be considerable variability in learning styles and preferences across students with disabilities from diverse multicultural backgrounds (Clark, 2008; Lynch & Hanson, 1998; Parette et al., 2008; Roseberry-McKibbin, 2008), it is important that education professionals design and implement curricula that are sensitive to such differences, particularly with regard to technology-based curricula supports. An important framework for developing and delivering appropriate technology-supported learning experiences for these students is universal design for learning (UDL; Rose, Gravel, & Domings, 2010; Rose & Meyer, 2006; van Garderen & Whittaker, 2006).

Curricula and learning activities that employ UDL principles are proactive and are designed to provide all children in any classroom with multiple means of (a) engagement (i.e., piquing learners' interests, challenging them appropriately, and motivating them to learn); (b) expression (i.e., providing alternatives for demonstrating what students have learned); and (c) presentation (i.e., giving students who have diverse learning styles various ways of acquiring information and knowledge (CAST, 2011; Rose & Meyer, 2006). If such principles are adhered to in developing classroom learning experiences, the needs of all students could conceivably be addressed more effectively and efficiently.

While there is a paucity of guidance for education professionals regarding how a UDL framework is applied toward multicultural education (Blum et al., 2011; CAST, 2011a; Courtad et al., 2010), a starting point would be to examine common values held across cultural groups that have been described in the literature for decades (cf. Battle, 2002; Lynch & Hanson,

TABLE 10.2 AT Applications That Can Support Multicultural Students With Disabilities

Web Site	URL	Description
Mont-gomery County Public Schools	http://www.montgomeryschoolsmd.org/departments/hiat/tech_quick_guides/	Provides a wide array of tutorials and study guides regarding widely used AT devices
Free Technology Toolkit for UDL in All Classrooms	http://udltechtoolkit.wikispaces.com/	Wiki having 13 page links to technologies designed to support writing, literacy, study skills, and math. Other pages provide links to audio book sites, research tools, graphic organizers, multimedia and digital storytelling tools, text-to-speech, collaborative tools, UDL, and "additional" tools.
Florida Department of Education Bureau of Exceptional Education and Student Services	http://www.fdlrs.com/docs/ent2010web.pdf	A comprehensive listing of AT resources compiled by the Florida Department of Education Bureau of Exceptional Education and Student Services
Assistive Technology Training Project Online	http://atto.buffalo.edu/	Provides information on AT applications that help students with disabilities learn in elementary classrooms. Links include AT Basics, AT Decision-Making, Tutorials and Resources.
National Center for Technology Innovation	http://www.techmatrix.org/	Contains instructional planning content and product descriptions for Writing, Reading, Science, and Math

1998; Parette, 1998; Roseberry-McKibbin, 2008; see Table 10.3). What this means is that teachers use an array of strategies and materials that go far beyond traditional 20th century approaches to teaching to ensure the active participation of all children—by providing students with "a wider variety of options to access, use, and engage with learning materials" (van Garderen & Whittaker, 2006, p. 13). The IDEIA (2004) clearly placed emphasis on UDL and its relationship to AT in stating each state's responsibility to "support the use of technology, including technology with universal design principles and assistive technology devices, to maximize accessibility to the general education curriculum for children with disabilities" [20 U.S.C. 611(e) (2) (C) (v)].

TABLE 10.3 Examples of Readily Available Technologies for Education Professionals Working With Multicultural Students With Disabilities

Free

Best Freeware Download	http://www.bestfreewaredownload.com/categories/download-education-kids-freeware-6-71-0-d.html	84 free programs available useful to support varying aspects of the curriculum.
Free Technology Toolkit for UDL in All Classrooms	http://udltechtoolkit.wikispaces.com/	Wiki having 13 page links to technologies designed to support writing, literacy, study skills, and math. Other pages provide links to audio book sites, research tools, graphic organizers, multimedia and digital storytelling tools, text-to-speech, collaborative tools, UDL, and "additional" tools.
Educational Freeware	http://www.educational-freeware.com/freeware/category-K-12.aspx	Presents a comprehensive listing of free, downloadable, Windows-compatible learning games designed for K-12 learners.

Low Cost

File Buzz Download	http://www.filebuzz.com/	Site providing downloadable low cost programs that have relevance to Activities in the curriculum.

Off the Shelf

iPad Touch	http://www.apple.com/ipad/	iPad is the first tablet computer developed by Apple Inc. and is part of a device category between a Smartphone and a laptop computer.
iPod	http://www.apple.com/ipod/	Palm-sized, electronic device primarily created to play music, although it can serve as a backup device, a basic organizer, and an alarm clock.
iPhone	http://www.apple.com/iphone/	An Internet-enabled Smartphone that combines features of a mobile phone, wireless Internet device, and iPod into one device

Familiar to Users

Microsoft® PowerPoint™	http://office.microsoft.com/en-gb/powerpoint/	Presentation software having an array of features to enhance the delivery of content, including animation.

(continued)

TABLE 10.3   Examples of Readily Available Technologies for Education Professionals Working With Multicultural Students With Disabilities (continued)

Microsoft® Word™	http://office.microsoft.com/en-us/word/	Word processing program having numerous features enabling manipulation of text and contrast, embedding sounds and Web links, and other features to support delivery of curricula.
Downloadable off the Internet		
Spectronics Activity Exchange	http://www.spectronicsinoz.com/activities	Collection of activities designed for use with a number of popular software programs, including Clicker 5, Intellitools Classroom Suite, Boardmaker with Speaking Dynamically Pro, and the Communicate series.
Classroom Suite Activity Exchange	http://aex.intellitools.com/	Contains downloadable teacher-made activities designed specifically for use with the Intellitools Classroom Suite.
ZAC Browser	http://www.zacbrowser.com/	Browser designed for the PC and specifically for children who lie along the autism spectrum.
Photo Story 3 for Windows	http://www.microsoft.com/windowsxp/using/digitalphotography/photostory/default.mspx	Enables students to create slideshows using digital photos, enhanced with an array of effects features, sound tracks, and capability to record voice.
Free Apps for Kids	http://bestappsforkids.com/	An array of free apps, selected by parents, that hold potential for facilitating learning.
Moms with Apps	http://momswithapps.com/apps-for-special-needs/	A site collaborative group of family-friendly developers seeking to promote quality apps for children and families. Links to a wide array of apps are provided.
Web site accessible		
Starfall	http://www.starfall.com/	Web site presenting an array of animated and interactive activities designed to develop phonemic awareness
Dovewhisper	http://dovewhisper.com/index.htm	Links to wide variety of technology activities organized by content areas.

(continued)

TABLE 10.3 Examples of Readily Available Technologies for Education Professionals Working With Multicultural Students With Disabilities (continued)

Widely available on computers

Microsoft® PowerPoint™	http://office.microsoft.com/en-gb/powerpoint/	Presentation software having an array of features to enhance the delivery of content, including animation.
Microsoft™ Word™	http://office.microsoft.com/en-us/word/	Word processing program having numerous features enabling manipulation of text and contrast, embedding sounds and Web links, and other features to support delivery of curricula.

Technologies often available for use

Clicker 5	http://www.cricksoft.com/us/products/clicker/index.htm	Authoring software providing reading and writing supports; used in many schools throughout the U.S.
Intellitools Classroom Suite 4	http://store.cambiumlearning.com/ProgramPage.aspx?parentId=074003925&functionID=009000008&site=itc	Authoring software providing reading, writing, and math supports; contains embedded assessments to monitor progress.

Operating system feature

OS X Accessibility Features	http://www.apple.com/accessibility/macosx/vision.html	Description of various accessibility features on the Apple OS X including voiceover, screen magnification, cursor magnification, high contrast and reverse video, Safari reader, finder views, view options, dock magnification, talking alerts, talking calculator, talking clock, converting text to speech, and cascading style sheets.
Accessibility in Windows XP	http://www.microsoft.com/enable/products/windowsxp/default.aspx	Description of various accessibility features on Windows XP including display and readability, sounds and speech, keyboard and mouse options, accessibility wizard and utilities.
Accessibility in Windows 7	http://www.microsoft.com/windows/windows-7/features/accessibility.aspx	Description of various accessibility features on Windows XP including speech, magnifier, on-screen keyboard, and narrator and visual notifications.

Source: H. P. Parette, Adapted with permission

Presented in Figure 10.1 is a framework for technology integration that has been introduced to professionals. This framework assumes that education professionals (a) understand the curriculum and its associated standards, (b) select specific benchmarks/indicators associated with the standards when designing a planned classroom activity, (c) select specific technologies to support attainment of the benchmarks/indicators (activities and materials) in the planned activity, (d) select instructional strategies to teach the planned activity (e.g., direct instruction), and (e) assess student performance. IT and ICT provide support for the latter three facets of this process because they are digital, flexible, shared, dynamic, and interactive (Blum et al., 2011). These characteristics enable both the development and delivery of curricula that accommodate the learning needs and preferences of multicultural students with disabilities.

Clark (2008) observed that current and emerging technologies can be used to facilitate children's development self-awareness, explore their role

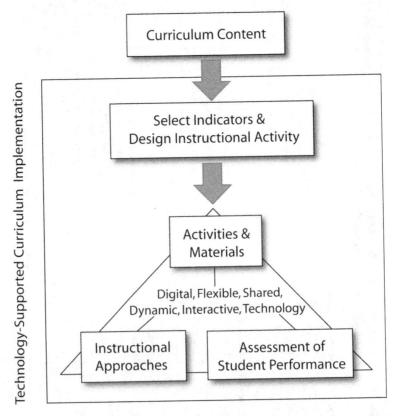

Figure 10.1 Technology-supported curriculum implementation framework. © 2010, H. Parette, G. R. Peterson-Karlan, & C. Blum. Used with permission.

in a larger cultural group setting, and build a sense of identity with others in the classroom. These broad facets of multicultural education have an array of corresponding IT, ICT, and AT supports that can support participation within the curriculum designed around UDL principles using such a technology integration framework presented in Figure 10.1.

CLASSROOM TECHNOLOGY SUPPORTS CONTRIBUTING TO THE MULTICULTURAL UDL CURRICULUM

While many technologies are available to education professionals who work with multicultural students with disabilities, it is important to understand that a "core infrastructure," or toolkit, is necessary for readily available technology, including AT, to be effectively and efficiently used (Hourcade, Parette, Boeckmann, & Blum, 2010; Parette, 2011a; Parette & Wojcik, 2004; Sadao & Robinson, 2010). These core tools may include (a) a computer with Internet access, (b) LCD projector and/or SmartBoard, (c) printer, (d) flatbed scanner, and (e) digital camera (Blum et al., 2011; Parette, 2011a). Admittedly, there are many classrooms that have little or no technology supports to help education professionals deliver their curricula to multicultural learners having disabilities. However, 21st century demands and the technology skills required of today's students have placed increasing pressure on schools to provide such supports—both to students and for the delivery of instruction (Partnership for 21st Century Skills, 2009; U.S Department of Education, 2010). More than a decade ago, Sivin-Kachala and Bialo (2000) noted "A growing body of research shows... that the effectiveness of educational technology depends on a match between goals of instruction, characteristics of learners, the design of the software and technology implementation decisions made by educators" (p. 15). With these core classroom infrastructure tools in place, many readily available technologies may then be accessed to support the educational experiences of multicultural students with disabilities.

SOFTWARE

Many schools provide software for the development and delivery of instructional activities. There are several software applications that afford education professionals maximum flexibility to include multicultural students with disabilities. These include (a) Microsoft® PowerPoint™, (b) Clicker 5 (Crick Software, Inc.2011b), (c) Boardmaker with Speaking Dynamically Pro (Mayer-Johnson, 2011), and (d) Voicethread (2011).

PowerPoint Presentations vice-versa

Microsoft® PowerPoint™

Providing dynamic, flexible, and interactive presentation capability, Microsoft® PowerPoint™ has increasingly been recognized as a readily available software program in many of today's classroom settings (Grabe & Grabe, 2007; Parette, Blum, Boeckmann, & Watts, 2009; Parette, Hourcade, & Blum, 2011). PowerPoint™ provides education professionals with features to communicate information to multicultural learners in a structured, engaging, and transitory manner (Grabe & Grabe, 2007), while also allowing content to be delivered either in a linear or branching format (Forcier & Descy, 2008; Newby, Stepich, Lehman, Russell, & Ottenbreit-Leftwich, 2011). Additionally, PowerPoint™ allows the education professional working with multicultural students to manipulate (a) varying types of pictures (static and animated); (b) symbols/text; (c) type of voice output (synthesized or digitized); (d) symbol size, shape, and position; and (e) color or black and white display. The array of options available thus accommodates a range of potential learning styles and preferences regarding how instructional content is delivered. For example, since recorded voices, music, and other audio may be embedded in slides created, a connection can be made to the cultural backgrounds of specific students. Graphic images representing an array of cultural groups can easily be inserted, thus creating a connection between the multicultural learner and the content. Audio recordings can be made by individual students on slides, thus providing voice inflections/accents that reflect sensitivity to linguistic differences among multicultural students. Emphasis features allow text to be "typed" and highlighted and synchronized to a recorded voice. Links may be embedded to Web sites to connect students to external content. The Power-Point™ presentation can also be used individually or in group formats. Of particular importance when using PowerPoint™ are the animation features available which can be used to create prompts and emphasize the entrances and exits of text and graphics (Blum et al., 2011; Parette, Blum et al., 2009; Parette et al., 2011; see Figure 10.2). For example, use of prompting features (e.g., a letter "grows" or changes colors following a question delivered to the student who must choose a correct response from three letters presented; a hand appears and points to a correct response). PowerPoint™ also has a text-to-speech feature that allows students to highlight text and have it pronounced (File>Options>Quick Access Toolbar>Commands Not in the Ribbon>Speak>Add). Office 2010 has a multilingual text-to-speech feature (see Figure 10.3) such that different languages may be added and spoken in PowerPoint™.

The education professional is limited only by creativity and degree of understanding regarding how these features may be used in the context of UDL classroom activities (Carson & Kennedy, 2006). Additionally, resource

Figure 10.2 Adapted from Parette, H. P., Blum, C., & Hourcade, J. J. (2010, January). *Using PowerPoint prompting strategies coupled with direct instruction to teach students with developmental disabilities.* Paper presented to the 12th International Conference on Autism, Intellectual Disabilities & Other Developmental Disabilities, Maui, HI. Used with permission. Hand image © Howard Parette, used with permission. Dog image courtesy of Fotolia.com, used with permission.

sites are available where teacher-made presentations have been archived and easily downloaded and modified for classroom use (cf. Provincial Centre, n.d.; see Figure 10.4).

Clicker 5

Clicker 5 (Crick Software, Inc., 2011b) is a reading and writing software program used in most school settings in the U.K., and increasingly in K–12 education venues in the United States. Its utility in helping students develop emergent literacy skills and standards-based content knowledge is emerging (Karemaker, Pitchford, & O'Malley, 2008; Parette, Hourcade, Dinelli, & Boeckmann, 2009). Its conceptual foundation of "grid writing" allows for the sequential and systematic presentation of groups of words or iconic symbols on a computer screen (Blum et al., 2011; Parette, 2011a; see Figure 10.5). Multicultural students can then make writing choices from the options listed in the grid (Parette et al., 2009). Words, phrases, sentences, numbers, and pictures can be inserted into grids to allow multicultural to demonstrate rudimentary writing skills through simple mouse clicks (Dell et al., 2008). The software also supports use by students from linguistically diverse backgrounds by allowing multiple languages to be

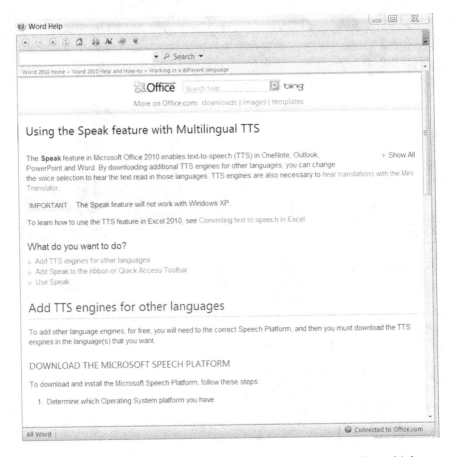

Figure 10.3 Text-to-speech features are available in PowerPoint™ for multiple languages.

used (see Figure 10.6). It also supports reading by enabling the education professional to create talking books (Crick Software, 2011b). The talking word processor feature in the software allows children to hear words spoken before and after making selections within the grids. Children who are English Language Learners would benefit from hearing each word (or even each letter) read out loud in English or other languages in a realistic (non-robotic) voice as it is entered (Hourcade et al., 2010).

Boardmaker™ With Speaking Dynamically Pro®

Boardmaker™ with Speaking Dynamically Pro® (Mayer-Johnson, 2011) is one of the most commonly used software programs in public school

Figure 10.4 Accessible talking books that can be downloaded and modified from the Provincial Centre website.

settings in the United States (Cohen, 2004). Using Picture Communication Symbols (PCS) in this software package, teachers can flexibly create a variety of customized visual supports (e.g., activity schedules, routine task sequences, Power Cards) for multicultural students. From a UDL perspective, many multicultural students with disabilities, particularly those with cognitive disabilities, may prefer pictures to text in learning activities. If used in conjunction with an LCD projector or Smart Board, activity sheets can be created that embed a diverse array of symbols relevant to varying groups of children.

Dynamically Pro® also provides templates for use with a wide range of augmentative and alternative communication (AAC) boards (Dell et al., 2008). If the education professional wishes to pair "text strings" with pictures, the Symbolate button can be used in Boardmaker™ Plus (see Figure 10.7).

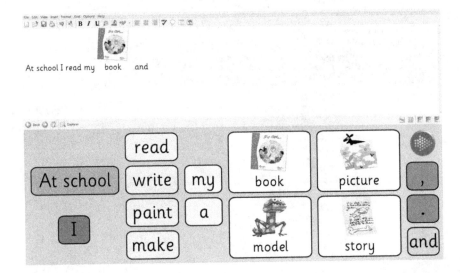

Figure 10.5 Clicker 5 enables customizable "grids" of text, graphics, video, and audio to be presented to multicultural students.

Other features of Boardmaker™ with Speaking Dynamically Pro® include word prediction capability and abbreviated expansion, which further supports AAC options. Boardmaker™ with Speaking Dynamically Pro® also provides a talking word processor and a speech output device with natural-sounding voices, which serve as powerful instructional adjuncts for multicultural readers. Education professionals can create customized talking communication boards, as well as other activities to support specific curricula (Dell et al., 2008; Mayer-Johnson, 2011). Additionally, the widespread use of Boardmaker™ with Speaking Dynamically Pro® has resulted in a range of support sites being accessible to education professionals to download and/or share pre-made activities (cf. Dynavox Mayer-Johnson, 2010; Spectronics, 2011; Websites for Free Boardmaker Downloads, n.d.).

Voicethread

Web 2.0 tools have great potential for supporting the instructional needs of multicultural students with disabilities. These tools generally enable users to add and edit content, including text, graphics, audio, video, and Web links. One particularly useful technology that has a wide variety of uses is Voicethread (Voicethread LLC, 2011). Designed initially for purposes of collaboration, Voicethread allows multiple users (identified by uploaded photos or icons) to comment on content that is posted by a "designer" or

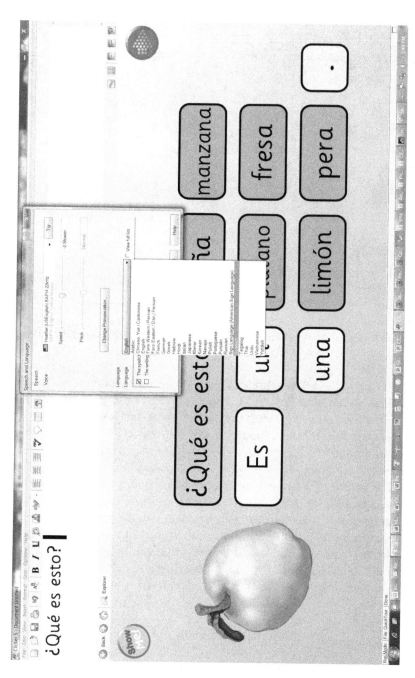

Figure 10.6 Multiple language formats are available when creating grids within Clicker 5.

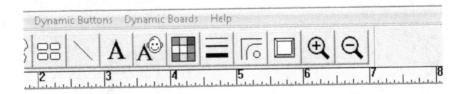

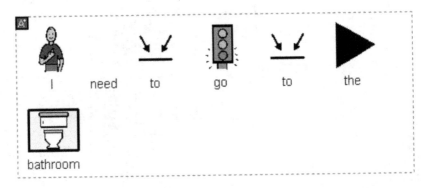

Figure 10.7 Using the Symbolate button tool in Boardmaker™ Plus allows print to be paired with symbols by drawing a text box and typing.

creator of a particular Voicethread. PowerPoint™ presentations, Microsoft® Word files, photos, and Web links. The multiplicity of formats for content would allow for students to select their own photos/images related to a particular project and to be included in the Voicethread. The multiple formats for "commenting" include text, audio, video (webcam), or phone. Thus, multicultural students who do not want to be heard or seen (due to their accents or nature of disability) can simply add text and still be included in the group (see Figure 10.8). If several or more students have similar cultural backgrounds, a Voicethread can be created to allow specific students to interact with one another. Content can also be uploaded as a means of assessment (i.e., instruction would be provided and images, video, or text regarding the instructional content added, thus allowing students to comment and demonstrate their knowledge or understanding).

CONCLUSION

While more traditional perspectives of multicultural education continue to focus on differences across cultural groups, and thus individual differences,

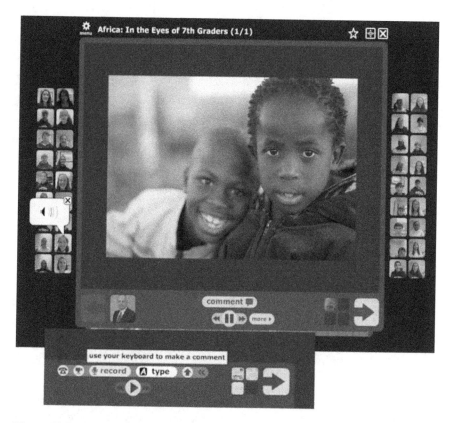

Figure 10.8 Voicethread enables all members of a group or classroom to have a "presence" and add/edit content.

the challenge to education professionals in 21st century settings is how to best design instructional materials and activities that meet the needs of as many individuals in the classroom as possible. When a UDL framework is used in designing classroom activities, all learners—including multicultural students with disabilities—can potentially have a floor of educational opportunity presented to them.

REFERENCES

Bakken, J. P., & Parette, P. (2007). Using technology to advance multicultural special education. In F. E. Obiakor (Ed.), *Multicultural special education* (pp. 272–289). Upper Saddle River, NJ: Merrill-Prentice Hall.

Banks, J. A. (1997). Multicultural education: Characteristics and goals. In J. A. Banks & C. A. M. Banks (Eds.), *Multicultural education: Issues and perspectives* (3rd ed., pp. 3–31). Boston: Allyn and Bacon.

Banks, J. A., & Banks, C. A. M. (2001). *Multicultural education: Issues and perspectives* (4th ed.). New York: Wiley & Sons.

Battle, D. E. (2002). *Communication disorders in multicultural populations* (3rd ed.) Boston: Andover Medical.

Blum, C., Parette, H. P., & Travers, J. (2011, April). *Future of instructional technology in early childhood special education.* Paper presented at the Council for Exceptional Children 2011 Convention and Expo, Washington, DC.

Bray, M., Brown, A., & Green, T. D. (2004). *Technology and the diverse learner. A guide to classroom practice.* Thousand Oaks, CA: Corwin.

Cambium Learning. (2006). *Classroom suite activity exchange.* Retrieved from http://aex.intellitools.com/

Carson, E., & Kennedy, M. (2006). From evaluation to innovation: How to emulate dynamic display using PowerPoint. *Closing The Gap, 24(6),* 28–29.

CAST. (2011). *What is UDL?* Retrieved from http://www.udlcenter.org/aboutudl/whatisudl

CAST. (2011a). *UDL guidelines-Version 2.0.* Retrieved from http://www.udlcenter.org/aboutudl/udlguidelines

Center for Technology in Education, Johns Hopkins University; and Technology & Media Division [TAM] of the Council for Exceptional Children. (2005). *Considering the need for assistive technology within the individualized education program.* Columbia, MD: Author.

Clark, K. (2008). Educational settings and the use of technology to promote the multicultural development of children. In G. Berry, M. Ellis, & J. Asamen (Eds.), *Handbook of child development, multiculturalism, and media* (pp. 411–417). Newbury Park, CA: Sage Publications.

Cohen, S. R. (2004). Boardmaker: Visual supports for all students. *Closing the Gap, 23(4),* 30–31.

Cook, A. M., & Hussey S. M. (2002). *Assistive technologies. Principles and practices* (2nd ed.). St. Louis, MO: Mosby.

Cools, E., Evans, C., & Redmond, J. A. (2009). Using styles for more effective learning in multicultural and e-learning environments. *Multicultural Education and Technology, 3(1),* 5–16.

Courtad, C. A., Watts, E. H., Parette, H. P., & Kelly, S. M. (2010, November). *Be the model: Preparing teachers and fostering universal design for learning (UDL).* Paper presented to the Council for Exceptional Children Teacher Education Division 33rd Annual Conference, St. Louis, MO.

Crick Software, Inc. (2011). *Clicker home page.* Retrieved from http://www.cricksoft.com/us/products/clicker/index.htm

Crick Software, Inc. (2011b). *Clicker in the curriculum.* Retrieved from http://www.cricksoft.com/us/products/tools/clicker/curriculum/talking-books.aspx

Dell, A. G., Newton, D. A., & Petroff, J. G. (2008). *Assistive technology in the classroom. Enhancing the experiences of students with disabilities.* Upper Saddle River, NJ: Pearson Merrill Prentice Hall.

Dynavox Mayer-Johnson. (2010). *Welcome to Boardmaker share!* Retrieved from http://www.boardmakershare.com/

Forcier, R. C., & Descy, D. E. (2008). *The computer as an educational tool: Productivity and problem solving* (5th ed.). Boston: Allyn & Bacon.

Gorski, P. (2001). *Multicultural education and the Internet: Intersections and integrations.* Boston: McGraw-Hill.

Grabe, M., & Grabe, C. (2007). *Integrating technology for meaningful learning* (5th ed.). New York: Houghton Mifflin.

Grant, K. B., & Ray, J. (2010). *Home, school, and community collaboration: Culturally responsive family involvement.* Thousand Oaks, CA: Sage.

Griffiths, M. (2010). Excessive online computer use and learning disabilities. *Australian Journal of Dyslexia and Other Learning Disabilities, 5,* 31–34.

Hedrick Hudson School District v. Rowley, 458 U.S. 206, 102 S. Ct. 3051 (1982).

Hourcade, J. J., Parette, Jr., H. P., Boeckmann, N. M., & Blum, C. (2010). Handy Manny and the emergent literacy toolkit. *Early Childhood Education Journal, 37,* 483–491.

Individuals with Disabilities Education Improvement Act, 20 U.S.C. §§ 1400 et seq. (2004)

International ICT Literacy Panel (2007). *Digital transformation: A framework for ICT literacy.* Retrieved from http://www.ets.org/Media/Tests/Information_and_Communication_Technology_Literacy/ictreport.pdf

Kalyanpur, M., & Harry, B. (1999). *Culture in special education: Building reciprocal family-professional relationships.* Baltimore: Brookes.

Karemaker, A., Pitchford, N. J., & O'Malley, C. (2008). Using whole-word multimedia software to support literacy acquisition: A comparison with traditional books. *Educational and Child Psychology, 25,* 97–118.

Kemp, C., & Parette, H. P. (2000). Barriers to minority parent involvement in assistive technology (AT) decision-making processes. *Education and Training in Mental Retardation and Developmental Disabilities, 35,* 384–392.

King, T. W. (1999). *Assistive technology: Essential human factors.* Boston: Allyn & Bacon.

Lynch, E. W., & Hanson, M. J. (1998). (Eds.). *Developing cross-cultural competence. A guide for working with young children and their families* (2nd ed.). Baltimore: Brookes.

Mayer-Johnson. (2011). *Boardmaker with Speaking Dynamically Pro.* Retrieved from http://www.mayer-johnson.com/boardmaker-with-speaking-dynamically-pro-v-6/

Mesch, G. S. (2011). Minority status and the use of computer-mediated communication: A test of the social diversification hypothesis. *Communication Research* [Online journal]. Retrieved from http://crx.sagepub.com/content/early/2011/02/17/0093650211398865.full.pdf+html

Newby, T. J., Stepich, D. A., Lehman, J. D., Russell, J. D., & Ottenbreit-Leftwich, A. (2011). *Educational technology for teaching and learning* (4th ed.). Boston: Pearson.

No Child Left Behind Act of 2001, 20 U.S.C. §§ 6301 et seq

Obiakor, F. E. (Ed.). (2007). *Multicultural special education. Culturally responsive teaching.* Upper Saddle River, NJ: Pearson Merrill Prentice Hall.

Parette, H. P. (1998). Cultural issues and family-centered assistive technology decision-making. In S. L. Judge & H. P. Parette (Eds.), *Assistive technology for young children with disabilities: A guide to providing family-centered services* (pp. 184–210). Cambridge, MA: Brookline.

Parette, H. P. (2011a, May). *Readily available technology integration in an early childhood education preservice curriculum: Issues and strategies.* Paper presented to the 13th Annual International Conference on Education, Athens, Greece.

Parette, H. P. (2011b, March). *A confluence of culture, technology, and education: Challenges of integrating new tools in 21st century classrooms.* Keynote presentation to the Illinois State University Council for Teacher Education Spring Colloquium, Normal, IL

Parette, H. P., Blum, C., Boeckmann, N. M., & Watts, E. H. (2009). Teaching word recognition to young children using Microsoft® PowerPoint™ coupled with direct instruction. *Early Childhood Education Journal, 36,* 393–401.

Parette, H. P., Brotherson, M. J., & Huer, M. B. (2000). Giving families a voice in augmentative and alternative communication decision-making. *Education and Training in Mental Retardation and Developmental Disabilities, 35*(2), 177–190.

Parette, H. P., Hourcade, J. J., & Blum, C. (2011). Using animation in Microsoft® PowerPoint™ to enhance engagement and learning in young learners with developmental delay. *Teaching Exceptional Children, 43*(4), 58–67.

Parette, H.P., Hourcade, J. J., Dinelli, J. M., & Boeckmann, N. M. (2009). Using Clicker 5 to enhance emergent literacy in young learners. *Early Childhood Education Journal, 36,* 355–363.

Parette, H. P., Huer, M. B., & Brotherson, M. J. (2001). Related service personnel perceptions of team AAC decision-making across cultures. *Education and Training in Mental Retardation and Developmental Disabilities, 36,* 69–82.

Parette, H. P., Huer, M. B., & Peterson-Karlan, G. R. (2008). Working with persons with developmental disabilities across cultures. In H. P. Parette & G. R. Peterson-Karlan (Eds.), *Research-based practices in developmental disabilities* (2nd ed., pp. 143–167). Austin, TX: Pro-Ed.

Parette, H. P., Huer, M. B., & Scherer, M. (2004). Effects of acculturation on assistive technology service delivery. *Journal of Special Education Technology, 19*(2), 31–41.

Parette, H. P., Huer, M. B., & VanBiervliet, A. (2005). Cultural issues and assistive technology. In D. L. Edyburn, K. Higgins, & R. Boone (Eds.), *The handbook of special education technology research and practice* (pp. 81–103). Whitefish Bay, WI: Knowledge by Design, Inc.

Parette, H. P., & Peterson-Karlan, G. R. (2007). Facilitating student achievement with assistive technology. *Education and Training in Developmental Disabilities, 42,* 387–397.

Parette, H. P., & Peterson-Karlan, G. R. (2010a). Assistive technology and educational practice. In P. Peterson, E. Baker, & B. McGraw (Eds.), *International encyclopedia of education* (3rd ed., Vol. 2, pp.537–543.) Oxford, UK: Elsevier.

Parette, H. P., & Peterson, G. R. (2010b). Using assistive technology to support the instructional process with students with disabilities. In F. E. Obiakor, J. P. Bakken, & A. F. Rotatori (Eds.), *Current issues and trends in special education: Research, technology, and teacher preparation* (Vol. 20, pp.73-89). Bingley, UK: Emerald Group Publishing Limited.

Parette, H. P., Peterson-Karlan, G. R., Wojcik, B. W., & Bardi, N. (2007). Monitor that progress! Interpreting data trends for AT decision-making. *Teaching Exceptional Children, 39*(7), 22-29.

Parette, H. P., Watts, E. H., & Courtad, C. A. (2010, November). *Technology for all education majors: A unique course and lessons learned.* Paper presented to the Council for Exceptional Children Teacher Education Division 33rd Annual Conference, St. Louis, MO.

Parette, H. P., & Wojcik, B. W. (2004). Creating a technology toolkit for students with mental retardation: A systematic approach. *Journal of Special Education Technology, 19*(4), 23–31.

Partnership for 21st Century Skills. (2009). *Framework for 21st century learning.* Washington, DC: Author. Retrieved from http://www.p21.org/documents/P21_Framework.pdf

Peterson-Karlan, G. R., & Parette, P. (2005). Millennial students with mild disabilities and emerging assistive technology trends. *Journal of Special Education Technology, 20*(4), 27–38.

Provincial Centre. (n.d.). Free books for you. Retrieved from http://www.setbc.org/setbc/accessiblebooks/freebooksforyou.html

Rose, D. H., Gravel, J. W., & Domings, Y. M. (2010). *UDL unplugged: The role of technology in UDL.* Wakefield, MA: National Center on Universal Design for Learning. Retrieved from http://www.udlcenter.org/sites/udlcenter.org/files/notech_final2.pdf

Rose, D. H., & Meyer, A. (2006). *A practice reader in universal design for learning.* Cambridge, MA: Harvard University Press.

Roseberry-McKibbin, C. (2008). *Multicultural students with special language needs* (3rd ed.). Oceanside, CA: Academic Communication Associates.

Sadao, K., & Robinson, N. M. (2010). *Assistive technology for young children: Creating inclusive learning environments.* Baltimore: Brookes.

Sivin-Kachala, J., & Bialo, E. R. (2000). *2000 research report on the effectiveness of technology in schools* (7th ed.). Washington, DC: Interactive Educational Systems Design, Inc. Retrieved from http://www.siia.net/estore/pubs/ref-00.pdf

South Carolina ETV Commission. (2011). *Welcome to knowitall.org.* Retrieved from http://knowitall.org/

Spectronics. (2011). *Boardmaker activities to print.* Retrieved from http://www.spectronicsinoz.com/activities/boardmaker-activities-to-print

Sullivan, A. L., & Thorius, K. A. K. (2010). Considering intersections of difference among students identified as disabled and expanding conceptualizations of multicultural education. *Race, Gender & Class, 17,* 93–109.

Torres, L. M. (2009). *Multicultural education and technology.* Retrieved from http://www.slideshare.net/lotorres09/multicultural-education-and-technologyppt

Trumbull, E., Rothstein-Fisch, C., Greenfield, P. M., & Quiroz, B. (2001). *Bridging cultures between home and school.* Mahwah, NJ: Erlbaum.

U.S. Department of Education. (2010). *Transforming American education: Learning powered by technology.* Washington, DC: Author. Retrieved from http://www.ed.gov/sites/default/files/netp2010.pdf

Van Garderen, D., & Whittaker, C. (2006). Planning differentiated, multicultural instruction for secondary inclusive classrooms. *Teaching Exceptional Children, 38*(3), 12–20.

Voicethread LLC. (2011). *Express your presence with incredible flexibility.* Retrieved from http://voicethread.com/

Websites for Free Boardmaker Downloads. (n.d.). Retrieved from http://www.region10.org/specialeducation/documents/boardmakerwebsites2.pdf

Wilson, P. (2011). *iPhone and iPod touch apps—Childhood disability [Blog].* Retrieved from http://www.bellaonline.com/articles/art62136.asp

IMPLEMENTING CULTURALLY RESPONSIVE BEHAVIOR MANAGEMENT TECHNIQUES TO TEACH CULTURALLY AND LINGUISTICALLY DIVERSE LEARNERS WITH SPECIAL NEEDS

Cheryl A. Utley and Anthony F. Rotatori

ABSTRACT

This chapter examines culturally responsive classroom/behavior management techniques for culturally and linguistically diverse (CLD) learners with special needs. The current research literature provides numerous examples of CLD children with special needs that have different behavioral patterns that frequently result in (a) a misdiagnosis of behaviors, (b) inappropriate interpretations of behaviors, (c) deterioration of interpersonal respect between teachers and students, (d) increased attention to controlling student behavior, (e) poor use of instructional time, (f) ill-defined classifications and labels, and (g) dysfunctional educational programs. Therefore, it is recommended

Multicultural Education for Learners with Special Needs in the Twenty-First Century, pages 175–196
Copyright © 2014 by Information Age Publishing

that general and special educators infuse culturally responsive principles into effective behavioral strategies designed to strengthen and facilitate positive behaviors in CLD children with special needs.

INTRODUCTION

It has become very clear that there is greater cultural and linguistic diversity within our nation and within the United States public school system than ever before. According to a report by the National Center for Educational Statistics, Institute of Education Sciences (2010) entitled *Status and Trends in the Education of Racial and Ethnic Minorities,* the demographic pattern of the

> Hispanic population is expected to grow at a faster rate than most other races/ethnicities. In the year 2025, about 21% of the population is expected to be of Hispanic ethnicity. In addition, the growth rate for Whites is expected to be slower than the rate for other races/ethnicities, decreasing their share of the total population. In 2025, the distribution of the population is expected to be 58% White, 21% Hispanic, 12% Black, 6% Asian, 2% two or more races, 1% American Indian/Alaska Native, and less than 1% Native Hawaiian or Other Pacific Islander. (p. 1)

In addition, current statistics show that 1 in 5 children live in poverty and about 1 in 10 children have limited proficiency in English.

General and special educators are faced with the challenges of implementing protections provided by the Individuals with Disabilities Education Improvement Act (IDEIA, 2004) to guarantee that culturally and linguistically divers (CLD) students are not disproportionately represented in special education programs. Despite the implementation of this law, educational, socioeconomic, sociocultural, and sociopolitical factors have contributed to the disproportionate representation of Culturally and Linguistically Diverse (CLD) students with special needs in terms of (a) education and placement classification, (b) least access to programs, services, and resources, (c) an individualized general education curriculum, and (d) design and implementation of effective instruction and classroom management procedures (Adelman & Taylor, 2011; Artiles, Rueda, Salzaar, & Higareda, 2005; Salend, Duhaney, & Montgomery, 2002; Utley, Obiakor, & Bakken, 2011; Utley & Salend, 2006). According to Garcia and Conroy (2002) and Kewalramani, Gilbertson, Fox, and Provasnik (2007), five prevalent trends in national data are evident: (a) once identified, CLD students from every major racial/ethnic group are more likely than white students with disabilities to be removed from general education classrooms for all or part of their school day; (b) African American students are most often overidentified in the disability categories that have the highest correlation with isolation from the general education setting, mental retardation and emotional disturbance; (c) Hispanics have substantially lower risk for mental retardation and emotional disturbance compared to Whites, and even lower compared to African American, even though Hispanics and African American share a far greater risk for poverty, exposure to environmental toxins and low academic achievement; (d) there are large disparities in cognitive disability identification rates between boys and girls generally, and especially between African American boys and girls; and (e) school suspensions are being used with increasing frequency, in a disproportionate manner relative to CLD students, and for infractions that should be handled with less intensive disciplinary strategies.

In examining the cognitive and behavioral competence of CLD students, scholars have argued that on the ability–achievement continuum, judgmental and nonjudgmental (also referred to as high incidence) categories of disability are artificial and variable (Donovan & Cross, 2002). Within the schooling context, several factors affect where CLD students fall along the continuum, in particular, the overreliance on the ability–achievement discrepancy approach (Hale, Kaufman, Naglieri, & Kavale, 2006). For CLD students with academic and behavioral difficulties in school and who do not have a medically-diagnosed disability, key aspects of the context of schooling itself, including administrative, curricular/instructional, and interpersonal factors, may contribute to their identification as having a disability and may contribute to the disproportionately high or low placements of CLD students in special education (Losen, 2002; Losen & Welner, 2002). Consequently, these factors have not led to the successful implementation of classroom management/behavior management techniques in inclusive and special education classrooms. In addition, studies have indicated that school traditional schooling procedures (e.g., suspensions) are not successful in decreasing students' academic problems and chronic and inappropriate behaviors (Mendez & Knoff, 2003).

The teaching profession is continually scrutinized for not addressing the achievement and cultural gaps of CLD students with special needs that exist in general and special education classrooms. Nationwide teacher shortages in special education have resulted in the pervasive use of unqualified personnel in classrooms for students identified for special education services. The majority of general and special educators have indicated that they have not mastered the skills needed to accommodate the academic and behavioral needs of CLD students with special needs. Furthermore, there is a dearth of teachers from CLD backgrounds in such programs. While 38% of students identified for special education services are from CLD backgrounds (Irvine, 2003), only 14% of teachers serving these students are from historically underrepresented groups (Tyler, Yzquierdo, Lopez-Reyna, & Flippin, 2002).

Numerous problems arise when general and special educators fail to consider the role of culture and the experiences CLD students may bring to school. Gay (2000) remarked that most [teachers] do not know how to understand and use the school behaviors of CLD students, which differ from their normative expectations, as aids to teaching. Therefore, they tend to misinterpret them as deviant and treat them punitively. As Gay noted:

> Most curriculum designs and instructional materials are Eurocentric. They are likely to be more readily meaningful and to have a greater appeal to the life experiences and aspirations of Anglo students than to those of ethnic minorities. Thus, when attempting to learn academic tasks, Anglo students do not have the additional burden of working across irrelevant instructional materials and methods. A high degree of cultural congruency exists between middle-class and Anglo students' culture and school culture. These students do not experience much cultural discontinuity, social-code incompatibility, or need for cultural style shifting to adjust to the behavioral codes expected of them in school. (pp. 182–183)

The primary purpose of this chapter is to describe culturally responsive teaching techniques, with an emphasis on classroom and behavior management for CLD students with special needs. We begin by discussing different perspectives about the role of culture in education followed by key ideas describing culturally responsive theory, pedagogy, and principles. Finally, we present culturally responsive classroom management and behavior management techniques for CLD students with special needs.

THE ROLE OF CULTURE IN EDUCATION

Within the last decade, educational definitions of the concept of culture embrace a broad perspective. Culture refers to a system of shared knowledge and beliefs that shape human perspectives and social behavior (Gay, 2000; Ladson-Billings, 1995; Shade, Kelly, & Oberg, 1997). Those who have adopted this definition recognize that our cultural background influences the way we act, believe, perceive ourselves and others, and judge the world around us. Culture is referred to as a worldview that is shared by a cultural group. Human behaviors and interactions are a result of the underlying cultural assumptions that shape the worldview of individuals. Culture is more than just one characteristic, such as race or ethnicity; culture reflects the unique blending of characteristics among individuals within groups and may include variables such as socioeconomic status, life experiences, gender, language, education, sexual orientation, psychological state, and political viewpoints (Bodley, 2010). Families represent a valuable source for the transmission of cultural norms, knowledge, and values. So, when

CLD students enter the classroom, they have developed attitudes, communication patterns, a perceptual orientation, learning and behavioral styles based on the transmission of cultural values. Since culture influences interpersonal relations and behaviors, children's social competence cannot be generalized outside the culture in which they are obtained. To understand the influence of cultural factors on children's behavior, researchers must conceptually and empirically validate cultural frameworks that reflect the dynamic interactions between children and their cultural contexts. For several decades, distinct culturally influenced social behaviors have been found among CLD and European American children (Cartledge & Milburn, 1996). To a great extent, maximizing CLD students' learning outcomes depend upon a host of factors, including but not limited to (a) positive teacher beliefs about learning, (b) interactive and experiential teaching, (c) contextually-embedded curriculum and materials, and (d) appropriate instructional techniques. It is, therefore, critical that general and special educators develop an awareness of the profound and pervasive influence of culture and culturally responsive pedagogy in the classroom.

CULTURALLY RESPONSIVE TEACHING THEORY

Culturally responsive teaching is a foundational concept of multicultural education and involves many things: curriculum content, learning context, classroom climate, student–teacher relationships, instructional techniques, and performance assessments (Gay, 2002). Three educational perspectives of culturally responsive teaching have been visible in the literature. The first educational perspective by Ladson-Billings (1995) defined culturally responsive teaching as an approach that empowers students intellectually, socially, emotionally, and politically by using cultural referents to impact knowledge, skills, and attitudes of students. The second perspective by Gay (2000) defined "culturally responsive teaching as using the cultural knowledge, prior experiences, and performance styles of diverse students to make learning more appropriate and effective for them; it teaches to and through the strengths of these students" (p. 29). The third perspective is by Nieto and Boder (2008) which defined culturally responsive teaching as learning that is "actively constructed, connected to experience, influenced by cultural differences, developed within a social context, and created within a community" (p. 3). They noted that the conditions in U.S. society and schools have been consistently, systematically, and disproportionally unequal and unfair for students who are different from the mainstream. Therefore, a personal and collective transformation of teachers is needed, which includes learning from and with CLD students, and challenging bias within both oneself and one's school.

The culturally responsive teaching framework does not replace the use of (a) academic data to monitor school progress, (b) effective instructional strategies, and (c) use of effective educational principles and practices. It requires general and special educators to create structured learning environments, develop and implement supportive classroom environments, and provide access to opportunities and resources for CLD students with special needs, regardless of their CLD backgrounds. For general and special educators to be effective practitioners, they must have a working knowledge of these dimensions and their interactive effects on how to conduct assessments and teach in a culturally responsive and affirming manner.

CULTURALLY RESPONSIVE PEDAGOGY

The merits of culturally responsive pedagogy are continually discussed and debated by general and special educators (Schmidt, 2000, 2003, 2004, 2005). Irvine and Armento (2001) identified seven characteristics for the successful implementation of culturally responsive teaching that include:

1. *High expectations*—supporting students as they develop the literacy appropriate to their ages and abilities.
2. *Positive relationships with families and community*—demonstrating clear connections with student families and communities in terms of curriculum content and relationships.
3. *Cultural sensitivity–reshaped curriculum, mediated for culturally valued knowledge*—connecting with the standards-based curriculum as well as individual students' cultural backgrounds.
4. *Active teaching methods*—involving students in a variety of reading, writing, listening, speaking, and viewing behaviors throughout the lesson plan.
5. *Teacher as facilitator*—presenting information; briefly giving directions; summarizing responses; and working with small groups, pairs, and individuals.
6. *Student control of portions of the lesson or "healthy hum"*—talking at conversation levels around the topic being studied while completing assignments in small groups and pairs.
7. *Instruction around groups and pairs, low anxiety*—completing assignments individually, but usually in small groups or pairs with time to share ideas and think critically about the work.

CULTURALLY RESPONSIVE TEACHING PRINCIPLES

Culturally responsive teaching principles encompass three dimensions: (a) academic achievement—making learning rigorous, exciting, challenging, and equitable with high standards; (b) cultural competence—knowing and facilitating the learning process in different cultural and linguistic groups; and (c) sociopolitical consciousness—recognizing and assisting CLD students in the understanding that education and schooling do not occur in a vacuum (Gay, 2002; Nieto & Boder, 2008). This strategy facilitates and supports the acquisition of new knowledge, skills, and achievement outcomes for CLD students with special needs.

Building culturally responsive teaching principles require general and special educators to (a) build trust among their students, (b) become culturally literate, (c) use appropriate diagnostic and assessment approaches, (d) use culturally sound questioning techniques, (e) provide effective feedback, (f) analyze content in instructional materials, and (g) establish positive home–school–community relationships (Algozzine, O'Shea, & Obiakor, 2009; Nieto & Boder, 2008; Obiakor, 2007). Validating cultural and linguistic experiences of CLD students with special needs in the schooling process, curriculum, and instructional content is a way to affirm their self-identity. The cultural lens of validating cultural and linguistic experiences creates multiple ways of seeing and perceiving meaningful experiences of individuals in a culturally diverse society (LeMoine, Maddahian, Patton, Ross, & Scruggs, 2006). In the end, culturally responsive teaching uses the students' cultural beliefs, language, and prior learning experiences to build bridges to new knowledge and the understanding of skills for success in school.

CULTURALLY RESPONSIVE TEACHING AND CLD STUDENTS WITH SPECIAL NEEDS

To establish a culturally responsive classroom/behavior management program, appropriate behaviors for CLD students with special needs must be given serious attention so that global teacher judgments and interpretations are not magnified. More than two decades ago, Kauffman (1989) argued that:

> Nearly all behavioral standards and expectations—and therefore nearly all judgments regarding behavior deviance—are culture-bound; value judgments cannot be entirely culture free. In our pluralistic society, which values multicultural elements, the central question for educators is whether they have made sufficient allowance in their judgment for behavior that is a function of a child's particular heritage. (p. 212)

Multicultural aspects of rules and standards must address two important questions: (a) "Whose standards?" and (b) "What culture?" Responses to these two questions may vary—depending upon an individual's culture and school contexts (Obiakor, Harris-Obiakor, Obi, & Eskay, 2000).

Culturally responsive teaching has critical features that could benefit CLD students with special needs (Cartledge & Kourea, 2008; Cartledge & Lo, 2006; Cartledge & Milburn, 1996; Obiakor, 2007; Utley, Greenwood, & Douglas, 2007). The most recent report by the National Center for Learning Disabilities (2011) stated that in the differential diagnostic process, "cultural and linguistic factors do not preclude the possibility that an individual also has LD" (p. 9); a comprehensive assessment must address all issues of suspected disability, including cultural sensitivity, knowledge, and skill on the part of team members to understand the interactive factors of language and literacy development in bilingual students. Formal assessment instruments and procedures must be nondiscriminatory, nonbiased, and address language needs that are responsive to the CLD students' needs Individuals with Disabilities Educational Improvement Act (IDEIA, 2004). The interpretation of results must be done cautiously with consideration of all of the culturally and linguistic factors that may impact these student's abilities to learn. The multidisciplinary team must make an informed and data-based decision, which includes knowledge about the cultural and causal factors impacting CLD students' learning and behavioral problems.

CULTURALLY RESPONSIVE CLASSROOM MANAGEMENT TECHNIQUES

Cultural and linguistic diversity cannot be ignored in the classroom and behavior management of CLD students with special needs because the social context of learning and the attitudes, values, and behaviors of the family, peer group, and community profoundly influence student's emotional, behavioral, moral, and cognitive development. Obiakor, Enwefa, Utley, Obi, Gwalla-Ogisi, and Enwefa (2004) noted that CLD students with special needs have "different behavioral patterns that frequently result in inappropriate interpretations, classifications, and labels and dysfunctional educational programs" (p. 16). Therefore, before judging behaviors as deviant, general and special educators must acknowledge culture and the social environment as critical factors when developing effective educational practices. General and special educators must develop effective and efficient classroom management and behavior management techniques. Scholars such as Cartledge and Kleefeld (2010), Ewing (1995), Gay (2002), Obiakor et al. (2004), noted that CLD students with LD have different behavioral patterns that frequently result in (a) a misdiagnosis of behaviors, (b) inappropriate interpretations of behaviors, (c) deterioration of interpersonal respect between teachers and students, (d) increased attention to controlling student behavior, (e) poor use of instructional time, (f) ill-defined classifications and labels, and (g) dysfunctional educational programs.

Over the past few years, a considerable amount of work has illustrated how culturally responsive pedagogy and classroom and behavior management theories can be integrated into school and classroom practices (Utley & Obiakor, 2012). Infusing culturally responsive principles into proactive classroom management practices is a multifaceted process (Duda & Utley, 2004; Ewing, 1995; Grossman, 2004; Metropolitan Center for Urban Education, 2008; Sullivan & A'Vant, 2009; Utley, Obiakor et al., 2011). Culturally responsive discipline is for teachers to create caring and nurturing relationships with students, grounded in cooperation, collaboration, and reciprocity rather than current teacher-controlling, student-compliance patterns (Gay, 2002). Caring is a foundational pillar of effective teaching and learning [and] the lack of it produces inequities in educational opportunities and achievement outcomes for ethnically different students (Gay, 2000).

Bacon, Banks, Young, and Jackson (2007) examined the perspectives of 19 African American boys (5 students from elementary school; 14 students from middle school) on topics related to culturally responsive teaching (e.g., qualities of good teachers), cultural discontinuity (e.g., respect among peers, grades), and differential treatment (e.g., fairness). African American boys had high suspension rates and had been identified as having chronic behavior problems. In a group meeting, several questions were asked:

1. Tell me about the things you like best in school.
2. Tell me about some good teachers that you know.
3. What makes them good teachers?
4. How can you tell if teachers care about you?
5. How do teachers show disrespect to students?
6. How do students show disrespect to students?
7. How do students show respect to students?
8. Do students get treated fairly in your school?
9. What do teachers do or say that makes it hard for you to follow the school rules?

The conclusions drawn from this study revealed the following: (a) culturally responsive teachers provide assistance, give clear explanations, are persistent in expectations that they do their work, and help them stay out of trouble; (b) cultural discontinuity between teachers and African American students occurs because teachers do not understand the importance of respect in their interactions with them, that it is necessary to stand up for yourself, and that fighting and scolding are a part of daily life in the neighborhood; and (c) differential treatment occurs because teachers rely on student labels and white students are not punished and suspended for the same school infractions committed by African American students.

Characteristics of Culturally Responsive Classroom Management (CRCM)

Weinstein, Tomlinson-Clarke and Curran (2004) developed a culturally responsive multicultural counseling and care, which includes the following components: (a) recognition of one's own cultural lens and biases, (b) knowledge of students' cultural backgrounds, (c) awareness of the broader social, economic, and political context, (d) ability and willingness to use culturally appropriate management strategies, and (e) a commitment to building caring classroom communities. Table 11.1 describes the essential elements of CRCM.

Hershfeldt, Sechrest, Pell, Rosenberg, Bradshaw, and Leaf (2009) developed a professional development program aimed at assisting general and special educators to interpret their own behavior when faced with problematic behaviors of CLD students. The five components of the Double-Check program consists of (a) reflective thinking about children and their group membership, (b) efforts made to develop authentic relationships, (c) effective communication, (d) connection to the curriculum, and (e) sensitivity to student's cultural and situational messages. Table 11.2 describes the components of the Double-Check professional development program.

A culturally responsive classroom environment, as defined by Shade et al. (1997), requires general and special educators to have strategies that build strong teacher–student relationships and reduce behavior problems. Prescriptive culturally responsive behavior management programs to prevent discipline problems in CLD students with special needs are a prerequisite to good teaching (Ewing, 1995). Table 11.3 presents proactive culturally responsive behavior management strategies.

POSITIVE BEHAVIOR INTERVENTION AND SUPPORT PROGRAMS

One educational approach to solving problem behaviors in CLD students with special needs is the implementation of school-wide positive behavior intervention and support (SWPBIS) (Sugai, Fallon, & O'Keefe, 2011; Utley & Obiakor, 2012). Features of a successful SWPBIS program includes implementing (a) positive behavioral expectations, (b) specific methods to teach these expectations to staff and students, (c) proactive supervision

TABLE 11.1   Essential Elements of CRCM

Principles	Integrating Cultural Knowledge	Understanding Cultural Differences in Behavior	Understanding Linguistic and Communication Patterns	Creating a Caring Environment
1. Use of effective instructional and behavioral strategies to build positive and supportive school and classroom learning environments. 2. Make informed academic and behavioral adaptations that match and build upon the learner's prior knowledge, experiences, skills, and beliefs. 3. Ensure that learning and behavioral outcomes are meaningful, relevant, useful, and important to each child.	1. Cultural knowledge is an understanding of the importance of culture in affecting students' perceptions, self-esteem, values, classroom behavior, and learning. 2. Culturally responsive behavior management and instruction clearly shows that the knowledge of students' family, community, and socio-ethnic cultures—their languages, literacy practices, and values—can help teachers address the interests and build on the skills of their students.	1. Behavioral patterns and actions considered to be different vary by culture. 2. A lack of appreciation and understanding of behavior that is different from our own culture leads to misinterpretations and a subsequent referral to special education. 3. Teachers' expectations and attitudes impact how children learn and behave in school. A mismatch may occur between conventional management strategies and students' cultural backgrounds. 4. To effectively teach culturally and linguistically diverse children, teachers must have understand how students' patterns of communication (verbally and nonverbally) and various dialects their classroom learning.	Culturally responsive discipline is for teachers to create caring and nurturing relationships with students, grounded in cooperation, collaboration, and reciprocity rather than current teacher controlling-student compliance patterns. Caring is a pillar of effective teaching and learning [and] the lack of it produces inequities in educational opportunities and achievement outcomes for ethnically different students .

(continued)

TABLE 11.1   Essential Elements of CRCM (continued)

School Entry—Account for language readiness skill gaps through student screening	Instructional Format—Provide immediate/ urgent and intensive instruction through	Multi-tiered Levels of Support
• Access early school skills • Organize student grouping • Structure classroom activities on the basis of screening outcomes • Identify at-risk students early enough	• Structuring classroom activities with empirical support for CLD students. • Accounting for the importance of movement and verve with such activities that include ample academic responding opportunities, brisk pacing, positive reinforcement, and corrective feedback. • Monitoring the progress of at-risk students weekly. • Maintaining high expectations and affirming students cultural beliefs.	*Tier 1—Whole Classroom Instruction* • CLD students continue receiving structured/ dynamic instruction. • Student performance monitored quarterly. *Tier 2—Small group instruction* • CLD students who show low responding receive additional small-group instruction to increase response rates and peer-mediated activities. • Student performance monitored weekly.

Source: Adapted from: Cartledge, G., & Kourea, L. (2008). Culturally responsive classrooms for culturally diverse students with and at risk for disabilities. *Exceptional Children, 74*(3), 351–371.

TABLE 11.2 Components of Double-Check Professional Development Program

Reflective Thinking About the Children and Their "Group Membership"
- I understand culture and why it is so important.
- I reflect on how my actions contribute to chains of behavior.
- I am aware of other groups and how histories and present circumstances contribute to my behavior interacting with others.
- I make tangible efforts (reading, home visits, interviews, student inventories) to "reach out" and understand differences.
- I have positive and constructive views of difference.

Efforts Made to Develop an Authentic Relationship
- I display tangible evidence of warmth, care, and trust.
- I recognize special talents.
- I encourage positive interactions.
- I provide positive adult attention.
- I take genuine interest in the activities and personal lives of others.
- I display a professional and personal orientation toward students.

Effective Communication
- Consistently communicates high expectations
- Displays professionalism, civility, and respect in all communications
- Communicates with care and persistence of effort
- Communicates with credibility, dependability, and assertivenes
- Aware and facile with "code switching"
- I communicate without judging others

Connection to Curriculum
- Instruction contains exemplars from the backgrounds of my students
- Able to highlight cultural differences positively during instruction
- Uses learning activities reflective of the background of students, their families, and the community

Consider Cognitive Style Differences
- Understand and apply the concept of teacher and student vs. the content
- Sensitivity to student's cultural and situational messages
- Awareness of how situations influence behavior (e.g., health, poverty, dress, neighborhood expectations)
- Aware of the students' needs to address multiple constituencies
- Ability to emphasize resiliency, choice, and internal locus of control
- Ability to recognize students' social and political consciousness

Source: Hershfeldt, P. A., Sechrest, R., Pell, K. L.,Rosenberg, M. S., Bradshaw, C. P., & Leaf, P. J. (2009). Double-Check: A framework of cultural responsiveness applied to classroom behavior. *TEACHING Exceptional Children Plus, 6*(2) Article 5. Retrieved from http://escholarship.bc.edu/education/tecplus/vol6/iss2/art5

TABLE 11.3   Proactive Culturally (Responsive) Behavior Management Strategies

- Employ teacher movement patterns in an unintrusive manner rather than in an aversive manner.
- Use peer mediators or peer jury to facilitate dispute resolution occurring between peers.
- Use role-playing techniques that actively involve culturally diverse students in developing alternative solutions aimed at producing acceptable behavior.
- Carefully select timing and use of time-out procedures in order to eliminate feelings of alienation, powerlessness, and peer estrangement.
- Use praise to reinforce acceptable behavior only if approved by the student.
- Use culturally sensitive counseling techniques. The educator's understanding of the student's world view, values, beliefs, and behaviors that are deeply rooted in their culture will be enhanced, thus minimizing the misinterpretation of culturally-based behavior.
- Recognize accomplishments and employ public (e.g., name on bulletin board) recognition as positive reinforcement.
- Avoid confronting, reprimanding, and criticizing students in front of peers. Allow student to save face in presence of peers.
- If aversive disciplinary approach is used, discuss and implement in privacy. Humiliation can wound pride and erode peer respect.
- Select social reinforcers that focus on affective, group-conscious, and cooperative activities.
- Use modeling with careful consideration of various psychosocial variables (gender, race, ethnicity, social class).

Source: From "Culture: A Neglected Factor in Behavior Management Strategies" by N. Ewing, in F. E. Obiakor & B. Algozzine (Eds.), *Managing problem behaviors: perspectives for general and special educators*, (pp. 96–114), Dubuque, IA: Kendall Hunt, 1995.

or monitoring of behaviors, (d) contingency management systems to reinforce and correct behavior, and (e) methods to measure outcomes and to evaluate progress. The SWPBIS model has three tiers with specific core elements at the (a) *primary prevention/school-wide*, including universal school-wide management strategies to reduce disruptive behavior and teach prosocial skills to all students; (b) *secondary prevention*, including targeted or group-based intervention strategies for students at risk of developing more serious antisocial behaviors (about 5% to 10%); and (c) *tertiary prevention*, including functionally derived treatment strategies for the small number of students (about 1%–3%) who engage in more chronic patterns of antisocial behavior (Horner, Crone, & Stiller, 2001).

Sugai et al. (2011) described the "universal tier" as the level where "risk factors," such as low achievement, truancy, high student mobility, office discipline referrals (ODR), and histories of suspensions or expulsions of CLD students at risk for special education services are documented and supports for all students are implemented. In the "secondary tier" behavioral analysis and empirically supported behavioral interventions in smaller groups are applied to the CLD students who are at-risk for special education and who are not responsive to the universal supports provided to all students. In the third tier, CLD students, who need additional interventions and supports beyond the universal and secondary tiers, are exposed to highly specialized, FBA-informed interventions by specialized teams of special educators, behavioral interventionists, school psychologists, and counselors. The multidisciplinary team makes determinations about which CLD students with special needs require more intensive behavioral interventions and supports are made by Positive Behavior Intervention Support (PBIS) teams consisting of members who represent multiple grade levels in the school and are based on the monitoring of a number of data sources and outcomes, ODRs, in a given time period and location by student and staff member, attendance, tardiness, suspension, and academic outcomes (e.g., standardized test scores and patterns of course failure rates).

The multitiered model in Culturally Responsive (CR) PBIS is based on the notion that behavior management practices at each level should be based on scientific evidence about "what works." In addition, it is essential to find out specifically "what works" with whom, in what classroom contexts, and under what conditions/circumstances with CLD students with special needs. Important questions must be asked before we move forward in the field of special education: What should the first tier look like for CLD students with special needs? What behavioral management techniques should be implemented at the second tier? In what ways, do the behavioral techniques vary and how should this be determined? How can we make sure that behavioral techniques are culturally responsive to the needs of CLD students?

Culturally responsive PBIS (CR-PBIS) frameworks are designed and implemented in terms of the four tenets of PBIS: a) outcomes, b) empirically validated practices, c) data-based decision making, and d) systems change (Sugai & Horner, 2002). In addition, according to Utley, Kozleski, Smith, and Draper (2002), a CR approach to PBIS engages the cultures that students, families, and school personnel bring with them to school and the culture of schooling that predominates in U.S. public schools. Therefore, the SWPBIS programs must identify, teach, promote, and foster prosocial behaviors (Sugai et al., 2011). A CR approach to PBIS specifically acknowledges and values the unique social and cultural contexts of the school. While PBIS programs are designed to teach and positively reinforce appropriate behaviors through a continuum of universal, group, and individual prevention and culturally appropriate behavior interventions (Sugai et al., 2011), a CR approach to PBIS focuses on effective, respectful, supportive relationships and the use of cultural responsive principles and practices. This focus creates a CR environment that supports the unique instructional and behavioral needs of the school and eliminates the cultural mismatch that often occurs between school personnel and students. Therefore, CR-PBIS programs infuse cultural responsive principles of teaching and student learning, intergroup relations, school governance/organization, assessment (Banks, 2006; Shade et al., 1997; Utley et al., 2007) classroom management (Weinstein et al., 2004), and approaches in character education, social skill instruction, and discipline procedures with positive behavior intervention and support features (Fenning & Rose, 2007; Jones, Caravaca, Cizek, Horner, & Vincent, 2006; Osher, Dwyer, & Jackson, 2004).

Functional Behavioral Assessment

CLD children with special needs may be vulnerable to significant behavioral challenges. Depending upon the situation, it may be more effective to redirect inappropriate behavior on the part of CLD students with special needs than to discuss it with them, particularly within the context of a classroom situation. CLD students with special needs may not fully understand comments made by general and special educators concerning their behavior. It is also important not to draw attention to misbehavior since this may prove reinforcing or may prove embarrassing to CLD children with special needs. The key to effective behavioral analysis is to look at what motivates the behavior and consider what environmental factors are promoting the behavior. It is important when developing a behavior plan to look at ways to prevent inappropriate behaviors and what skills students need to learn to avoid the behavior. It is important when developing a behavior plan to look at ways to prevent behaviors from happening and what skills the CLD student needs to learn to avoid the behavior. CLD children with special needs whose behavior interferes with their learning or the learning of the other students should have a behavior plan. The individualized educational plan (IEP) team should meet and complete a functional behavioral assessment (FBA). Best practice for an FBA should involve all the IEP team members in a brainstorming session to discuss the specific behaviors of CLD children with special needs so that all the IEP team members agree on inappropriate student behaviors. Salend and Taylor (2002) highly recommend professionals who are culturally sensitive to the CLD student's background in order for the team to learn about the student's cultural perspectives and experiential and linguistic background and to determine whether the student's behavior has a sociocultural explanation. Furthermore, Garcia and Ortiz (2008) noted that when strategies are implemented with CLD students with special needs, it is critical that the prereferral, assessment, and intervention phases be culturally and linguistically responsive; that is, educators must ensure that CLD students' sociocultural, linguistic, racial/ethnic, and other relevant background characteristics are addressed at all phases, including (a) collecting assessment information, (b) reviewing student performance, (c) considering reasons for student difficulty or failure,

(d) designing alternative interventions, and (e) interpreting assessment results (Basterra, 2011; Henderson, 2008).

The next step is to gather data including: duration, frequency, and intensity of the behavior. The IEP team should collect data on the actual behaviors, interview parents and other individuals about the history of the behavior and if it happens in other settings, and review school records. Important questions that must be addressed are (a) When, where, and with who does the behavior most often occur? (b) When, where, and with whom does the behavior seldom, if ever occur? (c) What happened just before and after the behavior? (d) What did the school staff do in response to the behavior? (e) Is this a "hidden" reward? (f) What are the environmental factors involved in the students behavior? (g) Are there any health or medical factors related to the behavior (i.e., change in medication, illness, dental issues, etc)? (h) Are there any factors at home related to the behavior (i.e., death, divorce, etc.)? (i) Why does the team think the student is doing the behavior? and (j) What need is the behavior fulfilling for the student? A positive behavior support plan (PBSP) is a proactive way to address a specific behavior that incorporates positive strategies and supports designed to increase appropriate replacement behaviors. It should include two parts. The first part is a list of intervention strategies the school can do to prevent or decrease the likelihood of inappropriate behaviors occurring (see Table 11.3). The second part is to look at what skills CLD students with special needs must learn in order to get their needs met in an appropriate way. It is very difficult to change a behavior if you have not helped them get their behavioral challenges met in a culturally responsive and appropriate way. A good PBSP also includes (a) a plan to phase out behavioral intervention techniques, (b) a schedule of follow up meetings to determine if the plan is successful and to make changes, (c) a discussion of how the plan will be implemented outside of the school setting, and (d) how the plan relates to goals on the student's IEP.

CONCLUSION

This chapter has discussed the role and importance of culture in designing and implementing culturally responsive classroom and behavior management techniques for CLD children with special needs. The current research literature provides numerous examples of CLD children with special needs that have different behavioral patterns that frequently result in (a) a misdiagnosis of behaviors, (b) inappropriate interpretations of behaviors, (c) deterioration of interpersonal respect between teachers and students, (d) increased attention to controlling student behavior, (e) poor use of instructional time, (f) ill-defined classifications and labels, and (g) dysfunctional educational programs. It is, therefore, critical that general and special educators consider cultural and contextual factors in culturally responsive behavioral programs in the monitoring disproportionality in office discipline referrals (ODRs) between dominant and nondominant groups through analysis of trends in data disaggregated across student demographic characteristics (i.e., race/ethnicity). In addition, the implementation of culturally responsive behavioral techniques and positive behavioral interventions and supports highlight the strengths and are designed to improve the problem areas of CLD students with special needs.

REFERENCES

Adelman, H., & Taylor, L. (2011). *Moving beyond the three tier intervention pyramid toward a comprehensive framework for student and learning supports.* Retrieved from http://smhp.psych.ucla.edu/pdfdocs/briefs/threetier.pdf

Algozzine, B., O'Shea, D., & Obiakor, F. E. (2009). *Culturally responsive literacy instruction.* Thousand Oaks, CA: Corwin Press.

Artiles, A. J., Rueda, R., Salzaar, J., & Higareda, I. (2005). Within-group diversity in minority special education disproportionate representation: The case of English language learners in California's urban school districts]ts. *Exceptional Children, 71,* 283–300.

Bacon, E., Banks, J., Young, K., Jackson, F. R., (2007). Perceptions of African American and European American teachers on the education of African American boys. *Multiple Voices, 10* (1 & 2), 166–172.

Banks, J. A. (2006). *Race, culture, and education: The selected works of James A. Banks.* New York, NY: Routledge.

Basterra, M. (2011). Cognition, culture, language, and assessment: How to select culturally valid assessments in the classroom. In M. Basterra, E. Trumbull, & G. Solano-Flores (Eds.), *Cultural validity in assessment: Addressing linguistic and cultural diversity* (pp. 72–79). New York, NY: Routledge.

Bodley, J. H. (2010). *A baseline definition of culture.* Retrieved from http://www.wsu.edu/gened/learn-modules/top_culture/culture-definition.html.

Cartledge, G., & Kleefeld, J. (2010). *Working together: Building children's social skills through folktales, Grades 3–6* (2nd ed.). Champaign, IL: Research Press.

Cartledge, G., & Kourea, L. (2008). Culturally responsive classrooms for culturally diverse students with and at risk for disabilities. *Exceptional Children, 74,* 351–371.

Cartledge, G., & Lo, Y. (2006). *Teaching urban learners: Culturally responsive strategies for developing academic and behavioral competence.* Champaign, IL: Research Press.

Cartledge, G., & Milburn, J. F. (1996). *Cultural diversity and social skill instruction: Understanding ethnic and gender differences.* Champaign, IL: Research Press.

Donovan, S., & Cross, C. (2002). *Minority students in special education.* Washington, DC: National Academy Press.

Duda, M., & Utley, C. A. (2004). Positive behavior support for at-risk students: Promoting social competence in at-risk culturally diverse learners in urban schools. *Multiple Voices for Ethnically Diverse Learners, 8*(1), 128–143.

Ewing, N. (1995). Culture: A neglected factor in behavior management strategies. In F. E. Obiakor & B. Algozzine (Eds.), *Managing problem behaviors: Perspectives for general and special educator,* (pp. 96–114). Dubuque, IA: Kendall Hunt.

Fenning, P., & Rose, J. (2007). Overrepresentation of African American students in exclusionary discipline: The role of school policy. *Urban Education, 42,* 536–559.

Garcia, F., & Conroy, J. W. (2002). Double Jeopardy: An explosion of restrictiveness and race in special education. In D. Losen & G. Orfield (Eds.), *Racial inequity in special education* (pp. 39–70). Cambridge, MA: Harvard Education Press.

Garcia, S., & Ortiz, A. A. (2008). Preventing disproportionate representation: Culturally and linguistically responsive pre-referral interventions. *Teaching Exceptional Children, 38*(4), 64–68.

Gay, G. (2000). *Culturally responsive teaching: Theory, research, & practice.* New York, NY: Teachers College Press.

Gay, G. (2002). Culturally responsive teaching in special education for ethnically diverse students: Setting the stage. *International Journal of Qualitative Studies in Education, 15,* 613–629.

Grossman, H. (2004). *Classroom behavior management for diverse and inclusive schools* (3rd ed.). New York, NY: Rowman & Littlefield.

Hale, J. B., Kaufman, A., Naglieri, J. A., & Kavale, K. A. (2006). Implementation of IDEA: Integrating response to intervention and cognitive assessment methods. *Psychology in the Schools, 43*(7), 753–770.

Henderson, J. L. (2008). *Disproportionality in special education: The relationship between prereferral intervention teams and the special education process.* Dissertation from the Department of Counseling and Psychological Services, Dissertations, Georgia State University.

Hershfeldt, P. A., Sechrest, R., Pell, K. L., Rosenberg, M. S., Bradshaw, C. P., & Leaf, P. J. (2009). Double-Check: A framework of cultural responsiveness applied to classroom behavior. *Teaching Exceptional Children Plus, 6*(2), 2–18.

Horner, R. H., Crone, D. A., & Stiller, B. (2001). The role of school psychologists in establishing positive behavior support: Collaborating in systems change at the school-wide level. *NASP Communique, 29* (6). Retrieved from http://www.nasponline.org/publications/cq/cq296pbs.aspx

Individuals with Disabilities Education Improvement Act, P.L. 108–466 (2004, 2005). 34C.F.R. 300 (Proposed Regulations). Retrieved from http://www.a257.g.akamaitech. net/7/257/2422/01jan20051800/edocket.access.gpo.gov/2005/pdf/05-11804.pdf

Jones, C., Caravaca, L., Cizek, S., Horner, R. H., & Vincent, C. G. (2006). Culturally responsive school-wide positive behavior support: A case study in one school with a high proportion of Native American students. *Multiple Voices, 9,* 108–119.

Irvine, J. J. (2003). *Educating teachers for diversity: Seeing with a cultural eye.* New York, NY: Teachers College Press.

Irvine, J., & Armento, B. (2001). *Culturally responsive teaching: Lesson planning for elementary and middle grades.* New York, NY: McGraw-Hill.

Kauffman, J. M. (1989). *Characteristics of behavior disorders of children and youth* (4th ed.). Columbus, OH: Merrill.

Kewalramani, A., Gilbertson, L., Fox, M., & Provasnik, S. (2007). *Status and Trends in the Education of Racial and Ethnic Minorities (NCES 2007-039).* Washington, DC: U.S. Department of Education.

Ladson-Billings, G. (1995). Towards a theory of culturally relevant pedagogy. *American Educational Research Journal, 32,* 465–491.

LeMoine, N., Maddahian, E., Patton, D., Ross, R., & Scruggs, L. (2006, February). *Applying culturally relevant strategies to systemic reform: Los Angeles Unified School District.* Presentation at the National Center for Culturally Responsive Educational Systems Conference, Denver, CO.

Losen, D. J. (2002). Minority overrepresentation and underservicing in special education. *Principal, 81*(3), 45.

Losen, D. J. & Welner, K. G. (2002). Legal challenges to inappropriate and inadequate special education for minority children. In D. Losen & G. Orfield (Eds.), *Racial inequity in special education* (pp. 167–194). Cambridge, MA: Harvard Education Press.

Mendez, L. M., & Knoff, H. M. (2003). Who gets suspended from school and why: A demographic analysis of schools and disciplinary infractions in a large school district. *Education and Treatment of Children, 26(1),* 30–51.

Metropolitan Center for Urban Education. (2008). *Culturally responsive classroom management.* New York, NY: Author.

National Center for Education Statistics, Institute of Education Sciences (2010). *Status and Trends in the Education of Racial and Ethnic Minorities.* Washington, DC: U.S. Department of Education.

National Center for Learning Disabilities. (2011). *The state of learning disabilities: Facts, trends, and indicators.* New York, Author.

Nieto, S., & Boder, P. (2008). *Affirming diversity: The sociopolitical context of multicultural education* (5th ed.). Boston, MA: Allyn & Bacon.

Obiakor, F. E. (2007). Multicultural special education: Effective intervention for today's schools. *Intervention in School and Clinic, 42,* 148–155.

Obiakor, F. E., Enwefa, S., Utley, C. A., Obi, S. O., Gwalla-Ogisi, M., & Enwefa, R. (2004). *Serving culturally and linguistically diverse students with emotional and behavioral disorders.* Arlington, VA: The Council for Children with Behavioral Disorders. The Council for Exceptional Children.

Obiakor, F. E., Harris-Obiakor, P., Obi, S. O., & Eskay, M. (2000). Urban learners in general and special education programs: Revisiting assessment and intervention issues. In F. E. Obiakor, S. A. Burkhardt, A. F. Rotatori, & T. Wahlberg (Eds.), *Intervention techniques for individuals with exceptionalities in inclusive settings* (Vol. 13, pp. 115–131). Stamford, CT: JAI Press.

Osher, D., Dwyer, K., & Jackson, S. (2004). *Safe, supportive and successful schools: Step by step.* Longmont, CO: Sopris West Educational Services.

Salend, S., Duhaney, L., & Montgomery, W. (2002). A comprehensive approach to identifying and addressing issues of disproportionate representation [Electronic version]. *Remedial and Special Education, 23,* 289–299.

Salend, S. J., & Taylor, L.M. (2002). Cultural perspectives: Missing pieces in the functional assessment process. *Intervention in School and Clinic, 38*(2), 104–112.

Schmidt, P. R. (2000). Emphasizing differences to build cultural understandings. In V. J. Risko & K. Bromley, (Eds.), *Collaboration for diverse learners: Viewpoints and practices* (pp. 50–65). Newark, DE: International Reading Association

Schmidt, P. R. (2003, February). *Culturally relevant pedagogy: A study of successful inservice.* Paper presented at the annual meeting of the National Reading Conference, Scottsdale, AZ.

Schmidt, P. R. (2004, December). Supporting culturally relevant pedagogy: "It made the difference!" In R. Perry (chair), *Culturally responsive teaching and third space theory.* Symposium conducted at the annual meeting of the National Reading Conference, San Antonio, TX.

Schmidt, P. R. (Ed.). (2005). *Preparing educators to communicate and connect with families and communities.* Greenwich, CT: Information Age Publishing.

Shade, B. J., Kelly, C., & Oberg, M. (1997). *Creating culturally responsive classrooms.* Washington, D.C.: American Psychological Association.

Sugai, G., Fallon, L., & O'Keefe, B. (2011). *Culture, disability, & behavior: Let's have a conversation.* Retrieved from http://www.pbis.org schools. *Journal of Positive Behavior Interventions, 2*(3), 131–143.

Sugai, G. & Horner, R.H. (2002). The evolution of discipline practices: School-wide positive behavior supports. *Child & Family Behavior Therapy, 24*(1/2), 23–50.

Sullivan, A. L., & A'Vant, E. (2009, November). *On the need for cultural responsiveness.* National Association for School Psychologists Communiqué, 38(3). Retrieved from http://www.nasponline.org/publications/cq/mocq383culturalrespon-sive.aspx

Tyler, N., Yzquierdo, Z., Lopez-Reyna, N., & Flippin, S. (2002). *Diversifying the special education workforce (COPSSE Document No. RS-3E).* Gainesville, FL: University of Florida, Center on Personnel Studies in Special Education.

Utley, C. A., Greenwood, C. R., & Douglas, K, (2007). The effects of a social skills strategy on disruptive and problem behavior in African American students in an urban elementary school: A pilot study. *Multiple Voices, 10,* (1 & 2), 173–191.

Utley, C. A., Kozleski, K., Smith, A., & Draper, I. (2002). Positive behavior support: A proactive strategy for minimizing behavior problems in urban, multicultural youth. *Journal of Positive Behavioral Interventions, 4*(4), 196–207.

Utley, C. A., & Obiakor, F. E. (2012). Response to intervention and positive behavior intervention and supports: Merging models to improve academic and behavioral outcomes of culturally and linguistically diverse children with learning disabilities. *Insights on Learning Disabilities, 9*(1), 37–67.

Utley, C. A. Obiakor, F. E., & Bakken, J. P. (2011). Culturally responsive practices for culturally and linguistically diverse students with learning disabilities. *Learning Disabilities: A Contemporary Journal, 9*(1), 5–18.

Utley, C. A., & Salend, S. (2006). Working with multicultural learners with emotional and behavioral problems. In F. E. Obiakor (Ed.), *Multicultural special education: Educating teachers to work with all students* (pp. 97–109). New York, NY: MacMillan Publishers.

Weinstein C., Tomlinson-Clarke S., & Curran M. (2004). Toward a conception of culturally responsive classroom management. *Journal of Teacher Education,* 55(1), 25–38.

9 781623 965808